Preaching God's Word

Preaching God's Word

A Hands-On Approach
to Preparing, Developing,
and Delivering the Sermon

TERRY G. CARTER • J. SCOTT DUVALL • AND J. DANIEL HAYS

ZONDERVAN®

ZONDERVAN.com/
AUTHORTRACKER
follow your favorite authors

ZONDERVAN

Preaching God's Word
Copyright © 2005 by Terry G. Carter, J. Scott Duvall, and J. Daniel Hays

Requests for information should be addressed to:

Zondervan, *Grand Rapids, Michigan 49530*

Library of Congress Cataloging-in-Publication Data
    Carter, Terry G.
        Preaching God's word : a hands-on approach to preparing, developing, and delivering the
    sermon / Terry G. Carter, J. Scott Duvall, and J. Daniel Hays.
            p. cm.
        Includes bibliographical references and indexes.
        ISBN 978-0-310-24887-3 (hardcover, printed)
        1. Preaching. I. Duvall, J. Scott. II. Hays, J. Daniel, 1953- III. Title.
    BV4211.3.C37 2005
    251—dc22   2005007676

Interior design: Ruth Bandstra

Printed in the United States of America

13 14 15 16 17 18 /DCI/ 25 24 23 22 21 20 19 18 17 16 15 14 13 12 11 10 9 8

*To those from whom I feel the greatest love and support in
all my endeavors—my wife and best friend, Kathy Carter;
our greatest gift from God and wonderful daughter,
Tilly Gambill, and her husband, Brent,
a welcome addition to our family.*

*To Ashley, Amy, and Meagan Duvall, for being gracious and
encouraging to their dad, who is also their preacher.*

*To my dad, Jim Hays. His preaching edified, inspired, and
entertained me as a boy, and his powerful yet folksy sermon
illustrations still live on in my memory. His preaching has
always been the standard by which I have evaluated the
homiletics of others.*

Contents

Acknowledgments

One would think that three authors would be able to handle all the details of writing a book. However, all writing projects require the assistance of many others, and so it is only appropriate to recognize some of those friends who made this work possible. First, we offer our deep appreciation to the encouraging people at Zondervan, and especially to our editor Jack Kuhatschek, for their vision and patience in the project. With their help and encouragement the emphasis on biblical preaching continues. As part of the process, Zondervan enlisted Ryan Padzur to read through the book and make appropriate suggestions for improvement. We offer gratitude to Ryan for taking the time and effort to review the manuscript and direct us to better ways of communicating the material. He helped us produce a better book.

As professors at the same institution, we are grateful that Ouachita Baptist University allows us the freedom and flexibility to write and contribute to various aspects of Christian studies. Writing demands time, encouragement, and freedom. Ouachita is a good place for this endeavor. In a similar vein, writing takes a great deal of time from families, and we want to thank our families for being so patient and encouraging throughout the process—that is especially true of our wives. We thank God for them daily.

Finally, we are daily reminded of the grace of God present in our lives that allows us to engage in the work of writing. We are ever indebted for all the blessings and abilities he has bestowed on us, and we hope the book helps you fan into flame your gifts.

Terry G. Carter, J. Scott Duvall, and J. Daniel Hays

Preface

How This Book Came to Be

Several years ago we (Scott Duvall and Danny Hays) struggled to find a hermeneutics textbook to use in our classes here at Ouachita Baptist University that was appropriate and effective for teaching students how to study and interpret the Bible. There were lots of advanced books on hermeneutics, but we could not find any that really taught our students a practical, hands-on approach to reading, interpreting, and applying the Bible. We found ourselves changing textbooks each semester and developing our own material to supplement the textbooks.

Eventually we discussed this problem with Jack Kuhatschek at Zondervan, and he encouraged us to try to produce such a practical text. A few years later *Grasping God's Word: A Hands-on Approach to Reading, Interpreting, and Applying the Bible* was published. It did indeed seem to fit the niche and now is being used regularly in numerous Christian universities, seminaries, and churches. We are appreciative of all the positive feedback that we have received from professors, students, pastors, and laypeople from all over North America who have been using *Grasping God's Word*.

Meanwhile, our colleague Terry Carter, who regularly teaches homiletics at Ouachita Baptist University, also struggled to find a homiletics textbook appropriate for his students that was practical and contemporary, yet still focused on *biblical* preaching. One afternoon the three of us (Carter, Duvall, and Hays) were at Zondervan's book booth at an Evangelical Theological Society (ETS) conference, chatting casually with the Zondervan staff. The topic of preaching came up, and all of us reaffirmed how important it was that preaching be *biblical* and follow sound hermeneutical principles like those presented in *Grasping God's Word*. The Zondervan staff noted that there was a real need for a basic, introductory homiletics book that integrated sound hermeneutical principles into the practical aspects of sermon development and delivery. They suggested that perhaps the three of us could produce such a textbook.

With little time at that moment to give the idea serious consideration, the three of us soon scattered to attend various conference sessions (and Carter went to play golf). Later that night we gathered together again at the annual ETS banquet dinner. Over a thousand people were at the banquet, and dozens of waiters scrambled to serve the large crowd. The food looked great, and as far as we could tell, everyone in the banquet hall ate well—except Terry and Scott. They waited patiently for their food for quite some time, watching everyone else get served and begin to eat. Finally the waiters sheepishly told them that all the food was gone; they couldn't be served. They were quite hungry by this time, so in spite of the $20 banquet tickets, they simply slipped out and drove to the nearby IHOP. While eating pancakes there, they recalled the conversation at the Zondervan booth that afternoon and began discussing ideas for a practical homiletics textbook designed to teach students how to develop and deliver powerful *biblical* sermons. On a napkin at the IHOP they sketched out the chapter outline for this book.

The Nature of *Preaching God's Word*

First and foremost, this book teaches students that preaching must be *biblical*—sermons must be based on a solid exegetical study of the Bible. In this sense *Preaching God's Word* is a companion text to *Grasping God's Word*. In *Grasping God's Word* the student learns how to use standard evangelical exegetical approaches to studying the Bible. Throughout *Preaching God's Word* we build on this hermeneutical foundation, making frequent references to *Grasping God's Word* in regard to the details relating to interpretive issues. But *Preaching God's Word* focuses on communicating God's Word. It teaches the students to take the results of their exegesis, develop them into a strong, coherent sermon, and then deliver that sermon in a powerful manner that connects with today's audiences.

We realize that not everyone using this book has studied *Grasping God's Word*, and we have, therefore, structured *Preaching God's Word* so that it is still beneficial to those who are unfamiliar with the earlier book. Indeed, chapter 2 in *Preaching God's Word* provides a good short summary of *Grasping God's Word*, designed especially for those who need a review of the nuts and bolts of exegesis.

The subtitle sums up the book succinctly: *A Hands-On Approach to Preparing, Developing, and Delivering the Sermon*. "Hands-on" points to the practical orientation of the book. "Preparing, developing, and delivering" underscore that this book teaches both sermon development and sermon delivery. But from beginning to end, we stress that if sermons are to carry any authority, they must be firmly grounded in the Word of God.

The Organization of *Preaching God's Word*

Part 1 of this book focuses on developing and preaching a biblical sermon. It deals with critical issues common to most biblical sermons. In teaching this material the book presents a ten-step process:

Step 1	Grasp the Meaning of the Text in Their Town
Step 2	Measure the Width of the Interpretive River
Step 3	Cross the Principlizing Bridge
Step 4	Grasp the Text in Our Town
Step 5	Exegete Your Congregation
Step 6	Determine How Much Background Material to Include
Step 7	Determine the Sermon Thesis and Main Points
Step 8	Develop Text-Centered Applications
Step 9	Find Illustrations
Step 10	Write Out the Sermon and Practice Delivery

After learning the basic biblical sermon development and delivery, the student moves on to analyze the unique challenges and opportunities when preaching from specific biblical genres. Thus, part 2 deals with New Testament genres: New Testament letters,

Gospels and Acts, and Revelation. Part 3 covers the Old Testament genres: Old Testament narrative, law, prophets, and psalms and wisdom literature. We cover preaching from the New Testament first because for most students, the New Testament is easier, and we find that learning progresses best when the student moves from the less difficult to the more difficult.

Target Audience for *Preaching God's Word*

Preaching God's Word is targeted primarily for beginning students. Especially in part 1, this book assumes that the reader knows little about preaching and has little experience. Likewise reflecting the "classroom" tone are the assignments at the end of each chapter. If you are a professor using this book for a homiletics class, we also encourage you to require your students to watch great preachers on video and to evaluate their sermons. Thus, we make reference in a few places to the video series *Great Preachers*.

However, biblical preaching is a challenging enterprise, and we know that many, many preachers already active in a preaching ministry are interested in improving their sermons and their preaching skills. Perhaps you fall into this category. We think that this book will be helpful to you as well, and we have included a significant amount of material that may be new and helpful (e.g., how to exegete your audience). Moreover, within sermon development, the issue of biblical hermeneutics—how to move from the biblical text to valid but relevant and powerful application in the lives of people today—is a huge challenge. Perhaps this book can assist you in that process. Regardless of your experience level, you will probably find part 2 ("Preaching the New Testament") and part 3 ("Preaching the Old Testament") particularly helpful.

Introduction

I felt God call me into the ministry when I was fifteen years old. Having been in my home church since I was in preschool, everyone was pleased and sought to help me in every way possible. The pastor took it upon himself to help the "preacher boy" and offered advice and a chance to preach. So it was set on the calendar—my first of many preaching events.

Where should I start? With no clue at all to the process for preparing and delivering a sermon, I did the best I could. I found a book of sermon outlines and selected one that seemed to fit the bill— simple and easy. I worked hard with great anxiety, finding a few lightweight commentaries in my deacon father's library and reading several minutes about the text. After all, no one wants to embarrass himself in front of an audience and certainly not on the first try. It was an ominous task. The title of my sermon was "Christian Resources and Responsibilities." If you are wondering how I remember, it's because that sermon still resides in my file as an ever-present reminder of where I started and where I never want to return.

The event occurred on a Sunday evening, probably because few pastors will readily give up Sunday morning to a rank novice. After what I considered days of preparation (it was probably a couple of hours) and lots of worry, I stood to preach the first sermon of my ministry career. As the title suggests this sermon determined to cover virtually everything one could imagine in the Christian life. To be honest, I have had a career preaching the same sermon in smaller chunks—about a thousand altogether. Maybe I was just starting with the general and then spent the rest of my preaching career on the specifics.

All this is to say that the sermon lacked focus—it rambled everywhere. The delivery could only be described as stellar if stellar means

Biblical preaching is perhaps the most urgent need of our day.

eyes down, tied to notes, speaking pace at breakneck speed, and gripped by fear at every breath. Having been given thirty minutes to preach, I gave back twenty; finishing that sermon in a short ten minutes. I doubt seriously if anyone in the audience understood anything. It was an inauspicious beginning.

Well, you guessed it. I had no idea what I was doing. Preaching is hard and scary. But in that sermon I also sensed its immense importance. Maybe that's why it mattered so much to me to do well. I had to learn something if I was going to spend a lifetime doing this. So the journey that I am still on began that night in a small West Texas church.

What did I need to learn? Well, where does the list end? How do I exegete a text? At that time the word "exegete" never entered my mind but the concept did. How do I put information into a sermon? How can I say it so it makes sense? Where can I find those illustrations pastors use every Sunday? What should I be trying to accomplish with my sermon? How long should I preach? How should I deliver the message? Questions like these plague all beginning preachers, and many veteran ones as well. So what about the answers?

Are there others struggling as I did? We see student preachers every year with the same questions. They do what I did—just imitate what they have seen and heard, sometimes from bad role models. How can they find the answers and improve their preaching? We offer in this book one way it can be done. We believe *Preaching God's Word* will help all preachers by providing a hands-on approach to sermon preparation, beginning with solid biblical exegesis and culminating in a well-crafted sermon that communicates the greatest story ever told to today's audience.

Our primary goal, then, is to promote the preaching of biblical sermons (i.e., sermons that flow out of the biblical text). To some degree, we are motivated to write this book from hearing sermons that had little serious connection to the biblical text. Biblical preaching is perhaps the most urgent need of our day. More and more preachers are realizing that congregations are desperately hungry for a genuine word from God. People also look to sermons to model for them how to understand and apply the Bible for themselves. And preachers themselves need realistic examples of how to discover, develop, and deliver that word from God.

We do not believe that our goal of preaching relevant, biblical sermons is a pipe dream; rather, it is a matter of learning how to do so. We hope *Preaching God's Word* can lead you to preach biblical sermons that will quench the thirst of your audience. If you preach a biblical text to them in a way that communicates the truth, your audience will appreciate it and might rise up and call you blessed.

So what is the game plan? We begin by defining the goal—a biblical sermon. The first chapter ends with a Ten-Step Process for accomplishing the goal, and the following seven chapters flesh out those steps. We will provide a key at the beginning of each chapter to keep you in step. The steps include exegesis, incorporating the biblical data into your sermon, exegeting your audience, translating the truth to your audience, applying the spiritual principles, illustrating them, and then finally delivering the sermon. All these steps build up to a solid biblical message that truly communicates what the text of God's Word is about to your audience. In parts two and three (chs. 9–15) we offer you advice on how to develop biblical sermons from various types of material found in the Bible (New Testament letters, Old Testament prophets, etc.). We think you will find the journey beneficial.

So let's get to it. Get ready to work because biblical preaching is hard work. Prepare to take the text seriously. Learn to incorporate its truth into your sermons using powerful illustrations and relevant applications. Seek through preaching to interest and grow your audience as they listen week after week. God gives you the gift of preaching. We merely want to help you fan it into flame by discovering a process that results in relevant, biblical preaching.

Part 1
Developing and Preaching a Biblical Sermon

Step 1 Grasp the Meaning of the Text in Their Town

Step 2 Measure the Width of the Interpretive River

Step 3 Cross the Principlizing Bridge

Step 4 Grasp the Text in Our Town

Step 5 Exegete Your Congregation

Step 6 Determine How Much Background Material to Include

Step 7 Determine the Sermon Thesis and Main Points

Step 8 Develop Text-Centered Applications

Step 9 Find Illustrations

Step 10 Write Out the Sermon and Practice Delivery

Preaching a Biblical Sermon

1

Defining a Biblical Sermon
Beginning the Sermon Process
Elements of a Biblical Sermon
The Form of the Sermon: Deductive versus Inductive
Summary and Review Questions
Sermon Prep Guide
The Ten-Step Sermon Process

Have you ever experienced the preaching of John R. W. Stott or Eugene Lowery or Tony Campolo? Stott is calm in presentation and fills sermons with background information from biblical times. He is intentional in his outline and lays out the truths clearly. Lowery is free in his approach and fills his sermon with narrative and colorful language to lead the audience in discovering the truth from the text. Campolo is a whirl of activity and excitement, filling his sermons with stories of exploits of radical ministry. In our homiletics classes we want our students to be exposed to preachers like these. Each of these preachers possesses a style of preaching so different from the other two that one wonders how in the world what each does in the pulpit can be called preaching in the same sense. And yet each continues to enthrall audiences with unique presentations of God's Word.

How can these three men be so different and yet so effective with their preaching ministries? What common feature in their sermons endears them to congregations and continues to place them in the category of great preachers? For that matter, what will it take for you with your own unique style to establish an effective preaching ministry? We think we have an answer to those questions, and that is the purpose of this textbook on preaching. We believe all three of these men, and many more like them, exhibit an understanding of biblical

*A biblical sermon
is one that carries
biblical authority.*

preaching. They approach it in different ways and present sermons their own way, but in the end they all arrive at the same place.

Good preaching is biblical preaching. You are now probably asking yourself what that means. What is biblical preaching and how can I imitate great preachers? This textbook seeks to show you the way— or at least a way to that kind of preaching. Our goal is to help you develop a process that will allow you to preach biblical sermons week in and week out in your own way—sermons that challenge and encourage growth in your congregation. So where do we start?

Defining a Biblical Sermon

In the 1960s, in *A Quest for Reformation in Preaching*, H. C. Brown declared that Protestant preaching in America was in a crisis because too many ministers held to "inadequate and inferior concepts about the ministry in general and preaching in particular."[1] Unfortunately this "inadequate and inferior concept" of preaching has probably plagued the church throughout much of its history. Until preachers grasp the goal of the preaching event and come to a clear understanding of how structure and content contribute to that goal, the people in our churches will continue to suffer under weak and ineffective preaching. Therefore, it is imperative in a textbook on homiletics that we come to grips with the most basic building blocks of biblical preaching—how to develop an effective biblical sermon.

Obviously a biblical sermon is necessary for biblical preaching. But what exactly is a biblical sermon? One way to define it is to connect the sermon to the concept of biblical authority. In other words, a biblical sermon is one that carries with it high biblical authority. In such a sermon the biblical text serves as the basis of the sermon, and the message communicated through the sermon follows closely the intended meaning of the biblical text, thus drawing its authority from that text.

Brown classifies sermons according to how well they reflect the intended meaning of the text. *Direct biblical sermons* are the best, for they "employ the natural and logical meaning of the text in a direct,

[1] H. C. Brown, *A Quest for Reformation in Preaching* (Nashville: Broadman, 1968), 16.

straightforward fashion." *Indirect biblical sermons* tend to depart from the intended meaning of the text and stray from the central idea in the scriptural passage. *Casual biblical sermons*, continues Brown, utilize Scripture in a rather "free and loose" way. The *combination biblical sermon* attempts to combine all of the above categories, while the *corrupted biblical sermon* intentionally or unintentionally abuses the Scripture.[2]

The *direct biblical sermon* carries the highest level of biblical authority. If our goal is to preach with the authority of "thus says the Lord," then it is critical that we ground our sermons firmly and directly in the Bible. That is, we should endeavor to develop and preach *direct biblical sermons*.

Beginning the Sermon Process

A biblical sermon first requires a text. The Latin term for text (*textus*) comes from a root word connected to the concept of weaving a fabric.[3] As the original inspired human authors of the Scriptures wove together the words of God to declare his message, so we, too, strive to declare this same message. In biblical preaching the text becomes the material or fabric to be woven into the sermon. When we declare a text from the pulpit, the sermon to follow should reflect that biblical passage in its points, theme, and message. It should be clear to the audience that the scriptural passage is the foundation and material of the sermon.

A sermon is not a biblical sermon if a passage is merely read and then ignored while the preacher tells funny stories or deals with other unrelated issues. As we discuss in this book, there are different effective styles or types of preaching, but all of them must be grounded in God's Word, and their message must flow from that Word if we are to preach with biblical authority.

A few weeks ago I visited a church and sat through two sermons. In both cases the preacher set up a text and stated clearly to the audience that he intended to use that text as a basis for the sermon. After reading it, he began to ramble through a series of subjects from

[2]Ibid., 36–37.

[3]John C. Traupman, *The New College Latin and English Dictionary* (New York: Bantam, 1966), 311. It is related to our word "textile" and can denote "woven cloth."

morality to ethics to church. Not once did he ever refer us back to the text, make a point from it, explain it, or even give us cause to look at the Bible again. In other words, we could just close our Bibles and listen, which is what several of us did after a while. Neither sermon possessed a text. Neither showed evidence of the weaving of biblical information or truth. They were not biblical sermons. He missed the idea of a sermon text. We don't want that to happen to you or your audience.

But how do you get the meaning of the text? The details of this process appear in the next chapter of this book, but some preliminary considerations are necessary here. In order to utilize a Scripture passage as the text and foundation of a biblical sermon, an exegesis of the text is necessary. To exegete means to work through the text sufficiently to "bring out" the meaning. The fruit of good exegesis provides more than enough fascinating and relevant material to fill any sermon with principles originating from God. In the exegesis of the text and sermon process you discover the meaning of the text "in their town," determine the similarities and differences between our situation and that of the biblical audience, find universal biblical principles, and begin to translate that meaning to your congregation.

How do you select a text for preaching? Various preachers answer this question in different ways, but perhaps a summary of some options will prove helpful to you.

(1) *Personal reading and study of Scripture.* Many preachers discover their sermon texts as they perform their own personal study of the Bible. Certain passages speak to them or cause a personal point of growth in their spiritual life. From this encounter with the text and the passion that results, they select a passage for preaching. One strength of selecting a sermon text in this manner is that such texts excite and interest the preacher, which leads to better sermons. In addition, the preacher finds motivation to share what he has personally learned from the truth found in a certain passage. But there is a weakness in this method as well. Sermons developed from these passages may or may not meet the needs of the congregation, and the preaching schedule rests on the preacher's personal study habits and

Selecting a Sermon Text

1. Personal reading and study of Scripture
2. Needs of the congregation
3. Book or theme series
4. Church calendar or events

breadth of study. Avoid allowing this method to lead you into preaching only to your own needs and interests.

(2) *Needs of the congregation.* Some preachers simply observe and evaluate the congregation to determine what themes or spiritual truths they most need to hear. The preacher then searches for biblical passages that address those needs. This option depends on spending time with the people to understand their needs. Obviously, congregations benefit from good sermons targeted to them and their areas of needed growth. But be careful with this option because it may result in a preaching ministry that neglects large sections of Scripture. Try to preach the entire Bible while meeting the needs of the congregation. Chapter 4 provides help with this.

(3) *Book or theme series.* Some preachers select a biblical book or theme and preach through it. This narrows the search for texts and allows a focus of study time in one area. This makes the preaching process a little easier for the preacher, but it can result in missing some of the real needs of the congregation. Using this method does not solve all problems in text selection. The preacher still must find sections in the book to preach or passages dealing with preferred themes. Moreover, often people grow weary of long series or only working through books. They sometimes feel this method does not meet them where they live.

(4) *Church calendar or events.* Regardless of what other options preachers may use for choosing texts, most of us will occasionally land in this category. Things happening in the church or Christian calendar demand the selection of texts representing certain truths. Christmas, Easter, and other special times of the year focus our sermons on certain themes and lead us to those passages. Events like stewardship week or missions emphases also require special texts for preaching. We look for and find texts that speak to the issue at hand. But we must be careful with this option as well. Often these sermons are less passionate because we have to preach about the subject. These sermons are often some of the hardest to keep fresh and to present a word that the congregation hasn't already heard a million times.

The public reading of the Bible should be prepared, practiced, and well-delivered.

In summary, do not choose one of these options to the exclusion of the others. Each has strengths and weaknesses, and the preaching task calls for variety. Each of the above-mentioned options is appropriate at different times in preaching ministry. The next chapter contains information that allows you to narrow the text selection to a manageable passage that can be preached in one sermon.

Elements of a Biblical Sermon

Remember, the goal of our preaching is to translate the meaning of the text in the time of the biblical audience to the meaning of the text in our time, connecting this meaning in a relevant and contemporary way. Our congregations need a word from God, and that word must be put into terms the people can understand and be structured in a manner they can follow and comprehend. What elements in a sermon help us do that?

Most effective sermons include the following: a reading of the text, introduction, text explanation, main points, illustrations, applications, and conclusion. These elements appear in a structure designed by the preacher. Sermons need to be coherent, and structure is beneficial because it helps your listeners follow along and grasp the biblical message and respond. Experienced preachers often incorporate structure into their sermons intuitively because they have been crafting biblical sermons for so long they often don't consciously think about it. But most preachers, and especially those early in their preaching careers, need to pay close attention to the actual structure of the sermon. Let's look in more detail at some of the elements normally found in a biblical sermon.

Read the Text

As already noted, the Scripture text is essential to a sermon. Unfortunately, sometimes we give little attention to reading the Word of God, and in many sermons it appears to be an afterthought. Since the biblical text is central to all that follows in a truly biblical sermon, this demands a public reading of the text that is prepared, practiced, and well-delivered. More will be said about this later in chapter 8, "Delivering a Biblical Sermon." Note that the reading of the text does not necessarily precede the introduction. Sometimes it follows the introduction, or it can even be interspersed throughout the sermon points. Yet an effective reading of the biblical passage plays an important part in communicating biblical truth.

Introduce the Sermon

All sermons begin some way; we generally call that an introduction. This part of the sermon engages (or ought to engage) the audience to remain with you for the duration of the sermon. What a tragedy to spend countless hours developing a Bible-based sermon only to lose the attention of the congregation in the first few minutes of your delivery.

You accomplish several things in these initial moments. (1) You introduce the audience to the connection between the biblical text and the sermon to follow. The introduction must make clear that this sermon attempts to fulfill their expectation to hear a word from God. This suggests that the theme of the sermon might at least be summarized or alluded to in this section. What exactly is the sermon's purpose and role? What do you expect to accomplish with it? "This sermon is about. . . ." In the case of an inductive sermon, the introduction might not clearly state the main idea of the sermon. (Don't worry, we will discuss various types of sermons, such as "inductive," later.) But you might say: "Let's think about . . ." or "Have you considered . . . ?"

(2) Introductions convince your audience that what is about to be discussed is somehow of interest to them. They establish relevance. Why should the audience listen to you? What difference will this message make in the listener's life? An effective introduction addresses these questions. Chapter 4 ("Exegeting the Audience") gives insight into developing the kind of introductions that connect to specific congregations in particular settings.

(3) An interesting, well-designed introduction generates interest on the part of the audience. Audiences are enticed into listening to our sermons. Eugene Lowery describes the entire sermon as "evocation."[4] The process of evocation begins in the introduction. Inexperienced

[4]Eugene Lowery, *The Sermon: Dancing the Edge of Mystery* (Nashville: Abingdon, 1997), 39.

preachers (and occasionally even veterans) sometimes imagine that every person in the congregation is sitting on the edge of the pew waiting with rapt anticipation to hear the sermon. Oh, if that were so! Our task would be much simpler.

However, reality contradicts that notion. You spend hours during the week diligently working with the text and the sermon, growing in excitement about all the spiritually helpful information you now share with the congregation. Your audience, however, has spent the week worrying about problems at work, sick children, bills, mowing the lawn, needed house repairs, tensions with the in-laws, or why their favorite team is losing so badly. A good introduction must grab the attention of the congregation, convincing them that the upcoming twenty or thirty minutes of listening activity are interesting and relevant to life.

Many teachers of preaching suggest that the introduction be written last. This makes good sense. First, try introducing something that has not yet been written. Writing the introduction first may result in an interesting introduction but one that fails to integrate with the sermon to follow. Often our beginning students find a great story or illustration they feel will make a great introduction and then are compelled to use it even if it doesn't really introduce the rest of the sermon. Writing the introduction last makes that mistake easier to avoid. Moreover, writing the sermon body first helps you recognize the relevance of the text to the audience, thus enabling that connection to be made clear in the introduction. In fact, your own understanding of the sermon's theme increases through the sermon-writing process, making the writing of a good introduction easier.

Since the succeeding chapters do not address introductions in more depth, perhaps an example or two at this point will help you see what an introduction should do.

Goals for Your Introduction

1. Show connection to the biblical text.
2. Establish relevance.
3. Generate interest.

Text: Luke 5:12–32.

Sermon: Hope in Times of Hopelessness

Introduction: In 1963 Kurt Vonnegut wrote a book entitled *Cat's Cradle* in which the narrator and main character, John, sought to write a book about the day the world ended. He was prompted to do so by the nuclear bomb at Hiroshima. Vonnegut's fiction book deals with the technological ability of the human race combined with its stupidity. In the process of his research and travels, John comes across a book related to his new religion. The title was *What Can a Thoughtful Man Hope for Mankind on Earth, Given the Experience of the Past Million Years.* It doesn't take John long to read it because it consists of only one word followed by a period: "Nothing."[5]

Vonnegut's book reveals what many in our world today think—there is no hope. Incidents like the tsunami in Southeast Asia, the genocidal activity found in many countries in the last couple of decades, and the daily death rates of HIV patients cause people to question where the hope is. Does Christianity have anything to say in this situation? Does the church have a message of hope in this apparent hopelessness? The three stories found in our passage reveal that Jesus does have something to say about hope in situations that seem void of it. Let's learn how the church can broker that message of hope to a hurting and despairing world.

[Note: This introduction establishes the issue to be addressed, tries to interest the audience in the message, attempts to establish relevance, and connects the text to the main sermon theme of hope.]

[5]Kurt Vonnegut, *Cat's Cradle* (New York: Dell, 1963), 199.

Text: 2 Corinthians 5:7

Sermon: Live by Faith, Not by Sight

Introduction: When was the last time you visited the zoo? Do you remember seeing an African impala in one of the pens? These animals are very unusual. Experts tell you that they are capable of jumping ten feet into the air and as far as thirty feet in distance. However, when you look at the pen that surrounds them, it will often have only a three-foot fence. How can that keep them in? Because the impala will not jump unless he can see the landing spot. They live by sight only.

Often we live that way. We want to know the exact details of a situation. We want assurances and security and no risks. We want to make sure things will turn out the way we want them to. We want to know how much money it will take and how much we have in the bank. Like the impala we tend to live by sight. But Paul suggests another option for the believer. He states, "We live by faith, not by sight." What could that possibly mean? Let's investigate.

Make a Point

The main points of the sermon grow out of the exegetical work to be discussed in the next chapter. These points relate to the key theological truths or principles discovered in your study of the text. Some preachers prefer to write out and state each point clearly in an outline form, while others take a more inductive or narrative approach, allowing the listener to discover the main points as the sermon progresses. Regardless of the approach, every sermon needs at least *one point*. What is the main lesson from God found in this text? What truths need to be applied to the life of the congregation? These principles become evident in some form in every sermon.

Sermon Points

- Tied to the Scriptures
- Directed at the audience

Sermon points possess certain characteristics, some of which are obvious and some not. First of all, the point addresses the listening audience in a present tense manner. It is fine to say that Paul understood what it means to live by faith instead of sight (2 Cor. 5:7), but the point in the sermon directs the relevancy of that truth to our listeners' lives today. Phrases such as "we should" or "believers today need" make it clear that the message is for this church now, today.

Furthermore, the points of the sermon tie directly to the passage in a recognizable way. Each point grows out of the text or perhaps is even directly stated in the text. The scriptural words need not be used verbatim but the spiritual truth should be clearly based on the text so that audiences see and comprehend how each point was derived from the text. Points not arising from the text belong in another speech, but not in your sermon. Biblical preaching always involves points—stated, developed, or implied—that come from the biblical passage being proclaimed. Chapter 5 ("Communicating the Meaning in Our Town") focuses on the process of discovering the points and how sermon points should be developed and preached.

Explanation *demonstrates the biblical authority of the point.*

Explain It

The explanation segment of the sermon tightly connects to the points of the sermon. If the point noted is a spiritual truth from the text, then the audience seeks to know how that point was derived from the text. Are there some words, phrases, nuances, historical facts, or theological understandings from the first century that clarify the passage and therefore the point? Further discussion on this appears in chapter 3 ("Preaching the Meaning in Their Town"). For now, just remember that explanation reflects and demonstrates the biblical authority of the point. In this segment of the sermon you delineate between your words or opinions and that of the text. This section probably ranks as the most important part of the sermon and comprises the bulk of information surrounding a point. Take great care in this section to keep facts accurate and the truth clear.

Tell the Audience What to Do with It

In the application section of the sermon you suggest to the audience how they might embody the spiritual truth of the sermon in real life and then challenge them to respond obediently. Application needs to be simple, doable, and relevant. Every time you preach, your people ask from the very start how this sermon can make a difference—a practical difference—in their individual lives. Sermons that stop short of powerful and relevant application fall into the category of mere telling of history rather than biblical proclamation. Effective application is crucial to effective biblical preaching, and we will address it again in more detail in chapter 6 ("Applying the Message").

Make It Clear

Illustrations serve as illuminators of truth in the sermon. They clarify the meaning of a point through simple pictures, stories, or analogies. Often a spiritual truth needs clarification or simplification. Jesus taught this through example. He mastered the use of illustrations in preaching and teaching situations to make theological truth easier for people to grasp. Jesus utilized parables, object lessons, analogies, and examples from nature to illuminate and explain his teaching. We do the same in our sermons by selecting images and stories familiar to our audiences that will clarify and connect our theological points to our listeners. Illustrations are important; they are discussed in more detail in chapter 7 ("Illustrating Biblical Truth").

Save some time and energy for a great ending!

Finish Well

The conclusion should do just what it implies—end the sermon. How that is done is critical to completed communication. Preachers often preach masterful, well-developed sermons that truly touch the congregation and then either cannot find a way to stop, resulting in a loss of audience attention, or else they just end haphazardly, deflating the resolve developed earlier in the listener. A conclusion wraps up the entire sermon. It includes all of the main points, not just the last point. For one-point sermons, such as some narrative or inductive sermons, the conclusion summarizes and concludes that point. This final segment of your sermon draws the audience to a point of decision.

Conclusions must be considered, developed, and practiced with as much care as the rest of the sermon. Unfortunately, sometimes preachers deplete all their energy, discipline, and time in the writing of the body of the sermon and then have nothing left to develop a solid, creative, and powerful conclusion. This is a tragedy that leaves the audience perplexed and unsure of the sermon's relevancy.

In order to accomplish its purpose, the conclusion should be concise and it must conclude. It does not introduce new points or information that causes the audience to think the sermon is starting again. It pulls all the main ideas of the sermon together and then challenges the audience to respond. Work on doing this in both interesting and unpredictable ways.

A favorite method for many of our beginning students is simply to repeat all the points one by one. This works, of course, but it lacks fire and often adds a boring end to an otherwise good sermon. Other creative options, such as a story, art, a song, a dramatic monologue, or an object lesson that sums up the sermon idea, offer more exciting and powerful ways to conclude. As with introductions, conclusions will not be discussed at length in the remainder of the book, so some examples here might clarify and help you in developing good conclusions.

Text: 1 Corinthians 4:16–17

Sermon: Being a Role Model

[Sermon based on Paul's statement to the Corinthians that they should imitate him.]

Conclusion: If you ask around, most people will agree that we need role models—people who will live out the truth in our presence so we can see and follow their example. But the real question is who will step up and do it. Many of you have heard the Aesop's fable about the mice and the cat.

> The mice had a council to consider how to handle the Cat. There were several suggestions, but finally a young mouse spoke up. "Our main problem is that the enemy sneaks up on us with no warning. If we had a way to signal her approach, we could easily escape her. I propose we get a small bell and tie it to a ribbon that will be placed around the neck of the Cat."
> Everyone liked the idea and agreed it was the answer until an old mouse took the floor. "That is all very well, but who will bell the Cat?" No one spoke up.[6]

We all agree to the need for some outstanding Christians who will model for us the way a believer should live, think, speak, and witness. But the question remains: Who will bell the cat? Will you step up and be the model for others to imitate?

Text: Numbers 14:17–19; Nehemiah 1:5–6

Sermon: The Basis of Our Prayer

[Sermon deals with Moses and Nehemiah praying to God because God is a forgiving, caring, powerful God.]

Conclusion: When we realize that the power in our prayer is based on the character and nature of God and not on our character, then we can pray with confidence. Nancy Spiegelberg said it effectively. "Lord, I crawled across the bareness to you with my empty cup, uncertain in asking any small drop of refreshment. If only I had known you better. I'd have come running with a bucket."[7] To truly know God is to realize that prayer works because of who God is—a loving, compassionate, powerful, awesome, forgiving, and merciful God. Pray, therefore, with this knowledge, and you will find power in prayer. Do you know God and the power of praying to him?

The Form of the Sermon: Deductive versus Inductive

Two general models of preaching appear in most pulpits regularly. The deductive model (e.g., John Stott) represents the most common and traditional approach to preaching. Many congregations hear this type of sermon every Sunday. Billy Graham popularized this style on

---

A deductive sermon declares the theme of the sermon and then presents propositions or points relating to that theme.

---

[6]*Aesop's Fables*, trans. Vernon S. Jones (New York: Franklin Watts, Inc., 1967), 4.

[7]Nancy Spiegelberg poem quoted in *Our Daily Bread*, "Bibles and Buckets" (Grand Rapids: Radio Bible Ministries, July 10, 1999).

Inductive preaching invites the congregation into the process so they can discover the truth as the sermon unfolds.

[8]Ralph L. Lewis and Gregg Lewis, *Inductive Preaching: Helping People Listen* (Wheaton, IL: Crossway, 1983), 81.

[9]Ibid.

the national and international scene. Deductive preaching moves from a general statement of sermon purpose to the more specific facts regarding that purpose. Often it declares the main idea for the sermon and then states propositions, points, or spiritual truths concerning that theme. For example, a sermon theme might be "Jesus is Lord" and the specific points: (1) Jesus is Lord over nature; (2) Jesus is Lord over death; (3) Jesus is Lord over life.

Ralph and Gregg Lewis, critical of this approach, describe deduction as starting with assertions, conclusions, or propositions and then defining, delimiting, and defending them. "Deductive sermons begin with the preacher's conclusions that are a result of sermon preparation—conclusions offered as *givens* to listeners who may or may not be ready to accept them and go on from there."[8] Lewis and Lewis, however, offer little support for their criticism. The deductive biblical sermon does seek to state what a passage is about and then attempts to expose the spiritual principles from the text related to that theme. The audience accepts or rejects the propositions based on the evidence presented in the sermon. So the deductive approach can be used in effective biblical preaching.

The inductive model of preaching (e.g., Eugene Lowery) also produces effective biblical preaching. Inductive sermons move from specific truths, examples, or ideas (particulars) in the text to the general truth of the sermon, which is normally revealed at or near the end of each unit in the sermon or at the end of the sermon itself. If based on sound exegesis, the particulars lead to correct assertions or statements of truth. Lewis and Lewis define the inductive method as seeking "to help listeners see the truth in such a way that they are ready to accept, agree with and respond to that truth at the end of the sermon."[9]

Inductive preachers invite the congregation into the process so they can discover the truth as the sermon unfolds and, hopefully, accept it at the end. Audience participation or involvement looms as a major goal for those arguing for inductive sermons. Preaching is leading or guiding the audience to discover the meaning of the text while the preacher may or may not ever declare a propositional truth.

For example, a sermon entitled "Faith" may present three examples in progressive order, followed by the concluding truths about faith. Furthermore, the inductive method allows the audience to see how each truth is derived from the biblical text, reaffirming for them that this truth is based on the authority of the Scriptures and not merely on the authority of the preacher.

New impulses in preaching have surfaced both as a reaction to the traditional deductive approach and as a series of creative tweakings of the inductive style; these impulses have been called the "new homiletic." Probably no one gives a better summary of the most common sermon forms than Thomas Long in *The Witness of Preaching*. In his discussion he refers to the deductive style as an outline approach or "a schematic diagram of the parts and order of the message."[10] This style represents the most endorsed form in textbooks of the past generations.

The inductive styles, Long continues, vary and are refined by several preachers. Long notes that Fred Craddock argues for an approach that follows the process the preacher uses when interpreting a passage through exegesis. He defines it as a process through which the preacher imagines a problem and then leads the congregation to solve it on their own.[11] Lowery approaches inductive preaching by beginning with a felt need and then moving to a gospel answer, but with some ambiguity. He poses the problem, diagnoses it, gives a clue to the gospel resolution, explains more clearly the gospel solution, and then projects future possibilities of that solution.[12] Perhaps the most unusual approach is that of David Buttrick, who argues that audiences listen like a camera taking pictures. Therefore, the preacher should set up pictures or vivid ideas for the audience. A sermon consists of a series of these ideas with the goal of leading the audience to a clear understanding of truth. Buttrick suggests that each picture or idea must be fully developed by stating it, elaborating on it, and then restating it.[13]

Obviously, varieties of both the deductive and inductive sermon forms exist. Each one has strengths and weaknesses. But which is best? Which communicates most effectively? We tend to agree with Long

[10]Thomas Long, *The Witness of Preaching* (Louisville: Westminster John Knox, 1989), 93.

[11]Ibid., 98.

[12]Ibid., 99–100.

[13]Ibid., 103.

that the form or structural arrangement of a biblical sermon should be determined by a combination of factors involving the preacher, the audience, and the situation. Long states it well. "A good sermon form grows out of the particularities of preaching this truthful word on this day to these people."[14] In other words, you may choose either of the two main forms available (including the many variations) in order to match a special group of people in a unique situation at a certain time. Either approach can produce effective biblical preaching so long as the sermon is still derived from a serious exegesis of the text and has main communication components (reading, introduction, main point or points, explanation, illustration, application, conclusion) incorporated within it either explicitly or disguised.

Each of the forms discussed highlights different sermon elements. Inductive sermons primarily utilize elements like stories, analogies, illustrations, questions and answers, experiences, examples, associations, visuals, object lessons, and imagination. Deductive sermons focus more on reasoning, proofs, explanations, logic, theological comparisons, definitions, language, context, propositions, and conclusions. We maintain that the best sermons often include elements of both forms. Inductive tools tend to spark audience interest and keep them in the text, providing movement and audience involvement that relates truth to life. Deductive tools seek to proclaim biblical truth and scriptural principles in a clear, concise manner, leaving the audience with valuable biblical information.

Learn to use all of these elements creatively while avoiding the overemphasis of one form to the exclusion of the other. But remember there is no such thing as good preaching without structure of some sort. Lowery argues that "content and form are inseparable. There is no such thing as formless content."[15] Deductive or inductive—you choose and then fashion the elements accordingly for the best communicative effect.

Our goal in this chapter has not been to endorse one form over another but to give an overview of what is normally included in a sermon, to outline the common styles of sermons, and to emphasize the connection of the sermon to a biblical text. Our best advice to you is

[14]Ibid., 105.

[15]Lowery, *The Sermon*, 56.

be flexible and try variety and creativity in your sermons. Avoid getting tied to one style exclusively, and make sure that the form you select matches your audience.

Howard Hendricks reminds us in his book *Teaching to Change Lives* of what he calls "the law of education": *The way people learn determines the way you teach.*[16] Each congregation consists of people who learn in different ways, and preaching needs to adjust. Some will be visual learners while others logical, analytical learners. Choose sermon forms that communicate the truth to hit your people. Since most congregations contain all kinds of learners, opt for variety in sermon form in order to speak to all of them regularly. But never let the form of a sermon lead you away from the textual basis of the sermon. We will further discuss adapting form and style to specific audience needs and audience orientation in chapter 4 ("Exegeting the Audience").

[16]Howard Hendricks, *Teaching to Change Lives* (Portland: Multnomah, 1987), 55.

Summary and Review Questions

Let's summarize. The criterion for a good biblical sermon includes the answers to several important questions.

1. Does the sermon grow out of a biblical text and does it connect closely to it?
2. Does the sermon have elements that generate interest, connect truth to real life, and engage the listener?
3. Does the sermon form leave the audience with clear, sound biblical truth that communicates to them and can be applied to life?
4. Does the sermon challenge them to make changes in life based on the principles found in the biblical text?

Sermon Prep Guide

We know this introductory chapter on the biblical sermon has probably raised more questions than it has answered. You may be feeling overwhelmed at this stage. How can I do all that a biblical sermon requires? How do I find applications and illustrations? Where do I even get started? We thought it would be good at this stage to simplify everything with an outline of the process for developing and delivering a biblical sermon. This step-by-step guide will serve as our foundation for the following chapters as we take you from an exegesis to a delivered sermon. We will refer to the outline in each chapter by highlighting the applicable step.

The Ten-Step Sermon Process

Exegesis

Step 1. **Grasp the Meaning of the Text in Their Town (original meaning).**

Read the text, notice details of text.

Consider genre.

Note literary and historical-cultural context; consult resources.

Translate passage from original language if possible.

Check commentaries.

Write out your "text thesis statement" and "text outline."

The Bridge to Your Audience

Step 2. **Measure the Width of the River.**

Define similarities and differences between biblical context and today.

Step 3. **Cross the Principlizing Bridge.**

Identify the universal, timeless theological principles.

Step 4. **Grasp the Text in Our Town.**

Observe the key elements of application for the original audience.

Think of parallel situations.

Make initial applications for today's audience.

Step 5. **Exegete Your Congregation.**

Determine spiritual maturity.

Determine biblical and theological literacy.

Determine social and cultural setting of audience.

Determine communication factors (formality level, gender issues, etc.).

Determine how to adapt to the level of congregation.

Step 6. Determine How Much Background Material to Include in the Sermon for Audience Understanding.

Look for culture-bound language, idioms, and issues that need translation.

Relate or re-create historical/theological setting.

Relate or re-create the literary context.

The Writing and Delivery

Step 7. Determine Sermon Thesis and Main Points.

Write out sermon thesis statement.

Develop main sermon points connected to thesis statement.

Decide on form of sermon.

Explain points of sermon from exegetical material.

Step 8. Develop Text-Centered Applications for Sermon.

Base them on the applications discovered in step 4.

Make the initial applications specific to your audience.

Avoid trite or legalistic applications.

Step 9. Find Illustrations to Make Points More Relevant to Audience.

Observe, read, and imagine illustrative ideas to make points clearer.

Let illustrations create transitions in the flow of the text.

Use appropriate illustrations.

Avoid lengthy illustrations.

Step 10. Write Out Complete Sermon and Practice Delivery.

Write out sermon in full form as you would say it.

Determine style of delivery (manuscript, memorization, extemporaneous).

Work on use of voice (pitch, pace, volume, articulation).

Pay attention to body language (gestures, facial expressions, eye contact, animation).

Work on conversational voice most natural to you (particularly with postmodern audience).

Work on variety, transitions, grammar, and dialect, memorization of certain portions of sermon, length.

Pay attention to time. Adjust your sermon as you practice to stay within the allotted time.

Now let's get to work developing a biblical sermon designed to deliver a fresh message from God.

Discovering Biblical Truth: The Interpretive Journey

2

The Interpretive Journey
Grasp the Text in Their Town
Measure the Width of the River
Cross the Principlizing Bridge
Grasp the Text in Our Town
An Example—Hebrews 12:1–2
Summary
Review Questions and Assignments

THE FOCUS OF CHAPTER 2:

Step 1	Grasp the Meaning of the Text in Their Town
Step 2	Measure the Width of the Interpretive River
Step 3	Cross the Principlizing Bridge
Step 4	Grasp the Text in Our Town
Step 5	Exegete Your Congregation
Step 6	Determine How Much Background Material to Include
Step 7	Determine the Sermon Thesis and Main Points
Step 8	Develop Text-Centered Applications
Step 9	Find Illustrations
Step 10	Write Out the Sermon and Practice Delivery

I have never been scuba diving, but I'm told that it's a blast. Strapping on those life tanks and exploring the water world below sounds like fun. I had a conversation once with a former navy diver about diving deep, really deep. He told me that he had been in situations so deep and dark that it was almost impossible to keep from becoming disoriented and confused. What a terrifying feeling—being under water, unable to see your hands in front of your face, not knowing which way is up, panic engulfing you. I immediately interrupted my friend, "So what did you do?" I knew he had survived the ordeal since he was standing there talking to me.

The first step toward meeting the needs of our listeners with a word from God is to learn how to interpret and apply the Bible ourselves.

"Feel the bubbles," he said.

"Feel the bubbles?" I asked.

"That's right. When it's pitch black and you have no idea which way to go, you reach up with your hand and feel the bubbles. The bubbles always drift to the surface. When you can't trust your feelings or judgment, you can always trust the bubbles to get you back to the top."

I do not intend to ever dive that deep and get myself into that situation, but it's nice to know that I could always "feel the bubbles" as a reality check. Apart from the experience of scuba diving, we need a way to determine what is real and true. Sometimes in life we get disoriented and desperate. At other times, we find ourselves drifting aimlessly. God knew that we would need advice and instructions about how to live. In the sixty-six books of the Bible we have a reality library—stories, letters, guidelines, and examples from God that tell us what is true and real. In a world that is changing faster than we can imagine, we have something stable, true, and real. The Bible is our Reality Book, an amazing gift from God who loves us deeply and desires a relationship with us.[1]

People who gather faithfully to hear a sermon need something more than noise generated by the surrounding culture; they need a word from God. Preachers with genuine compassion for their listeners live with the ongoing tension of preaching sermons that are simultaneously biblical and relevant. A biblical sermon that also connects with the audience starts with our own understanding of Scripture. If we cannot uncover the practical relevance of the Bible for ourselves, we will be hard pressed to discover and communicate a timely message to our listeners. As a result, the first step toward meeting the needs of our listeners with a word from God is to learn how to interpret and apply the Bible ourselves.

[1] Adapted from J. Scott Duvall, *Life Essentials*, Conviction 1, p. 1.

The Interpretive Journey

The process of reading, interpreting, and applying the Bible is similar to going on a journey. We have to take this *Interpretive Journey* because we are separated from the biblical world by culture and customs, language, situation, and a vast expanse of time. These differences form a barrier—a *river of differences* that disconnects us from the meaning of the text and often prohibits us from understanding and applying that meaning to our lives today. Any legitimate attempt to grasp the Bible's relevance for our lives involves trying to cross this river.

We need an approach to the Bible that is not based strictly on intuition, feeling, or guesswork.

Christians today attempt to cross the river in a variety of ways. While often unconscious of their interpretive method, some employ an *intuitive* or *feels-right* approach to interpretation. If the text looks as if it can be applied directly, they attempt to apply it directly. Others *spiritualize* the meaning of the text by attempting to find a hidden, more "spiritual" meaning. For example, they interpret Jesus' words to Simon Peter in Luke 5:4 to "put out into deep water, and let down the nets for a catch" to represent a "deep" theological or personal discovery on the part of Peter. In this case they spiritualize the word "deep." Other interpreters simply use *guesswork* or give up and move on in the sermon, ignoring the meaning of the text altogether.

None of these interpretive approaches will land you safely on the other side of the river. For example, those using the intuitive approach blindly wade out into the river, hoping that the water will not be more than knee deep. Sometimes they are fortunate and stumble onto a sandbar, but often they step out into deep water and end up washed ashore somewhere downstream. Those who spiritualize are actually trying to jump the river in one grand leap. They also end up washed ashore downstream with their intuitive friends. Simply ignoring a passage is to remain on your side of the river, content to gaze across without even attempting to cross.

What we need is a valid, accurate approach to the Bible that is not based strictly on intuition, feeling, or guesswork. We need an approach that derives meaning from within the biblical text, but one that is also able to cross the river of differences so that the message reaches Christians today. We also need a consistent approach that can be used on any passage and at the same time eliminate the habit of surfing through the Bible, picking and choosing passages that might apply. Our target is an approach that allows us to dig into any passage, determine its meaning, and then see how that meaning applies to us today. Following the steps of the *Interpretive Journey* will enable you to understand the meaning of the Bible, to transport that meaning from the world of the ancient audience across the river of differences, and then to apply it in our world today.

The Interpretive Journey consists of four main steps:

Step 1 Grasp the text in their town. What did the text mean to the biblical audience?

Step 2 Measure the width of the river to cross. What are the differences and similarities between the biblical audience and us?

Step 3 Cross the principlizing bridge. What is the theological principle in this text?

Step 4 Grasp the text in our town. How should individual Christians today apply the theological principle in their lives?

When interpreting a passage from the Old Testament, the river of differences widens even more. Between the Old Testament biblical audience and Christian readers today lies a change in the covenant. We as New Testament believers are under the new covenant, and we approach God through the sacrifice of Christ. The Old Testament people, however, were under the old covenant, and for them the law was central. The theological situation for the two groups is different. Because of the change of covenants between the Old and New Testaments, when interpreting an Old Testament passage, we must divide Step 3 into two separate steps.

Step 1 Grasp the text in their town.

Step 2 Measure the width of the river to cross.

Step 3a Cross the principlizing bridge.

Step 3b Cross into the New Testament. Does the New Testament teaching modify or qualify this principle, and if so, how?

Step 4 Grasp the text in our town.

Let's look more closely now at each phase of the Interpretive Journey.

Grasp the Text in Their Town

1. The journey begins with a careful and thorough reading of the text.

Even before we ask questions like "What does this text mean?" or "What do the commentaries say?" or "How does this apply to my life?" or "How can I preach this text?" (all important questions), we need to ask, "What does this passage actually say?" Often we read the Bible too quickly and skip over significant details that help us determine what the text means, how it applies, and how it can be preached.

The first step in grasping a biblical text is to read it carefully in its original context, looking for as many details as possible. Here we play the role of detective—searching, observing, discerning. Good interpretation takes time and effort. It cannot be short-circuited. At this beginning stage, try to refrain from exploring the implications of what you see. It will take a great deal of patience to read a text thoroughly without moving on to interpretation, application, and communication. Yet spending time just looking carefully at what the text says will pay rich dividends later in the process.

Moreover, we must not become caught in the trap of merely looking only for profound insights or sermon outlines. Instead, we should attempt to see everything we can, regardless of whether it seems significant or insignificant at the time. Later we will tackle the problem of significance and sorting through the details to determine what they mean.

Another important element to keep in mind in this observation stage is to analyze both small and large portions of text. We need to understand the small parts of the text (words, phrases, sentences) in order to understand the larger units (paragraphs, chapters, stories). However, the larger units of text also provide a critical context for understanding the smaller units. So the process requires a bit of both—reading the whole in order to get a general overview and then analyzing the parts in order to understand the nitty-gritty details.

> There is no substitute for reading a text thoroughly and carefully.

So, how do we develop the skill of reading the Bible carefully? It is fairly simple. We must know what to look for, and we must practice. Here are some things to look for in this first stage of observing the text.

- **Repetition of words:** Look for words and phrases that repeat.

   Do not love the *world* or anything in the *world*. If anyone loves the *world*, the love of the Father is not in him. For everything in the *world*—the cravings of sinful man, the lust of his eyes and the boasting of what he has and does—comes not from the Father but from the *world*. The *world* and *its* desires pass away, but the man who does the will of God lives forever. (1 John 2:15–17, italics added in all cases here and below)

- **Contrasts:** Look for ideas, individuals, and/or items that stand in contrast with each other.

   The wages of sin is *death*, but the gift of God is *eternal life* in Christ Jesus our Lord. (Rom. 6:23)

- **Comparisons:** Look for ideas, individuals, and/or items that are compared with each other.

   Like a muddied spring or a polluted well
      is a righteous man who gives way to the wicked.
                                            (Prov. 25:26)

- **Lists:** Any time the text mentions more than two items, identify it as a list.

   But the fruit of the Spirit is love, joy, peace, patience, kindness, goodness, faithfulness, gentleness and self-control.
                                            (Gal. 5:22–23)

- **Cause and effect:** Look for causes and the resulting consequences of those causes.

   For God so loved the world *that* he gave his one and only Son, that whoever believes in him shall not perish but have eternal life. (John 3:16)

- **Figures of speech:** Identify expressions that convey an image using words in a sense other than the normal literal sense.

   Your word is a *lamp* to my feet
      and a *light* for my *path*. (Ps. 119:105)

- **Conjunctions:** Notice terms that join units, like "and," "but," "for." Note what they are connecting.

  For God did not give us a spirit of timidity, *but* a spirit of power, of love *and* of self-discipline. (2 Tim. 1:7)

- **Verbs:** Note tenses, such as past and present, and voice, such as active and passive, etc.

  In him we were also chosen [passive], having been predestined [passive] according to the plan of him who works out [active] everything in conformity with the purpose of his will. (Eph. 1:11)

- **Pronouns:** Identify the antecedent for each pronoun.

  Whatever happens, conduct *yourselves* in a manner worthy of the gospel of Christ. Then, whether *I* come and see *you* or only hear about *you* in *my* absence, *I* will know that *you* stand firm in one spirit, contending as one man for the faith of the gospel without being frightened in any way by *those* who oppose *you*. *This* is a sign to *them* that *they* will be destroyed, but that *you* will be saved—and that by God. For *it* has been granted to *you* on behalf of Christ not only to believe on *him*, but also to suffer for *him*, since *you* are going through the same struggle *you* saw *I* had, and now hear that *I* still have. (Phil. 1:27–30)

- **General ←→ Specific:** Find the general statements that are followed by specific examples or applications of the general. Also find specific statements that are summarized by a general.

  So I say, live by the Spirit, and you will not gratify the desires of the sinful nature. (Gal. 5:16)

Note as well how the specific list of "acts of the sinful nature" in Gal. 5:19–21a is followed by "the fruit of the Spirit" in 5:22–23.

- **Questions and answers:** Note if the text is built on a question/answer format.

Look at the five episodes in Mark 2:1–3:6 that revolve around a question and an answer.[2] Jesus' opponents raise the first four

[2]See J. Scott Duvall and J. Daniel Hays, *Grasping God's Word: A Hand's-On Approach to Reading, Interpreting, and Applying the Bible*, 2nd ed. (Grand Rapids: Zondervan, 2005), 49.

questions and he answers them. Jesus asks the fifth question, but they do not answer him.

Question	Answer
Mark 2:7	Mark 2:10
2:16	2:17b
2:18	2:19
2:24	2:25, 27b
3:4	no answer

• **Dialogue:** Note if the text includes dialogue. Identify who is speaking and to whom.

Consider the serpent's conversation with Eve in Genesis 3 or Jesus' conversation with the Samaritan woman in John 4.

• **Purpose/result statements:** These are a more specific type of "means," often telling "why." Purpose and result are similar and sometimes indistinguishable. In a purpose statement, you usually can insert the phrase "in order that." In a result clause, you usually can insert the phrase "so that."

> You did not choose me, but I chose you and appointed you *to go and bear fruit—fruit that will last.* (John 15:16)

> I have hidden your word in my heart *that I might not sin against you.* (Ps. 119:11)

• **Means:** Note if a sentence indicates that something was done "by means of" someone/something (answers "how?"). Usually you can insert the phrase "by means of" into the sentence.

> How can a young man keep his way pure?
> By living *according to your word.* (Ps. 119:9)

• **Conditional clauses:** A clause can present the condition by which some action or consequence will result. Often such statements use an "if . . . then" framework (although in English the "then" is often left out).

> *If* we confess our sins, [*then*] he is faithful and just and will forgive us our sins and purify us from all unrighteousness.
> (1 John 1:9)

- **Actions/roles of God and actions/roles of people:** Identify actions or roles that the text ascribes to God. Also identify actions or roles that the text ascribes to people or encourages people to do/be.

  > Therefore, my dear friends, as you have always obeyed—not only in my presence, but now much more in my absence—continue to work out your salvation with fear and trembling, for it is God who works in you to will and to act according to his good purpose. (Phil. 2:12–13)

- **Emotional terms:** Does the passage use terms that have emotional energy?

  > I plead with you, brothers, become like me, for I became like you. You have done me no wrong. As you know, it was because of an illness that I first preached the gospel to you. Even though my illness was a trial to you, you did not treat me with contempt or scorn. Instead, you welcomed me as if I were an angel of God, as if I were Christ Jesus himself. What has happened to all your joy? I can testify that, if you could have done so, you would have torn out your eyes and given them to me. Have I now become your enemy by telling you the truth? (Gal. 4:12–16)

- **Tone of the passage:** What is the overall tone of the passage: happy, sad, encouraging, etc.?

  > "O Jerusalem, Jerusalem, you who kill the prophets and stone those sent to you, how often I have longed to gather your children together, as a hen gathers her chicks under her wings, but you were not willing. Look, your house is left to you desolate. For I tell you, you will not see me again until you say, 'Blessed is he who comes in the name of the Lord.'" (Matt. 23:37–39)

- **Connections to other paragraphs and episodes:** How does the passage connect to the one that precedes it and the one that follows it?

  See the example of Mark 4:35–5:43 in chapter 10, ("Preaching the Gospels and Acts").

Observation is the key to grasping the meaning of a text "in their town."

- **Shifts in the story/pivots:** Is the passage an important key to understanding a dramatic shift in the story or passage?

  Notice how Ephesians 4:1 marks a shift from the doctrinal matters of Ephesians 1–3 and the practical commands of Ephesians 4–6.

- **Interchange:** Does the passage shift back and forth between two scenes or characters?

  Notice how Luke uses interchange in the middle of Acts to show the transition between Peter and Paul as the chief human character.

As you can see from this sample list of things to observe, there is much to see in a biblical text. Our list of things to observe could be much longer. At this point, however, we must remember why it is so important to read a passage carefully. What's the point? Our goal here is to determine what the text meant to the biblical audience so that we can eventually determine how that meaning applies to our lives and how we can communicate that message to our audience. Observation is the key to grasping the meaning of a text "in their town." As a result, the Interpretive Journey starts with a thorough reading of the text.

2. Become familiar with the original context (literary and historical-cultural).

Context takes two major forms: literary context and historical-cultural context.

As we circle repeated words, observe contrasts, note emotional terms, and so on, we naturally wonder what it all means. The best way to get answers to those questions is to become familiar with the original context. As linguists will tell you, context determines meaning. For example, even the meaning of the common expression "I love you" depends on the context. Are these the affectionate words of a newly married groom to his bride, the soft words of a little girl to her kitty, or the energized words of a middle-aged man to his new Corvette?

Context takes two major forms: literary context and historical-cultural context (commonly referred to as "background"). *Literary context* relates both to the literary form or genre of your passage (e.g., narrative, law, poetry, prophecy, wisdom, gospel, letter, apocalyptic) and to the surrounding context (i.e., words, sentences, and paragraphs that come before and after your passage).[3] For example, to study the literary context of Romans 12:1–2 you must read the passage as part of a letter (the literary form) and take a close look at what comes before and what comes after these two verses (surrounding context).

What comes **before** your passage
Your passage
What comes **after** your passge

The power of the surrounding context to determine the meaning of your passage cannot be underestimated. Take, for instance, the popular promise found in Jeremiah 29:11: "'For I know the plans I have for you,' declares the LORD, 'plans to prosper you and not to harm you, plans to give you hope and a future.'" Most people are unfamiliar with the surrounding context of this promise (Jer. 29:10–14):

> This is what the LORD says: "When seventy years are completed for Babylon, I will come to you and fulfill my gracious promise to bring you back to this place. *For I know the plans I have for you," declares the LORD, "plans to prosper you and not to harm you, plans to give you hope and a future.* Then you will call upon me and come and pray to me, and I will listen to you. You will seek me and find me when you seek me with all your heart. I will be found by you," declares the LORD, "and will bring you back from captivity. I will gather you from all the nations and places where I have banished you," declares the LORD, "and will bring you back to the place from which I carried you into exile."

The popular understanding of this verse differs noticeably from the meaning communicated by the surrounding context. First, the "you" is not referring to an individual but to a group of people, the people of Israel. Second, God's plans do not follow some tragic accident or unexpected disaster, but God's deliberate discipline of his rebellious people. Later we read that God "banished" his people and "carried them into exile." The expression "seventy years" in the preceding verse refers explicitly to this time of divine discipline. The

[3]For more on why literary form makes a huge difference in how we interpret Scripture, see ibid., 116–17. See also 215–396, where the rules for reading each type of literary form are discussed in detail. For those who use Greek in New Testament exegesis, see George H. Guthrie and J. Scott Duvall, *Biblical Greek Exegesis: A Graded Approach to Learning Intermediate and Advanced Greek* (Grand Rapids: Zondervan, 1998), 113–14, for a discussion of how to identify the limits of the unit you are studying.

meaning of Jeremiah 29:11 in context is that when God's people disobey him and suffer his tough love, his purpose is ultimately redemptive—that is, his long-term intention is not to destroy them but to correct them, so that they will have a future. Context determines meaning.

The second type of context, *historical-cultural context*, is what we commonly refer to as the background of a text (e.g., What was life like for the Israelites as they wandered in the desert? What did the Sadducees believe about the resurrection? Where was Paul when he wrote Colossians?). This involves information about the biblical writer, the biblical audience, and any other historical-cultural elements touched on by the passage itself. In other words, this kind of context relates to just about anything outside the text that will help you understand the text itself. We need to study the historical-cultural context of the Bible because God chose to speak first to ancient peoples living in cultures that are radically different from our own. As we recapture the original context of God's Word, we will be able to grasp its meaning and apply that meaning to our lives.

In order to discover the historical-cultural context of a passage, you need to ask the right questions and then use reliable resources to find the answers. Here is a list of questions to help you become familiar with the background of your book and the specific text you are studying:

- Who was the author?
- What was his background?
- When did he write?
- What was the nature of his ministry?
- What kind of relationship did he have with the audience?
- Why was he writing?
- Who was the biblical audience?
- What were their circumstances?
- What was their relationship to God?
- What do you know about their relationship to the author and to each other?

- What was happening at the time the book was written?
- Are there any other historical-cultural factors that might shed light on the book?
- What specific historical-cultural issues are alluded to in the passage that we need to understand in order to really understand the passage?

To grasp the historical-cultural context of a particular book of the Bible, we first suggest that you read through the entire book containing your passage. The extra time it takes to read the entire book and grasp the big picture will be well worth it. You may want to write down some of your initial impressions about the major themes or emphases of the book as a whole. Whatever conclusions you come to after looking more closely at your passage will need to be consistent with what you see in your overview.

Second, we suggest that you supplement your overview of the book by learning more about the general background of the book (e.g., authorship, date and place of writing, situation, recipients, purpose, structure). The best way to become familiar with these introductory matters is to consult good study Bibles, Bible handbooks, Old and New Testament surveys or introductions, and the introductory portions of Bible commentaries. These resources will help you understand the author, his audience, and the basic message of the book.

Third, to get a better understanding of the specific historical, social, religious, political, and economic elements that shape your passage, take a look at Bible atlases, Bible dictionaries or encyclopedias, Bible commentaries, Bible background commentaries, Old and New Testament histories, and special studies.[4] As with most tools, you can usually locate a relevant discussion by looking up a key word or text in the book's index. Knowing the background of a passage can clarify its meaning and heighten your understanding of its relevance. Take a look at how historical-cultural context informs our understanding of the text in the following examples.

[4]See Duvall and Hays, *Grasping God's Word*, 107–16, for a detailed discussion of these Bible study tools and how to use them.

Have you considered studying Greek or Hebrew for yourself?

Text: Luke 10:30: "A man was going down from Jerusalem to Jericho."

Background: If you go down from Jerusalem to Jericho, you descend from 2,500 feet above sea level to about 800 feet below sea level. The twenty-mile journey takes you through some very rugged desert country that offered plenty of hiding places for thieves waiting to ambush a traveler.

Text: Acts 16:38–39: "The officers reported this [the beating and Paul's complaint] to the magistrates, and when they heard that Paul and Silas were Roman citizens, they were alarmed. They came to appease them and escorted them from the prison, requesting them to leave the city."

Background: It was illegal to publicly beat and imprison a Roman citizen, especially without a trial. The Roman officials acted quickly to apologize and cover their mistake. Paul and Silas demanded an escort out of town in order to make a public statement about their innocence for the benefit of the Philippian church.

Text: 2 Tim. 4:21: [Paul to Timothy] "Do your best to get here before winter."

Background: Paul is imprisoned in Rome awaiting trial as he writes to Timothy, who is leading the church in Ephesus. Travel by ship was dangerous from mid-September through the end of May and was closed from November through February. When Timothy received Paul's letter, he would have had little time to make the long journey to Rome. Paul seems to be saying "Put things in order in Ephesus and get on a ship as soon as you can. If you don't leave now before winter sets in, the shipping lanes will shut down and you won't arrive in time. Timothy, do your best to get here before they put me to death."

These few examples will help you to understand why studying the historical-cultural context of a passage is among the most practical things you can do when it comes to communicating and applying the message of the Bible.

3. Do a more in-depth analysis of the text itself (translation, parsing, structure).

In addition to observing the details of a passage and understanding its literary and historical context, part of "grasping the text in their town" involves doing more in-depth study of the text itself, including consulting secondary sources such as commentaries. We have used some of these resources before, but mainly to discover background information. Now we need their help to nail down the meaning of the text. Some of you are able to use Hebrew and Greek as you study the Bible, while others have yet to learn the original languages of Scripture. In the following section, we will try to mention resources that apply to both groups.

As you dig deeper into your passage, we recommend that you translate your passage from the original languages. If you are proficient in the biblical languages, now is the time to do the text-critical work, parse the key words,[5] and translate the passage. If you are limited to English in your study of the Bible, we recommend that you begin by comparing modern English translations to pinpoint the major exegetical difficulties.[6] Whenever translations differ considerably, this is a sure sign that exegetical difficulties lie buried beneath those differences. As you consult the commentaries, make sure that you read the treatment of those sections carefully. Also, when a commentator parses a word (e.g., describes the kind of word it is and the particular form it takes), pay attention to his or her explanation of the significance of this word form.[7]

Now that you have translated the passage and parsed the key words, you need to analyze the structure of the passage and determine how the words relate to each other (syntax). Grammatical and semantic diagramming will prove useful for helping you comprehend the structure of the passage.[8] (If you are working in English, you are much better off using a formal translation such as the New American Standard Version, English Standard Version, or Holman Christian Standard Version for your diagram.) The grammatical diagram of Romans 8:10 below clarifies the relationships between words, phrases, clauses, and sentences within this passage, while the semantic diagram captures how those grammatical relationships convey meaning.

[5]For help with translation and parsing New Testament texts, see William D. Mounce, *The Analytical Lexicon to the Greek New Testament* (Grand Rapids: Zondervan, 1993), and Cleon L. Rogers Jr. and Cleon L. Rogers III, *A New Linguistic and Exegetical Key to the Greek New Testament* (Grand Rapids: Zondervan, 1998).

[6]To make it easier to compare English translations in the New Testament, see John R. Kohlenberger III, ed., *The Evangelical Parallel New Testament* (Oxford: Oxford Univ. Press, 2003), or idem, *The Precise Parallel New Testament* (Oxford: Oxford Univ. Press, 1995).

[7]We believe that knowing just a little Hebrew or Greek is sometimes more dangerous than knowing no Hebrew or Greek at all. If you know only a bit about the biblical languages, you are much better off taking the advice of reliable experts found in respectable commentaries rather than drawing premature conclusions. For example, a lot has changed in the last twenty years with respect to our understanding of Greek verb tense. Those not familiar with these discussions could make some costly blunders in their preaching (e.g., assuming that the aorist tense always refers to past time).

[8]For diagramming in Greek, see Guthrie and Duvall, *Biblical Greek Exegesis*, 27–53, 122–28. For diagramming or "phrasing" in English, see William D. Mounce, *Greek for the Rest of Us: Mastering Bible Study without Mastering the Biblical Languages* (Grand Rapids: Zondervan, 2003), 55–79, 109–41.

Grammatical

conjunction →	But
conditional clause →	if Christ is in you,
main clause →	although the body is dead
prepositional phrase →	because of sin,
conjunction →	yet
main clause →	the Spirit is life
prepositional phrase →	because of righteousness.

Semantic

contrast with Rom. 8:9b →	But
basis (condition assumed true) →	if (since) Christ is in you,
concession "although" →	although the body is dead
reason for death →	because of sin,
contrast with concession →	yet
main truth →	the Spirit is life
reason for life →	because of righteousness.

4. Consult commentaries.

Probably the best time to consult commentaries is while you are analyzing the structure and syntax of a passage. For example, we learn the following about the grammar and syntax of Romans 8:10 from Doug Moo's commentary on Romans.[9] While you don't have to know Greek to understand these observations, you may need to brush up on your English grammar.

[9]Douglas Moo, *The Epistle to the Romans* (NICNT; Grand Rapids: Eerdmans, 1996), 492–93.

- The word "if" indicates a fulfilled condition as Paul assumes the reality of the Christian experience for his readers (i.e., "since").
- The first clause has a concessive idea ("although") with the main point coming in the second clause.
- The word "spirit" here probably refers to Holy Spirit rather than to human spirit.
- Christ indwells each believer since the "you" in the first clause is singular.

- The expression "because of sin" provides the reason for the deadness of the body, while the phrase "because of righteousness" explains why the Christian experiences deliverance from condemnation now and the future promise of resurrection life.

Commentaries can also prove helpful when checking the meaning of particular words.[10] The last step in the more comprehensive process is to check your work by consulting the standard word-study resources.[11] Some commentaries also fill this role when they discuss the meaning of words in the context of the flow of the entire book. For example, note the rich understanding of the term "body" in Romans 8:10 that Moo provides:

> In the first clause, "body" (*sōma*) might refer to the "person" as a whole, dead "with reference to" sin, in the sense of Rom. 6— that is, that the person has "died to," been freed from, the dominion of sin. But it is better to think of the body's "deadness" here as a negative condition, the state of condemnation—a condition that has come about "because of sin." And the "body" is probably the physical body specifically, its deadness consisting in the penalty of physical death that must still be experienced by the believer.[12]

Moo supports his conclusion by appealing to the context and Greek grammar (discussed briefly in a footnote). Since Moo's discussion of "body" is rooted in the context of Paul's argument in Romans, it actually goes beyond the standard word study resources.

Reliable commentaries are valuable tools that provide expert advice on just about every aspect of a passage—background, context, grammar, syntax, word studies, theology, and contemporary application. Because all commentaries are written from a particular point of view and since they differ in quality and scope, it is always a good idea to consult several and not just one. We recommend the following series as a reliable place to find good commentaries. There are certainly other fine commentaries (and some are not attached to a series), but this is a good place to start.[13]

Baker Exegetical Commentary. Grand Rapids: Baker.
Bible Speaks Today. Downers Grove, IL: InterVarsity Press.

Commentaries can be valuable tools. Learn how to use them well!

---

[10]You can learn how to do in-depth word studies by reading ch. 8 in Duvall and Hays, *Grasping God's Word*.

[11]For word studies in the Old Testament, see Ernst Jenni and Claus Westermann, eds., *Theological Lexicon of the Old Testament* (Peabody, MA: Hendrickson, 1997), and William VanGemeren, gen. ed., *New International Dictionary of Old Testament Theology and Exegesis* (Grand Rapids: Zondervan, 1997). For word studies in the New Testament, see Horst Balz and Gerhard Schneider, eds., *Exegetical Dictionary of the New Testament* (Grand Rapids: Eerdmans, 1993), and Verlyn D. Verbrugge, ed., *The New International Dictionary of New Testament Theology: Abridged Edition* (Grand Rapids: Zondervan, 2000).

[12]Moo, *Romans*, 491.

[13]See Duvall and Hays, *Grasping God's Word*, appendix, for commentary recommendations on every book of the Bible.

Expositor's Bible Commentary. Grand Rapids: Zondervan.

IVP New Testament Commentary. Downers Grove, IL: InterVarsity Press.

New American Commentary. Nashville: Broadman & Holman.

New International Commentary on the New Testament. Grand Rapids: Eerdmans.

New International Commentary on the Old Testament. Grand Rapids: Eerdmans.

NIV Application Commentary. Grand Rapids: Zondervan.

Pillar New Testament Commentaries. Grand Rapids: Eerdmans.

Preaching the Word. Wheaton, IL: Crossway.

Tyndale New Testament Commentaries. Grand Rapids: Eerdmans.

Tyndale Old Testament Commentaries. Downers Grove, IL: InterVarsity Press.

In addition, consider the following guidelines for choosing commentaries that are worth purchasing for your personal library:[14]

- Give preference to individual volumes rather than to entire series. Even though we recommend the above series, some of those volumes are stronger (or weaker) than others. Avoid old commentaries that you can buy at a bargain price (e.g., Matthew Henry).
- Survey the entire commentary to get a feel for level of detail and target audience. You can tell a lot by looking at the table of contents, the footnotes or endnotes, the bibliography, and the index. This is the time to make an educated guess about whether this commentary will meet your expectations.
- Check out how the commentary treats a small section of text that you have studied and preached recently. Does the author treat the difficult issues or skip over them? Does the commentator evaluate several interpretive options? Do they support their conclusions with sound reasons?
- Get advice from people you respect.

[14]For additional help on choosing and using commentaries, see D. A. Carson, *New Testament Commentary Survey*, 5th ed. (Grand Rapids: Baker, 2001); John Glynn, *Commentary & Reference Survey: A Comprehensive Guide to Biblical and Theological Resources*, 9th ed. (Grand Rapids: Kregel, 2003); Tremper Longman, *Old Testament Commentary Survey*, 3rd ed. (Grand Rapids: Baker, 2003). Every pastor should read "What Commentaries Are and Are Not" in Douglas Stuart, *Guide to Selecting and Using Commentaries* (Dallas: Word, 1990), 7–21.

To summarize, the first step of the Interpretive Journey consists of observing the details of a passage, understanding its literary and historical-cultural context, translating your passage (or comparing English translations), doing a more in-depth analysis of the passage, and consulting the commentaries to check your work and make decisions related to exegetical difficulties. The goal has been to grasp the meaning of the text for the biblical audience.

> *"Text thesis statement": a brief statement of what the text meant to the biblical audience*

To make sure that you understand the meaning of the text "in their town," we encourage you to synthesize the meaning of the passage for the biblical audience into one or two sentences, which we call the *text thesis statement*. In other words, simply write out what the passage meant for the biblical audience. Use past tense verbs and refer to the biblical audience (e.g., "God commanded the Israelites in Joshua 1 to ..." or "Paul exhorted the Ephesians to ..." or "Jesus encouraged his disciples by ..."). Be specific and avoid moving from the ancient world to the contemporary world for now. That is the goal of the next three steps.

Measure the Width of the River

In the second step of the Interpretive Journey, ask: "What are the differences and similarities between the biblical audience and us?" The Christian today is separated from the biblical audience by differences in culture, language, situation, time, and often covenant. This river of differences hinders us from connecting the original meaning directly to our situation. The width of the river, however, varies from passage to passage. Sometimes it is extremely wide, requiring an enormous bridge to cross. For example, the river is wide and deep in Leviticus 5:2–6, where we read about atoning for personal sin by sacrificing a lamb or goat as a sin offering. At other times, however, the "river" is only a narrow creek that we can easily hop over, such as when Paul commands the Ephesians in Ephesians 4:2 to "be patient, bearing with one another in love."

If you are studying an Old Testament passage, be sure to identify those significant theological differences that came as a result of the new covenant in Jesus Christ. For example, in Joshua 1:1–9, the people of Israel are preparing to enter the Promised Land. Moses has just died and Joshua has just been appointed to take his place. In this passage, God speaks to Joshua to encourage him to be strong and faithful in the upcoming conquest of the land. How does our situation differ from theirs? We are not entering or conquering the Promised Land. We are not the new leaders of the nation of Israel. We are not under the old covenant.

Yet, in spite of the differences, there are similarities to contemporary situations. We are not members of national Israel, but we are God's people because of the new covenant. While we are not the leaders of Israel, many of us are in leadership positions in the church. No, we are not invading the Promised Land, but we are seeking to obey God's will and to accomplish what he has commanded us to do. We need to identify differences and similarities between the ancient and contemporary audiences before we decide what the passage means to us. By measuring the width of the river, we establish boundaries that will frame and outline the theological principles of the passage.

Cross the Principlizing Bridge

Crossing the bridge poses the greatest challenge but also promises the greatest reward to the interpreter because here we cross from the ancient world to our world. The theological principle reflected in the meaning of the text allows us to cross from the biblical world to our world. Remember, this theological principle is tied to *meaning*. Our job is not to create the meaning but to discover the meaning intended by the author. As God gives specific expressions to specific biblical audiences, he is also giving universal teachings for all of his people through these same texts. Try to identify the timeless theological truths reflected in the text by writing out a present-tense statement summarizing what the text means. Then ask the following questions to determine whether your statement is truly a theological principle:

- Is the principle strongly tied to and reflected in the biblical text?
- Is the principle timeless and universal or is it attached to a particular situation?

- Is the principle transcultural or is it bound to only one specific culture?
- Is the principle harmonious with teachings of the rest of Scripture?
- Is the principle congruent with the similarities and differences between the two audiences?
- Is the principle relevant to both the biblical and contemporary audience?

Here are a few examples of theological principles:

Text: Jeremiah 29:11: "'For I know the plans I have for you,' declares the LORD, 'plans to prosper you and not to harm you, plans to give you hope and a future.'"

Theological principle: When God's people disobey him and encounter his loving discipline, they should know that his purpose is not to destroy them but to correct them so that they will have a future.

Text: Leviticus 5:2, 5–6: "Or if a person touches anything ceremonially unclean—whether the carcasses of unclean wild animals or of unclean livestock or of unclean creatures that move along the ground—even though he is unaware of it, he has become unclean and is guilty.... When anyone is guilty in any of these ways, he must confess in what way he has sinned and, as a penalty for the sin he has committed, he must bring to the LORD a female lamb or goat from the flock as a sin offering; and the priest shall make atonement for him for his sin."

Theological principle: God is holy, and his holiness demands that his people separate from unclean things. If they fail and become unclean, they must be purified by a blood sacrifice.

Text: Revelation 12:11: "They overcame him by the blood of the Lamb and by the word of their testimony; they did not love their lives so much as to shrink from death."

Theological principle: Christians can overcome Satan by living and proclaiming the gospel of Jesus Christ faithfully.

Remember that when interpreting Old Testament passages, we must add the step of crossing into the New Testament and asking how this principle is modified or qualified by the new covenant in Jesus

Christ. For example, when we cross into the New Testament with the principle from Leviticus 5 (see above), we notice that God no longer requires animal sacrifices to atone for sins because our sins are covered by the once-for-all sacrifice of Jesus Christ, the Lamb of God. God still demands holiness, but he expects us to rely on Christ's sacrifice rather than that of a goat or lamb. As a result, we must rephrase the theological principle in light of the New Testament—God is holy and expects us to stay away from sinful actions and impure thoughts. If we do sin, we must then confess this sin (1 John 1:9) and receive forgiveness through the blood of Jesus Christ.

This might be a good place to consider how your passage relates to the broader biblical and theological contexts. What are the true biblical parallels to your passage? You can find reliable parallels by looking at the cross references in a good study Bible, in the commentaries, in the Hebrew Old Testament, or in the Greek New Testament. Remember, you are looking for biblical parallels to the teaching or theology of the passage and not just to a single word found in the text or to a common topic. Pay attention to the context of the parallel texts and try to see how these parallels impact your understanding of the text you are studying.

You will also want to examine how the principles of your text fit into the broader arena of Christian theology. The best approach here is to look in the indexes of major works of theology to find relevant discussions.[15] Your aim here is to see how the theological principles in your passage relate to the whole of Christian theology.

Grasp the Text in Our Town[16]

In this fourth step we apply the theological principle to the specific circumstances of present-day Christians. Certainly we should apply the biblical text rather than leaving it stranded in the abstract, but application can be a tricky exercise.

We begin by noting the difference between *meaning* and *application*. The *meaning* of the text as reflected in its theological principle(s) does not change from reader to reader, but remains the same

[15]See, e.g., Millard J. Erickson, *Christian Theology*, 2nd ed. (Grand Rapids: Baker, 1998); James Leo Garrett, *Systematic Theology*, 2 vols. (Grand Rapids: Eerdmans, 1990, 1995); Stanley J. Grenz, *Theology for the Community of God* (Grand Rapids: Eerdmans, 2000); Wayne Grudem, *Systematic Theology: An Introduction to Bible Doctrine* (Grand Rapids: Zondervan, 1995).

[16]See Duvall and Hays, *Grasping God's Word*, ch. 13, for an extended discussion of the application process.

for all. This is because the meaning of a text is tied to what the author intended to communicate through the text. *Application*, by contrast, will vary from person to person because readers respond to the meaning of the text in various ways, depending on their current life situation and where they are in their relationship with God. Therefore, we should ask, "What does this passage mean and how do I apply this meaning to my life?" rather than, "What does this passage mean to me?" While this distinction between meaning and application may appear subjective and even picky, it does get to the heart of how we interpret the Bible.[17]

The process of applying a biblical text involves three phases. (1) Observe the key elements of how the theological principles in the text address the original historical-cultural situation. As you look carefully at the intersection between the theological principle in the text and the original situation, several key elements will emerge. In the Jeremiah 29:11 example as noted above, we see the following key elements:

- Element 1: A message is for the people of God.
- Element 2: A message is for God's people when they have deliberately disobeyed God and are experiencing his loving discipline.
- Element 3: God's promise of a future is for his disobedient people after they have been disciplined.

Think of a parallel situation in a contemporary context that includes all those same key elements.

(2) A situation is not really a parallel situation unless it includes all the key elements. The biggest mistake that people make when approaching Jeremiah 29:11, for example, is ignoring the second key element (i.e., people are encountering God's discipline because of their deliberate disobedience). When this element is ignored, the promise of Jeremiah 29:11 can be applied to all sorts of situations that go far beyond the intent of the author. When we move beyond the intent of the author, we put words in God's mouth and attempt to apply something that God never said. In Jeremiah 29:11 God is not promising a six-figure income or claiming responsibility for causing

We should ask, "What does this passage mean and how do I apply this meaning to my life?" rather than, "What does this passage mean to me?"

[17]For a deeper discussion on whether the author or the reader determines the meaning of a biblical text, see ibid., ch. 10.

A parallel situation must contain all the key elements.

an accident for some greater good. Rather, he is promising to restore his people after they have been disciplined for rebellion. Since many of us disobey God and find ourselves under his hand of discipline, we should not have a hard time finding a parallel situation.

(3) Make your applications specific. All the complaints about the Bible not being relevant come to a screeching halt here. At this point the Bible can become painfully relevant as we come face to face with what God says and how we are going to respond. The key here is to think of *specific* ways that the theological principles apply to the parallel situation. How should people think differently as a result of this text? What particular actions should people take? People not only need to know what to do, they also need to know how to do it. They need precise steps to take or specific examples to follow as they seek to live out these new beliefs and behaviors. We should make our applications specific so that people will know how the Bible applies to real life.

An Example—Hebrews 12:1–2

Most people need an illustration or example in order to understand clearly how the interpretive process works. Let's take Hebrews 12:1–2 through the four steps of the Interpretive Journey in order to clarify how the process works. The passage is as follows:

> Therefore, since we are surrounded by such a great cloud of witnesses, let us throw off everything that hinders and the sin that so easily entangles, and let us run with perseverance the race marked out for us. Let us fix our eyes on Jesus, the author and perfecter of our faith, who for the joy set before him endured the cross, scorning its shame, and sat down at the right hand of the throne of God.

Step 1. Grasp the text in their town. What did the text mean to the biblical audience?

1. Begin by reading the text carefully in its original context. Conduct a detailed observation of the text noting important words, lists, contrasts, comparisons, pronouns, purpose statements, figures of speech, conjunctions, emotional terms, "if-then" statements, and so on.

2. Identify the literary context of the passage. This entails noting the literary form of the passage as well as becoming familiar with what comes before and what comes after the passage (i.e., the surrounding context).

3. Use atlases, Bible dictionaries, background commentaries, and other resources to get a feel for the historical-cultural context.

4. Do more in-depth study of the passage (e.g., translation, grammar, syntax, word studies, and theology).

5. Finally, synthesize the meaning of the passage for the biblical audience into short statements, using past tense verbs.

The author of Hebrews uses the image of a long-distance race to challenge his audience to persevere in their commitment to Christ in spite of opposition. Rather than drifting away from Christ and reverting to Judaism, they needed to run the race with endurance, drawing inspiration from saints who had already endured, and to focus on Jesus, the ultimate example of perseverance under pressure.

Step 2. Measure the width of the river to cross. What are the differences and similarities between the biblical audience and us?

Most of us do not face the same level of persecution faced by the biblical audience, nor are most of us tempted to revert to Judaism in order to avoid opposition. But we do share several things in common. As Christians living after the death and resurrection of Christ in the midst of a hostile world, we too find ourselves in a long-distance race struggling to endure. We too have a wealth of faithful examples who have gone before, and we too will encounter temptation to unite with a more "acceptable" religious belief (e.g., pluralism) in order to avoid trouble.

Step 3. Cross the principlizing bridge. What is the theological principle in this text?

There are several significant theological principles found in Hebrews 12:1–2:

- The Christian life is like a difficult long-distance race, which requires both effort and endurance.
- The saints who have gone before supply us with valuable examples of endurance. We should look to them for inspiration and encouragement.
- To run the race successfully, we must reject things in life that hinder our progress, and, most importantly, focus on Jesus and our relationship with him.

Step 4. Grasp the text in our town. How should individual Christians today apply the theological principle in their lives?

There are numerous possible applications for each of the three principles mentioned above. Remember that while the meaning of the text is the same for all Christians at all times, the Holy Spirit will often lead individual Christians to apply the same meaning in a variety of ways.

Let's look more closely at the first principle: "The Christian life is like a difficult long-distance race, which requires both effort and endurance." What key elements emerge from the intersection between the theological principle and the original situation of the biblical audience? There are several:

- The runners are Christians and the race itself is life.
- The race is difficult, and we are tempted to take an easier route or even quit.
- Running a successful race requires both effort and endurance.

You will not have trouble finding a present-day situation that parallels the original situation (i.e., contains all the key elements). Any situation in which Christians are tempted to give up because they find it difficult to stay faithful to Christ in the face of worldly opposition will serve as a parallel situation. Once the parallel situation is identified, you need to make your application specific; this will depend a great deal on the person or group hearing the message. Here are a few suggestions about making your application specific:

- The youth group needs to hear that life is more like a marathon than a sprint. Perhaps this will entail a mission project to the same location for several years to give the students a sense of the long-term nature of the Christian walk.
- The newly married couple needs encouragement from Christian couples who have been married for twenty or thirty years about the need to endure as faithful partners even when life gets tough. Perhaps the mature couples could talk about situations where they were tempted to quit the faith and the marriage, and what helped them in such situations.
- The single college student needs encouragement to live a disciplined life, throwing off damaging habits and pursuing Jesus Christ wholeheartedly.

Summary

Preachers committed to God's Word and their congregations want to be both biblical and relevant. In order to be a "both-and" kind of communicator, the starting point is your own approach to Scripture. We have compared the process of reading, interpreting, and applying the Bible to going on a journey. Your journey begins in the town of the biblical audience as you attempt to grasp the meaning of the text for them. You do this by studying the text carefully in its original context. You compare translations, map out structure, study words, read commentaries, and do a host of other things as you seek to understand the meaning of the text for the biblical audience.

Next, you take into account the differences separating the biblical audience and the contemporary audience. You cross this "river of differences" using the bridge of theological principles. If you are interpreting an Old Testament text, you must remember to add the step of asking how the new covenant in Jesus Christ modifies or qualifies this principle.

Finally, you seek to apply the theological principle to the specific situations of Christians today. You observe key elements of intersection between the original situation and the theological principles.

You think of a parallel situation in our day that includes all those same key elements, and you make your applications specific. Whereas the meaning of a text is the same for all Christians, application will vary from person to person.

Biblical preaching begins with responsible biblical interpretation, a task that requires both time and effort. The outcome, however, makes it all worthwhile—we have the privilege of offering a healing, powerful, truthful word from God that will meet the deepest needs of our listeners.

Review Questions and Assignments

1. Why is biblical interpretation crucial to biblical preaching?
2. What are some ways that people attempt to cross the river of differences?
3. Describe the four steps of the Interpretive Journey.
4. What are the guidelines for developing and validating theological principles?
5. Describe the difference between meaning and application and explain the process for applying Scripture.

Preaching the Meaning in Their Town

3

The Preacher Grasps God's Word
From the Study to the Sermon
Summary
Review Questions and Assignments

THE FOCUS OF CHAPTER 3:

Step 1	Grasp the Meaning of the Text in Their Town
Step 2	Measure the Width of the Interpretive River
Step 3	Cross the Principlizing Bridge
Step 4	Grasp the Text in Our Town
Step 5	Exegete Your Congregation
Step 6	Determine How Much Background Material to Include
Step 7	Determine the Sermon Thesis and Main Points
Step 8	Develop Text-Centered Applications
Step 9	Find Illustrations
Step 10	Write Out the Sermon and Practice Delivery

I recently read a book on the lives of two of golf's greatest players, Harry Vardon and Francis Ouimet—men who helped make the game great. One grew up in poverty on the American east coast and the other in poverty on the island of Jersey in Great Britain. The book fascinated me not only because of my love for the game but also because the author helped me interpret the lives of these men by setting the unlikely and unusual context out of which grew their ability to excel in golf. Life in their time differed greatly from ours, and as I understood their situation, language, and equipment for the game compared to now, I saw them in a new light. Their equipment consisted of golf clubs made of hickory sticks and metal as well as golf balls made of rubber, feathers, and various skins. Nevertheless they could hit a golf ball farther than I can with my modern clubs.

Both men initially were kept from this elite game because of social status, except in the role of caddie. Virtually no breaks came their way except those they made themselves. They entered and stayed in golf as survivors and trailblazers. Without the information about context, history, and personal circumstances that the author so effectively wove into the storyline, I would have completely missed the power and passion of the story. In fact, all good storytelling demands some "filling in of the gaps" with story material to make it live for the listener.

Preaching consists of telling God's story. Because of the varying circumstances, language, and culture of the biblical times, it requires the same weaving of pertinent data from their circumstances to help your people understand the full story. In this chapter we consider what information to include in your sermons to make that story come alive. The kind of information we refer to here is "their town," which includes context, history, and the culture of the time. How much of this needs to be in your sermon? Where do you start with this information?

The Preacher Grasps God's Word

As you prepare a message, you undoubtedly acquire much more information on the passage you have chosen than will ever actually make it into the sermon. Why should you do this? Because short-circuiting your study can lead to disastrous results. Those who take shortcuts through the exegesis process limit their ability to fully grasp the text. The old adage is certainly true: "If there is a mist in the preacher's mind, there will be a fog in the congregation's."

As we argued in the previous chapter, it is imperative that preachers do thorough exegesis as a foundational step in their sermon preparation. A critical step in exegesis is grasping what the text meant to the original audience. If you skip this step, you will most likely misunderstand the biblical meaning; how then can you hope to communicate that meaning accurately and powerfully to your audience?

As I traveled back from a preaching engagement recently, I turned on the radio and caught a preacher dealing with the book of

Revelation. He said many things about this difficult book, but one thing stood out. His sermon consisted of attempting to explain the "secret codes" he found in the book, but he himself apparently didn't really understand the book of Revelation and also didn't have the details and background to communicate it correctly to his audience. Surely you want to do better.

"Their town" information includes context, history, and the culture of the time.

What kind of information are we talking about? Proper exegesis uncovers a great amount of material dealing with grammar, syntax, word meanings, historical background, theological issues, and contextual information, all of which help us understand what the inspired biblical writers were trying to say to the biblical audience. We call it the "their town" information because the original audience would have known or quickly perceived this pertinent material as they received the message. It communicated to them.

Even though much of this information never makes it into your sermon, you need it for your own knowledge and depth of understanding of the text. Good biblical preaching only occurs when you personally grasp the full meaning of God's Word. Guard against a "poor student mentality," which functions under the assumption that if it is not going to be "on the test" (in your case in the sermon), then why worry about it? Be a good student of the Scriptures in order to be a good preacher of truth. Look at chapter 2 again to review the more detailed instructions on how to find this information.

From the Study to the Sermon

After completing a thorough exegesis, you must now decide how much of this mass of exegetical material should reach the people in the pew. Although it is impossible to specify exactly what should or should not be mentioned in every sermon, we offer some basic guidelines here. First, ask a key question: How much of "their town" data does your audience need to know to really understand the passage's meaning? That is, how much of the "then" should you share to help them get the "now" meaning and see the connection? If your audience does not make the connection between the exegetical meaning

"Their town" information can make your sermon more interesting.

in the text and the applicational meaning you are proclaiming to them, your message loses its tie to biblical authority.

Much of the historical data you uncover during exegesis will undoubtedly interest your audience. Occasionally you may simply include information in a sermon just because it is interesting and will help to engage the mind of the audience with the text. But take care here because what is interesting to you, the preacher, is not always interesting to everyone. As we will discuss in chapter 4 ("Exegeting the Audience"), knowing the biblical knowledge level and spiritual maturity level of your congregation assists you in deciding how much and which historical material will be of interest to them.

Church people who have read and studied the Bible for years may enjoy some detailed historical background. They like to learn new things and expand their biblical knowledge. Newer believers, however, often struggle to grasp more basic concepts and may bore quickly with historical background explanations. Likewise, the "ivory tower issues" that theologians wrangle with evoke little interest with the layperson and should be avoided. Think more of the audience than of self. Yet without doubt, some "their town" information makes your sermons interesting and edifying to most people.

Look at some of the most popular television programs in the last several years. Shows built around the theme of forensic science, with ballistic and medical details scattered throughout, have gained a near cult following. Sometimes the same kind of details fit well into a sermon. For example, when dealing with a sermon on hope found in hopeless situations based on the stories found in Luke 5:12–26, you might include medical information on the types and seriousness of leprosy and paralysis to indicate the hopelessness felt by the main characters. This information gathered in the exegesis aids the communication of the message. So we will take some time to look at the varieties of "their town" details to be considered and perhaps included in the sermon for better preaching.

Cultural Language

Every culture contains certain expressions, ideas, and ways of communicating that are unique to that culture in that time. People who have tried to preach in other languages and other places quickly discover that reality. Just trying to give a word-for-word translation of certain phrases can result in an embarrassing moment. Words put together to form idioms often mean something completely different from the meaning of those same words taken literally.

This reality holds true for the biblical world and text as well. Explaining cultural-bound language, idioms, and parables is essential for a preacher dealing with a twenty-first-century audience. For example, Jesus frequently used hyperbole, a standard rhetorical technique recognized by the culture of his day. However, audiences today may misunderstand his use of hyperbole. For instance, Jesus states that we must "hate" our father, mother, wife, and children to be his disciples (Luke 14:26). Your listeners would question anyone using such language to make a point today. Imagine saying that to a non-Christian in your town. Even Jesus' disciples may have been shocked, but they undoubtedly recognized such language as a common rhetorical tool for making a point in their day. Explain in the sermon that Jesus was the consummate rabbi (teacher) who used exaggeration often and effectively to teach truth.

Scripture contains several other examples of hyperbole in Jesus' teaching (e.g., if your hand causes you to sin, cut it off). Explaining this rabbinic tendency helps your people see the emphasis Jesus intended in the exaggeration.

Historical Setting

Knowing the historical setting of a prophetic text like Jeremiah 29 (Jeremiah's letter to the exiles in Babylon) is essential for listeners to grasp God's revealed truth from this passage. What was happening then? Why did Jeremiah say what he said? How would the captives understand this letter? If you ignore questions such as these and just talk about what the words of the letter mean today, you risk missing the real force of the passage.

Jeremiah's letter, written over 2,500 years ago, was addressed to a certain people in a certain situation for a certain purpose. Failure to consider the context of that letter can lead the audience to miss proper application of an often-quoted passage, Jeremiah 29:11, thinking that this promise applies to any situation in which we find ourselves. Moreover, failure to discuss important background information to Jeremiah 29 also misses an opportunity to teach your people an important part of the biblical story. In this age of biblical illiteracy, preachers owe it to audiences to take every opportunity to help them learn more about the biblical story.

Thus, in a sermon on Jeremiah 29:1–14 it is important to include an overview of the historical setting. Provide a sketch of the conflict between Babylon and Judah that led to the taking of captives in 597 B.C. Describe the conditions in Babylon for the captives and their desire to return home. Explain to the audience about the false prophets who were telling the captives that God would not leave them long in captivity but that they would soon be returning home. This entire background overview can be done in only a paragraph of the sermon, but such information gives your listeners a proper understanding of Jeremiah's purpose and intent in the letter. As you preach "their town" material, share it in story form and not bullet outline form:

> Jeremiah faced a difficult situation. He wrote to his people who were captives while he himself remained free. They misunderstood the reason and extent of their captivity. They were taken because of God's judgment on them as a result of their sin, and Jeremiah had to tell them the truth. The captivity would last longer, but God would not forget them.

After setting the proper context, explain the content of Jeremiah's letter. The prophet sought to correct the misinformation of the false prophets. In contrast to those prophets, he proclaimed that the stay of the exiles in Babylon would last seventy years (an entire lifetime!). The long exile was not because God had forgotten them, Jeremiah points out, but rather because this discipline was part of God's good plan for them.

As we noted in the previous chapter, this historical context will help in the application portion of the sermon. We as Christians sometimes find ourselves in painful situations because of our rebellion and defiance against God. Sometimes we need to hear that God has not forgotten us regardless of the duration of our difficulty. He still guides and takes us through difficult times as we learn from the experience. Therefore, we feel encouraged to live life and trust God. This message and its application lack clarity and power apart from the historical context.

The message and its application lack clarity and power apart from the historical context.

Theological Context

Have you ever heard a sermon from the book of Job? This story deals with a man, his difficulties, and some intrusive friends with their own ideas about the theological background of Job's troubles. Did the preacher make that clear? How should this book be preached for maximum effect on the audience? Often a biblical passage is couched in a certain theological setting and context, which is the case with Job. A clear grasp of the overall theology of this book is crucial to understanding correctly the smaller passages being preached within the book.

Job, through no fault of his own, lost practically everything he had. His "friends," however, interpreted those tragic events according to the standard retributive theology of the day. They believed that good things happened to good people and bad things happened to bad people. They saw all reward and punishment as a "this life" event. As a result, Job's friends interpreted his troubles as the consequence of his sin. To them God was clearly punishing Job. In spite of Job's denials, his friends stressed again and again his need for repentance. Their theological preconceptions precluded any other interpretation of the events.

As you preach from a text that involves one of Job's friends, you must share those concepts with your congregation. These few lines explaining theological context will strengthen your audience's comprehension. Your listeners probably know people who have expressed similar beliefs during times of tragedy. Even some church members think all bad things must somehow be part of God's punishment or a reflection of God's will. As in Job's case, this belief does not always match reality. As God eventually pointed out, Job's friends were wrong. Tell your people this as you preach to them. It takes little time in the sermon to share this information, but the rewards in terms of communication are well worth it.

Biblical Language

When speaking with my wife about my attendance at dinner, the words I use count. If I say *I may be* home for dinner, the phrase leaves some doubt in her mind, and as a result she puts less effort into the meal. If I say *I will be* home for dinner, she expects me to be there. Word usage counts because it changes meaning.

This is also true in Scripture. Making the grammatical details clear becomes part of the preaching process. Sometimes there are important grammatical or semantic details in the biblical text that belong in a sermon. When necessary, present these explanations briefly and in a nontechnical way. For example, it is illuminating to point out how often a word or phrase is repeated in a passage. Don't shy away from sharing such details if the repetition indicates an important emphasis in the text.

What about the tense of a verb used in a sentence? Does it convey a special idea? Include a short, simple explanation when warranted. But be careful! Never get into an extended Greek or Hebrew lesson just to make a minor point or to impress everyone. Be sure you are illuminating an aspect of the passage that is important to the meaning. Then select an unpretentious way of communicating the information and quickly show its relevance. For example, an explanation of a verb tense in a sermon on 1 Timothy 4:16 might be: "The word 'watch' in this text is a present tense command and carries the idea of an ongoing, continuous action, implying that this is something that we should do continuously or constantly."

Likewise, share word meanings in your sermons to show how the original recipients would have perceived a particular word. What did this word mean in their world? Did it have multiple meanings? Your people will miss the meaning of a passage if the biblical words are misunderstood. Remember, you are preaching from a translation of the original text to people who don't speak or understand the biblical language. Different translations render meanings differently, often causing confusion and producing questions in the minds of your listeners. Surely a few lines of word meaning explanation in the sermon are justified and usually result in better understanding and, over a period of time, a better-educated congregation.

Let's look at Matthew 5:43–48 as an example. You may need to explain several words in this passage to allow your audience to grasp the force of the contrast Jesus underscores. For instance, in verse 47 Jesus states, "And if you greet only your brothers, what are you doing *more* than others?" The word translated "more" is a strong word, meaning "beyond, above or extraordinary."[1] Jesus expects his followers to go beyond unbelievers in the way they treat people. He commands us to be extraordinary in our actions compared to unbelievers. Define this word for your audience to help them see this.

That same passage ends with a more astounding command: "Be perfect, therefore, as your heavenly Father is perfect." At first glance this command seems impossible for believers to accomplish. Did the original audience understand the word translated "perfect" in a different way? Tell your listeners it can mean "perfect," but it also carries the idea of "completeness" or "needing nothing to be complete." It suggests something brought to its intended end or full growth.[2] Thus, the word translated "perfect" indicates more of a goal for believers than an immediate reality. This kind of information enlightens the congregation and makes application more possible. Your congregation will appreciate such "their town" information in a sermon. In fact, you may see in their eyes a first-time realization of the meaning of a passage.

Sometimes these explanations of grammar get a little more complicated. For instance, the Greek language includes several different types (identified by grammatical form) of conditional clauses. Often the meaning of a New Testament passage is much easier for audiences to grasp clearly if the specific type of Greek conditional clause is explained. Without any explanation, your audience assumes that the conditional term "if" introduces a regular English conditional clause, one that has no textual indicators as to whether the one who states it believes the premised condition or not. In the English sentence, "If

[1]Joseph Henry Thayer, *Greek-English Lexicon of the New Testament* (Grand Rapids: Zondervan, 1973), 506.

[2]Ibid., 618.

you are a believer, raise your hand," we have no way of knowing whether the speaker thinks that the addressee is or is not a believer; the conditional clause is neutral.

In Greek this neutral idea can be expressed, but Greek can also imply two other options—that the premise is true or that the premise is not true. For example, when Jesus states, "If you love me, you will obey what I command" (John 14:15), the Greek construction of the sentence indicates what is called a "first class conditional clause," a grammatical form that implies that the premise is assumed to be true or real, at least for the sake of argument.[3] Jesus is assuming that his disciples really do love him. His statement is not neutral on that point. Sharing this observation in the sermon is helpful to English-speaking audiences.

In some cases this "first class conditional clause" can better be translated (or explained) with the English word "since" instead of "if," thus indicating in English the intent of the Greek. For example, in the temptation experience of Jesus, Satan challenges Jesus with what (in English) appears to be doubt on Satan's part. "*If* you are the Son of God . . . throw yourself down . . . " (Matt. 4:6, italics added). In most English translations it can be read that Satan doubts Jesus' divinity and relationship to God. However, in light of the first class conditional clause used here, the text could perhaps be better translated, "*since* you are the Son of God. . . ." Letting your audience know this enlightens them to the dynamics of Satan's temptation of Jesus. Satan knows who Jesus is, and that is precisely why the temptations are unique. Jesus is God's Son, and surely—Satan taunts—God will save him if he jumps. Satan is using the reality of Jesus' divinity as the tempting reason to jump.

In other words, a few well-written sentences making this clear will work wonders for audience comprehension of what is actually transpiring between Satan and Jesus. But don't explain the entire Greek conditional clause system, an explanation that will quickly sink into irrelevance and probably bore your audience to tears. Yet a short explanation of the specific Greek conditional construction used in a particular passage can often clarify the text for today's audiences.

[3]Daniel B. Wallace, *The Basics of New Testament Syntax* (Grand Rapids: Zondervan, 2000), 309–10.

Of course, not every Greek grammatical construction requires explanation. In some cases the English translation conveys the proper idea. Jesus' statement in Matthew 13:9, "He who has ears, let him hear" communicates well to our audience without using sermon space to explain its grammar. But if a grammatical explanation helps your audience understand the passage better, if it relates to an important point and not a minor point, and if you can give it quickly, simply, and concisely, then provide one. If not, then don't waste valuable time in your sermon explaining it.

Literary context is critical to grasping the meaning of the text.

Literary Context

Recently my wife and I traveled to Texas with some friends. As normally happens on such trips, we found ourselves in an outlet mall. Because cell phones make it so easy to "reach out and touch someone," one of our friends was touched with a call from home. Standing in a crowded store, he engaged in a lively conversation that we and the other customers easily overheard. However, we could only hear his half of the conversation. He made statements such as, "You can borrow mine," "Be sure to use the bucket," and "How deep is it?" *What on earth was he talking about?* we all wondered. When he finished we asked him to explain it to us. It seems that a mutual acquaintance of ours managed to get his pickup stuck in the mud and my friend was offering the use of his tractor (with a bucket in the front) to help free the vehicle. Do you think that knowing the context of a conversation matters? It is the difference between getting it and missing it.

This is true when it comes to meanings in Scripture—the context surrounding a passage affects the meaning of the passage. How does the sermon text fit into the greater context of the chapter, book, or even the entire Bible? Although preachers often spend little time presenting this material in the sermon, when it helps to clarify the central theology, intent, or meaning of a text, you should include it. Literary context can prove to be your greatest ally in establishing the validity of theological meaning. It demonstrates that you are not proof-texting or taking things out of context. It also offers a helpful model for your congregation to follow in their own personal study, encouraging them to search out the context of the passage they are studying.

Suppose you are preaching on the parable of the prodigal son (Luke 15:11–32). Your sermon will focus on these twenty-two verses, but engaging the audience with the larger context is critical if they are to feel the intended impact of the passage. In two or three sentences explain that Jesus' audience consisted of many spiritually "lost" people who desperately needed to be "found"—tax collectors, sinners, Pharisees, and teachers of the law (15:1–2). Mention also that the entire chapter emphasizes through repetition the theme that God desires to save the lost and he takes the initiative to accomplish that. The other two parables in the chapter deserve a sentence or two as setup for your sermon text since they are stories about lost items that needed finding and whose recovery resulted in great celebration and joy (parable of the lost sheep, parable of the lost coin). Thus, the entire chapter is about God's passionate desire to seek and save the lost, and God himself rejoices when one of these lost ones is found. Once you point out the literary context, your audience stands a better chance of understanding the true meaning of the passage.

Some preachers may argue that there is no need to mention this type of information since audiences notice it on their own. But never assume too much of your audience in terms of diligence in searching out a context on their own. Perhaps some listeners will do contextual study, but many won't. In fact, many in churches today have not been trained to look for literary context when reading or listening to a passage. While mentioning the context strikes some as obvious, many listeners—even those who have been in church for years—are unaware of most contextual issues and will appreciate appropriate contextual information in your sermon.

Furthermore, when you make literary context a regular part of your sermon explanation, many listeners will adopt the practice themselves and incorporate this critical interpretive tool into their personal Bible study. We are not, of course, suggesting masses of contextual information that become laborious for both preacher and listeners, but rather concise and clear statements concerning the relationships and themes within the chapter or book. Many people come to church to gain more knowledge about Scripture, and a clear explanation of the literary context of a passage serves to deepen that knowledge and provide new (and accurate) insight into a passage.

Let's consider another example in which the literary context is not as easy to see as in Luke 15. In Ephesians 3:14–21 Paul prays for the Ephesian church. This prayer reveals his desire for the church to receive power and strength. If fulfilled, it will result in a powerful, dynamic church reflecting the awesome love of Christ and the fullness of God. While this text alone, even when taken somewhat "out of context," can be effective for preaching, an understanding of the entire book of Ephesians truly helps to enhance the message.

Ephesians 1–3 deals primarily with the spiritual blessings and privileges God has bestowed on the church, while chapters 4–6 focus on the spiritual responsibilities that the body of Christ should carry out *because of* those blessings and privileges. Chapters 1–3 are the cause and 4–6 are the effect or logical consequence. Paul's prayer in 3:14–21 links these two sections, summarizing the characteristics of the dynamic body of believers and reminding them of the awesome and powerful God who can do much more than they ever imagined. This passage orients us to the imperatives that are coming in Ephesians 4–6. This prayer is the critical connector between the two parts of the book. If you include just a few statements in the introduction of your sermon explaining this context and its significance, your listeners will see how this entire letter and the focused sermon passage are connected in theme and intent.

Summary

This chapter has included only selected samples of "their town" material, illustrating the type of exegetically derived material that may prove helpful in assisting your audience to understand a passage clearly. Although the decisions you make regarding which material to include in your sermon will vary, depending on your text and your audience, we do remind you of some of the basic guidelines that direct your work.

1. Only mention those things relating to grammar, word meaning, context (historical and literary), or any other "their town" data when that information clearly helps communicate the biblical truth to your specific audience.

2. Be careful not to turn the "their town" information in the sermon into a history or grammar lesson. Keep the data simple, brief, and connected to the sermon theme.

3. Always keep the focus of the sermon on "our town" where your audience lives. Sermons focused two thousand years ago tend to be dry and boring. Stay in the twenty-first century for the most part, but use "their town" information as supplemental sermon material for clarity and understanding. The goal is for people in "our town" to understand and apply the text and meaning from "their town."

4. Remember that you are teaching the Bible (and illustrating Bible study methods) every time you preach. Your people need to know pertinent information about culture, context, and historical theology to be well-informed believers. Include information that fulfills that role.

If you help your listeners see how the original audience would have understood the passage by including the relevant cultural, historical, theological, and grammatical issues from biblical times, they will be much better equipped to understand what it means to them personally. Furthermore, as they see the connection between the meaning that you preach to them and the meaning in the text for the original audience, they will be more likely to feel the imperative to change their lives according to the Scriptures rather than because of your persuasion. Allow the Bible to speak on its own authority.

Review Questions and Assignments

1. What kind of cultural/historical information might you include in a sermon to help your listeners understand the following passages? Ezra 1; Psalm 51; Isaiah 7:10–25; Habakkuk 1:12–17; 1 Corinthians 8; Hebrews 6:11–28; Revelation 2:12–17.

2. What words or phrases would most likely need to be defined or explained to your audience in a sermon on the following passages, and why? Amos 7:7–9; Matthew 5:1–11; Romans 5:1–11; Ephesians 4:7–16.

3. How does the literary context of the following passages affect the meaning and understanding of each? Deuteronomy 6:1–9; Isaiah 7:10–25; Luke 5:17–26; 2 Corinthians 9:6–14; Revelation 2:12–17.

4

Exegeting the Audience

THE FOCUS OF CHAPTER 4:

Step 1	Grasp the Meaning of the Text in Their Town
Step 2	Measure the Width of the Interpretive River
Step 3	Cross the Principlizing Bridge
Step 4	Grasp the Text in Our Town
Step 5	Exegete Your Congregation
Step 6	Determine How Much Background Material to Include
Step 7	Determine the Sermon Thesis and Main Points
Step 8	Develop Text-Centered Applications
Step 9	Find Illustrations
Step 10	Write Out the Sermon and Practice Delivery

Years ago I stood in a hot, stuffy room smaller than most of our average Sunday school classrooms and began to preach. This room functioned as a sanctuary for a small church in one of the poorest sections (barrios) of Salvador, Brazil. Earlier during the day as the pastor and I went to visit church members and prospects, we had walked through the poverty-stricken streets filled with sewage and other unimaginable things. As I started my sermon delivery, I wondered to myself whether my sermon message with its American illustrations and applications would speak at all to this Brazilian congregation. Would an illustration about a Texas ranch hand mean anything to these urban dwellers living in poverty? This group differed greatly from the Texas congregations I usually stood before. At that time I began learning a lesson that has continued to impress me. A sermon *must* be written and directed to the specific audience at hand in light of their unique situation and needs and qualities. So how do we interpret or exegete our audience?

> *Know and understand your particular audience.*

Knowing Your Audience

If you plan to connect the message of the Scriptures with your people in a meaningful and dynamic manner, you must know your people. In chapter 2 we spoke in general terms of "crossing the river" between the ancient world and ours. In this step you try to identify both the differences and the similarities between the ancient audience and the contemporary audience. However, in that chapter we spoke of today's audience in *general* terms. It is critical that you know and understand your *particular* contemporary audience in *specific* terms.

You must never assume that all contemporary audiences are the same. As part of your exegesis and sermon development process, not only do you need to understand the ancient situation that the Bible addressed, but you must spend time studying and reflecting on the spiritual, emotional, and educational situation of the specific audience you will preach to this Sunday (or Saturday night, etc.). What are the perspectives, presuppositions, issues, needs, concerns, and struggles of your people? What are their hopes, dreams, aspirations, fears, and challenges? One thing is certain: If you do not know your people—their needs, struggles, viewpoints, strengths, and weaknesses—you will struggle to preach effectively to them. Exegeting your audience, therefore, is a critical step if you are going to connect powerfully with them.

Many preachers in America today realize the need to exegete the biblical text. Certainly if preachers miss the scriptural meaning in the Bible, they will not deliver to their congregations a clear and correct word from God. Yet often they forget that they must exegete their audience as well. If they have ignored taking into account the situation of their audience, they may also fail at communicating God's

Word, misconnecting with their audience altogether. It is possible to understand the message of the text well but fail in the attempt to relate it to the audience. An example of this that occurs far too often in American churches is when pastors preach a steady diet of evangelistic sermons, calling for someone to convert, but directing the message to an audience populated with longtime believers. These pastors are missing the target.

Graham Johnston, in *Preaching to a Postmodern World*, deals with the specific issue of analyzing postmodern audiences. He suggests that we try to understand the assumptions, beliefs, and values of our postmodern listeners in order to be able to connect properly with them from the pulpit. Johnston compares the preacher's need to exegete the audience to the task that missionaries face on the mission field. Because of significant cultural differences, new missionaries are often unable to communicate well with the people they are trying to reach. They may actually employ strategies that simply will not work in the target culture. To cross this cultural gap, missionaries must first do an extensive study of the target people and their culture. Then, armed with a proper understanding of the culture, they can begin to develop a realistic strategy that will reach the target people and meet their needs.[1] All this has one primary goal—to communicate God's Word more effectively to people.

Duane Litfin suggests that by doing audience-exegetical work you are "emphasizing the need to take advantage of all the elements within any given speaking situation so that your audience, to the greatest extent possible, will be able to comprehend and be willing to act upon your ideas."[2] You want to know all you can about your listeners so you can preach more specifically to their situation.

I learned this more fully when I began to do interim ministry. After leaving a full-time pastorate for university teaching, the interim ministry became an important way for me to stay connected to the local church in a pastoral sense. Through the years I have served in numerous churches, which has exposed me to a wide range of congregations.

In one situation I preached to a young mission church that had a contemporary and casual approach to worship and ministry,

Graham Johnston, *Preaching to a Postmodern World* (Grand Rapids: Baker, 2001), 9–10.

Duane Litfin, as quoted by Johnston, *Preaching to a Postmodern World*, 65.

attempting to minister to people on the edge or even outside traditional religious practice. This church attracted people who had little or no background in church, the Bible, or religion in general. During one sermon from the Old Testament I talked about Abraham, but without giving an explanation as to his identity. I assumed that everyone was familiar with this great patriarch. One woman sitting next to my wife leaned over and asked her who Abraham was. Obviously, I assumed too much and failed to exegete my audience. I faced what Graham Johnston calls "biblically clueless" people and yet I had assumed that they were the same as lifelong churchgoers. Had I studied this congregation and learned where they were spiritually and biblically, I would have avoided such misguided assumptions. Knowledge of the audience strengthens effective preaching of God's Word.

Is there a biblical mandate concerning exegesis of an audience? In 1 Corinthians 9:19–23 Paul shares his own philosophy of ministry, including the need for a clear understanding of target groups and the need for him to make appropriate adjustments in order to reach these groups:

> To the Jews I became like a Jew, to win the Jews.... To those not having the law I became like one not having the law ... to win those not having the law. To the weak I became weak, to win the weak. I became all things to all men so that by all possible means I might save some. (1 Cor. 9:20–22)

This philosophy includes much more than just Paul's preaching ministry, but it certainly encompassed his preaching ministry. The apostle adjusted his style, language, and illustrations in order to adapt to each different audience. Just compare his sermon in Acts 13:16–41 (a typical synagogue audience) with his sermon in Acts 17:22–31 (a Gentile audience at the Areopagus). He never changed the message of the gospel, but he certainly adjusted his methods and style. Why? "I do all this for the sake of the gospel, that I may share in its blessings" (1 Cor. 9:23). Paul studied his audience and then adapted his preaching to hit his target audience. Shouldn't preachers in the twenty-first century do the same?

"To the Jews I became like a Jew, to win the Jews. . . ."

What do you need to know and how do you discover this information? Your goal is to find out what makes your audience different and unique from other congregations. What are their values? What do they desire and what do they hate? How do they occupy their time and how do they waste it? Answers to such questions will aid you in reaching your particular audience and will also save you from expending great energy trying to communicate in ways that will miss your target. So what specifically do you need to know about these people you stand before Sunday after Sunday?

Maturity of Your Audience

How spiritually mature is your congregation? Sometimes preachers face congregations that are mature spiritually. Mature Christians ask biblical questions that new believers (or immature believers) can't even imagine. Spiritually mature congregations usually spend time in the Bible on their own. They don't wait for the pastor to feed them, nor do they depend on the sermon to be their only source of spiritual nourishment. They read books dealing with serious spiritual issues and strive to grow and become even more spiritually mature. They are experienced in real ministry and bring a mature wisdom into the church to go along with their biblical knowledge. Congregations like these actively minister and are aware of theological and biblical issues. They are usually familiar with the basics of the faith and the basics of the Bible. They seek something stronger than spiritual milk on Sunday morning. If you find your congregation matching this description, acknowledge that maturity through your preaching ministry.

By contrast, you may encounter one of the many spiritually immature congregations that possess little information about the Bible or the Christian faith. Perhaps they are enthusiastic about learning, but their basic knowledge about the Bible is limited and their experience with ministry or mature Christian living minimal. Some of them easily get lost or confused in the midst of complicated sermons that use a lot of standard religious terminology. A wise preacher adjusts his sermon accordingly. You need to discern the spiritual situation of your congregation in order to tailor sermons suitable for them.

Yet be cautious about oversimplifying this matter of congregational spirituality into terms of only high or low. The truth is that most churches consist of people from all levels of spiritual maturity, and to neglect a group or to preach only sermons geared to one group often results in leaving some behind in confusion or boredom. Preach to challenge the mature while at the same time using a style and vocabulary that allows the immature to follow and grow.

How do you discover the spiritual maturity of a congregation? Know your people! Spend time in informal settings with church members in order to sense where they are spiritually. Probe spiritual issues with them and listen carefully to their responses. Eat with them, visit with them, talk to them, and most important, listen to them. In the process you will gain valuable information about their spiritual maturity and their biblical understanding. This information not only benefits you while you craft your sermons, but it also guides you in determining which sermon subjects address their true spiritual needs.

In addition, invest time with the leaders of the church. Talking to your leaders can help you in two ways. First, if you discover that the leaders are spiritually weak, it may indicate that the general spirituality of the church is likewise weak. Be careful in this analysis because sometimes people end up in leadership positions for reasons other than their spiritual maturity. However, in spite of this caution, knowing the spiritual maturity of your leaders is still useful. Knowledge like this directs you in choosing your sermon style as well as in selecting certain topics that address theological weaknesses in the church, thus building up both the congregation and its leadership. Growing a congregation spiritually requires more than just preaching, but certainly preaching is central to the process, and it is unlikely that your congregation will grow spiritually if your sermons do not touch on areas of need.

Second, leaders offer their own insight concerning the spiritual condition of the church and its spiritual needs. They usually know the people in the church better than you do. You as a preacher need such insight. Spend time with them. Question them about the spiritual climate in the church. Listen to them and pay attention. Your sermons will be more on target if you do.

Determine the spiritual situation of your congregation and tailor your sermons to meet their spiritual needs.

they will tell them things they won't tell you!

89

Another facet of evaluating the spiritual depth of your congregation is to study the church's history. Has the church been riddled with controversy and problems? Although not the final word on spirituality, this background gives some indication of spiritual strength. In most cases spiritually mature believers act spiritually mature and the result is usually growth, unity, and love. Conversely, spiritually immature believers normally leave a wake of brokenness behind in the form of splits and controversies. How has the church progressed? What do the church records reveal? How has the church recently handled difficulties? Knowing answers to these questions prepares you greatly to meet the needs of the congregation.

How does such information help in sermon preparation? First of all, knowing the spiritual needs of your congregation assists you in choosing sermon topics, thematic series, or biblical books to preach. In addition, this knowledge offers a background for planning and preparing the theological level of your sermons. New, immature congregations require some simple sermons until they reach more mature levels. They need to be fed milk. More knowledgeable and mature congregations are looking for serious meat from God's Word.

Paul faced similar situations in his ministry. When he dealt with the Corinthians, he met them where they were spiritually.

> Brothers, I could not address you as spiritual but as worldly—mere infants in Christ. I gave you milk, not solid food, for you were not yet ready for it. Indeed, you are still not ready. You are still worldly. For since there is jealously and quarreling among you, are you not worldly? Are you not acting like mere men? (1 Cor. 3:1–3)

Even though it frustrated Paul that the Corinthian believers were stuck in spiritual immaturity, he still communicated with them in a way they could understand. Surely you must do the same.

Knowledge of Your Audience

How well does your congregation know the Bible and the theological concepts in it? Those who ignore this reality and preach to all congregations in the same manner risk confusing, offending, or simply missing a congregation completely. Preachers usually possess a significant amount of biblical and theological knowledge, and sometimes they subconsciously forget that the congregation does not have this same knowledge.

It is true that many believers in America today possess a good grasp of biblical and theological knowledge. But in many areas and in many churches (especially in new or fast-growing churches) this situation is changing. You cannot automatically assume that the church member listening to your sermon grew up in the church and thus has a good understanding of the Bible. More and more people in our audiences today fall into the category of "unchurched postmodern listeners." Certainly we praise God for them, but such individuals often possess little knowledge of church, the Bible, or Christian theology. What knowledge they have may be incorrect or confused. The preaching event thus becomes critical in educating them and moving them along in biblical and theological understanding.

In addition, sometimes even among members who have grown up in the church there is biblical illiteracy. I have discovered that many of our students—even those who grew up in church hearing lots of sermons, attending Sunday school regularly, and participating in Christian summer camps—still don't know the basic biblical story and many of the central events. They recall lots of scattered biblical facts but are often unable to connect the facts in any kind of coherent understanding of the whole message or to put the facts into any kind of time frame. In all their exposure to the Bible the main storyline of the Bible somehow escaped them.

Some of this is the fault of the haphazard preaching they grew up with. Week after week their pastors picked topics from unrelated Scriptures, skipping around from one story to another without explaining the biblical context. This has resulted in a generation of young people who know a lot of stories and facts found in the Bible but who don't know the Bible or its story well. It is important to know exactly where your congregation is in regard to their knowledge and understanding of the Bible. Don't assume too much until you've done your homework.

> *More and more people in our audiences today fall into the category of "unchurched postmodern listeners."*

Keep in mind that often the congregation's *theological* understanding is limited, even when they know a lot about the Bible. Thus, be careful to avoid using complicated theological terms without properly explaining them. Using terms like sanctification, justification, or consubstantiation without some explanation either confuses your listeners or causes them to tune you out altogether.

Theological concepts are important, and certainly we do not propose you stay with a "milk" diet forever. As you seek to raise the level of theological understanding in your congregation, however, do it with clarity and often with simplicity. Awareness of the congregation's general theological knowledge enables you to preach on their level and plan sermons that help their knowledge and maturity grow. If you need help simplifying theological ideas, consult some good theology works that model this.[3]

[3]See Grudem, *Systematic Theology*; or Charles Swindoll, *Growing Deep in the Christian Life* (London: Hodder & Stoughtton, 1986); Bruce Shelley, *Theology for Ordinary People* (Downers Grove, IL: InterVarsity Press, 1993). Find a theology text that keeps it simple while still dealing with the difficult theological concepts.

Culture of Your Audience

Where and how do your people live? *Socioeconomic data* on an audience will prove beneficial to understanding a group of listeners and gearing sermons to them. What is the socioeconomic level of your congregation? Where do they shop? Where do they work? Are they poor, middle class, or affluent? Do they worry about how they will pay this month's electric bill, or do they worry about which investment banker to use? What kind of stresses do work and other economic issues put on them? How is the economy in your area? Are any factories closing? Layoffs? Transfers? The answers to such questions are important. No one lives in a vacuum. Everyone is influenced by social and economic pressures that they encounter in daily life. These pressures affect how people think. Understanding this helps you preach more effectively.

How do we obtain this socioeconomic information? Here again, spending time with the congregation in their homes and work settings is critical. Here you observe and experience the way they work, play, and shop. Such data will give you clues to their needs and everyday issues. Then address sermons to those needs.

Understanding the *culture* of a congregation also influences one's preaching ministry. What is the cultural background of the people in your church? Is the culture monolithic, or is there a diversity of cultures in the church? Is the culture in your area changing? Are there certain cultural ways of doing things and thinking? Are there culturally accepted communication practices, vocabulary, and ideas? Sometimes these appear obvious, but other times they require study and close observation.

America is becoming more and more culturally diverse, and you must adjust to that dynamic in your preaching.

Good missionaries are experienced at this form of audience exegesis. Effective sharing of the gospel with a people group from a different culture demands an understanding of how they function culturally. How do the people live, think, communicate, and function in everyday life? American preachers face similar issues. America is becoming more and more culturally diverse, and you must adjust to that dynamic in your preaching. The language you use, the idioms you employ, and the illustrations you describe are often culturally bound, making sense in one culture but not in another.

Several years ago I pastored a military-related church in Germany. I was confronted with a challenging cultural situation. My ministry targeted Americans who lived in Germany, but a large percentage of these Americans were part of a subculture—American military personnel and their families. The military proved to be a more unique culture than I expected.

I assumed at first that since these people were Americans, I could easily communicate and connect with them. Yet I found that they spoke their own "militarese" language, one that depended heavily on the use of military acronyms (SAC, CO, NCOIC, TDY, PX, etc.). Most of the soldiers and their families lived on the base in standard look-alike military housing, which created a conclave of sorts, isolating them from the rest of the surrounding culture. Few of them owned homes back in the United States. They depended on the military for medical and dental care as well as for the education of their children. The military even provided recreational areas and vacation spots.

These soldiers worked long hours and were often deployed on TDY (temporary duty at another place) away from their families.

When the first Gulf War erupted, most of the men were away for several months, resulting in unique family stresses and problems. As a preacher I made it a point to get close to these people and understand their subculture so that I might better minister to them. I spent time in their homes and workplaces in an intentional effort to comprehend their way of life since I was not in the military. My preaching often focused on issues faced by the military members of the church, such as family separation. During sermon preparation it was important for me to keep their subculture in mind and to craft points, illustrations, and applications in such a way that they would connect and find relevance with this particular audience.

At the same time, this American congregation shared a church building with a German congregation that I also occasionally preached to. What a difference in congregations! The German congregation expected a much more formal preaching style than I used with the American military people. I even tried *reading* my sermon manuscript, something that I had never done before (or since). I learned that many of the illustrations and applications that I had used successfully with the American congregation did not translate well to the German audience, so I had to make changes in the sermons. This experience illustrated firsthand just how much audiences affect sermon writing and presentation.

Culture plays a big role here in North America as well. Country folk and urban dwellers live and think differently. A congregation in New York City will be quite different from one in rural Oklahoma. Likewise, ranchers and loggers tend to think and act differently than engineers and accountants. Moreover, the ethnic composition of your community and your congregation is something that you must be aware of. Be cognizant of the total cultural dimension of your congregation and work hard at making proper changes in your preaching so that you can reach all of your people. The *message* of the gospel itself remains the same, but the form and style you use in *preaching* it must be adaptable to your target audience.

Other Considerations

Are there other considerations to think about when preaching to your audience? Wayne McDill suggests several other factors. For example, consider the size of an audience. The expectation of a large congregation regarding the sermon can be quite different from that of a small one, especially regarding the formality of the delivery.[4] Be cautious, however, because even on the issue of formal versus casual delivery, audience expectation varies widely. The size of the audience is not always the indicator. More casual approaches are more appropriate in some settings while more formal styles fit better in others. Also, the homogeneity of a group affects both your sermon delivery and your selection of texts and topics.

Preachers can also find themselves standing before youth groups or senior adult groups. The approaches to these two age groups differ greatly since each one has unique interests, needs, attention spans, and concerns. Be aware of the various types of people in the audience when you preach and tailor your sermon accordingly. When preaching to mixed groups (the most common situation), it is important to avoid focusing on only one specific group week after week. Try to connect with everyone in your audience.

Gender issues should also influence our preaching, although the mostly male population of preachers frequently overlooks this. Alice P. Mathews argues that since men and women are different both biologically and socially, those differences should affect how we preach to them. Mathews suggests that preachers should consider how women approach such issues as moral decision making, psychological wholeness, power, and leadership. Perhaps the most helpful chapter in Mathews' book is "Understanding Women as Listeners," in which she poses several questions that preachers (especially men) need to ask. "Does our language exclude women when we talk about humanity as a whole? . . . Do we use language that designates and describes men and women on equal terms?"[5]

Indeed, many (and often most) of your best listeners in the congregation are women. Spend more time trying to understand them

Many of your best listeners are women.

[4]Wayne McDill, *The Moment of Truth* (Nashville: Broadman & Holman, 1999), 127–28.

[5]Alice P. Mathews, *Preaching That Speaks to Women* (Grand Rapids: Baker, 2003), 160–61.

better as listeners. Sometimes male preachers use illustrations that are oriented primarily to men, such as stories about football, golf, hunting, or fishing. An illustration from football may be great for the men in the congregation, especially those who actually played the game, but it may fall short in connecting with the women in the crowd as well as with those men who did not play or do not take an interest in football. Thus, a detailed football illustration may totally miss two-thirds of your audience! The same is true for other male-dominated activities.

Are you conscious of the special situations that many Christian women deal with each day? Do your sermons speak to women who care for preschool children all day or to widows who now must face life alone? Do your applications relate to women struggling with relationships or facing inequities in the workplace? Certainly if you want to reach all of your people and help the entire congregation to grow, you must pay attention to both women and men in your sermons. Some preachers suggest you make a list of potential listeners and imagine what they are like and what their needs, their questions in life, and their ultimate issues are. Then fashion a sermon to speak to them.

Be Willing to Adjust

Are you a flexible person? Can you change? In order to be as effective in communicating the Word of God as possible, you must be open to adapting your preaching styles to match the needs of your audience. For many preachers, questioning their preaching style can be a touchy, personal subject. According to McDill, "style" includes all that is involved in a preacher's "characteristic manner of expressing his thoughts, whether in writing or in speech." He says that preachers often think of their current style as a "feature of divine creation."[6] This accusation strikes close to the truth for many, for often preachers believe that they cannot change the way they express themselves in their sermons because that is just who they are. But let us never forget that the Christian life consists of growth and change. If adjust-

[6]McDill, *The Moment of Truth*, 114–15.

ing your style of preaching communicates better to some audiences and results in better edification of the church, then be ready and willing to do so.

Most preachers normally use a deductive model of preaching, moving from the main idea of the sermon to making points about it. However, as you encounter more postmodern congregations (a different context and culture), try more inductive approaches, allowing the audience to discover the points or answers provided by the text as you walk them through it. Johnston argues that inductive preaching probably works best with today's postmodern audiences.[7] Try it and see.

The formality of your sermon presentation is integrally related to your style. In some settings, an informal preaching style communicates better with the audience than the traditional formal style. Often you do this naturally, modifying your level of formality to match your audience without even thinking about it. For example, most preachers are less formal on Sunday evening than on Sunday morning. Different audience contexts dictate the need for such adjustments. Also, keep in mind that many who did not grow up in church respond better to more conversational preaching styles. If you find yourself in a church comprised of a significant number of people who did not grow up in church, you probably need to consider a more informal conversational style (or at least experiment with it and get feedback from your congregation).

Be willing to adjust your preaching style!

[7]Johnston, *Preaching to a Postmodern World*, 151.

A Final Thought

In sermon preparation it is important to do exegesis on the biblical text that you are preaching. But it is also important to exegete your audience. As you prepare your sermons, first gain a clear understanding of the text and its historical background, but also try to comprehend the audience to whom you will proclaim the text. An important part of sermon preparation is reflecting on the situation of your people and adjusting your sermon to fit them and their needs so that the Word of God will impact their lives in a powerful way.

Review Questions and Assignments

1. Write a paragraph describing the character of your home church in as much detail as possible. Discuss spiritual and theological maturity, socioeconomic setting, and gender ratios. Based on your analysis, what kind of sermon would you preach to them next Sunday and why?

2. Exegete the homiletics class according to all the categories discussed in this chapter. What kind of sermon would you preach to them and why? What kind of illustrations might fit?

3. Take one of your sermons and ask the following question about it. How might this message, the illustrations, and application sound to a: young mother, fourth-grade girl, freshman soccer player, father who recently lost his job, recent widow, person struggling with an addiction, spiritual seeker, retired couple, and mature believer?

Communicating the Meaning in Our Town

5

Writing Out Your Sermon
Sermon Thesis Statement
Sermon Points
Other Options
Keep It Connected
Explain Yourself
Good Form
Summary
Review Questions and Assignments

THE FOCUS OF CHAPTER 5:

Step 1	Grasp the Meaning of the Text in Their Town
Step 2	Measure the Width of the Interpretive River
Step 3	Cross the Principlizing Bridge
Step 4	Grasp the Text in Our Town
Step 5	Exegete Your Congregation
Step 6	Determine How Much Background Material to Include
Step 7	Determine the Sermon Thesis and Main Points
Step 8	Develop Text-Centered Applications
Step 9	Find Illustrations
Step 10	Write Out the Sermon and Practice Delivery

We teach as professors in the School of Christian Studies (e.g., courses in homiletics, Old Testament, New Testament, Christian ministries) at a Christian liberal arts university. Other professors in the university teach other courses like organic chemistry, microeconomics, or abnormal psychology. Once a month we attend a gathering (colloquium) where a professor speaks to us concerning research in his or her field. This exercise develops camaraderie among the faculty and introduces the rest of us to different disciplines.

Write out your sermons! It will help you immensely.

Since our specialty is Christian studies, we stand a good chance of being as lost as a goose during a presentation from the organic chemistry professor. How does our faculty accomplish the purposes of the colloquium and communicate with everyone? The burden of that task lies with the presenter. He or she must organize the material in such a way that the rest of us can follow the line of argument with minimal background information. He or she must use terms and concepts we can grasp and use illustrations simple enough that even a homiletics professor can grasp. Sometimes presenters achieve that goal and sometimes they don't. When they miss, the presentation can be extremely boring.

In the same way, the burden of communication in the preaching event lies with you, the preacher. You have been trained, formally or informally, in biblical areas, and you must now present your findings of information and truth to an audience that wants to hear it. However, many among your listeners possess little background for understanding this material you call a sermon. The burden is on you to organize it in a way they can follow, say it in terms they understand, and illustrate it when needed for maximum listener comprehension. Learning to write out your sermon can help.

Writing Out Your Sermon

Haddon Robinson correctly states that writing the sermon before delivering it orally improves preaching because it allows you to work out (in advance) just the right words and clear ideas for communicating the message.[1] Some preachers only write out the sermon outline, and a few merely sketch rough outlines or scribble random ideas and notes. In our opinion, however, these latter practices force preachers to make a lot of quick decisions on their feet at the point of delivery. A few preachers are gifted enough to pull this off, but not many. We strongly encourage you to write out your sermons as part of your sermon preparation.

Writing is an excellent discipline that helps you in organizing, developing, and forming thoughts into words that communicate clearly and powerfully. You may not read your manuscript to the

[1]Haddon Robinson, *Biblical Preaching: The Development and Delivery of Expository Messages*, 2nd ed. (Grand Rapids: Baker, 1980), 183.

audience (see ch. 8, "Delivering a Biblical Sermon"), but writing it out will help you immensely.

Sermon Thesis Statement

Have you ever heard a sermon or a devotional talk that did not seem to have a main idea? After the speech, you aren't even able to explain what it was about, and you are not sure the speaker could either. You want your sermons to be different. You want to be able to focus your sermon and leave your audience with at least one powerful truth from the text.

Foundational to preaching a focused biblical sermon is the development of a *sermon thesis statement*. Every sermon needs one main idea. Few audiences will be able to follow sermons containing a number of central ideas unless those ideas are united into one main unifying theme. Keith Willhite argues that "developing a single idea in a sermon is the best way to preach, or at least, to learn to preach."[2] We heartily concur. Since the goal of this book is to teach you how to develop and preach a biblical sermon, it is important that you learn how to write out a sermon thesis statement that explains the one main sermon idea.

A sermon thesis statement is a clear, concise synthesis of what the sermon is all about. This statement should grow out of the central thesis of the text. The two statements are not identical, for the text thesis statement is grounded in the past meaning while the sermon thesis statement focuses on applying that meaning to the present audience.

In order to develop a sermon thesis statement, you must first return to your exegesis. In chapter 2 we suggested that at the end of the first exegetical step of the journey ("grasping the text in their town"), after you have completed your close observation and thorough study of the details in the passage and the context, you must "synthesize the meaning of the passage for the biblical audience into one or two sentences." That is, write out what "the passage meant for the biblical audience." This statement is called the *text thesis statement*. It should be written in past tense and focus only on what the inspired biblical author was saying to the original audience. You will

The text thesis statement *reflects what the text meant for the original audience. The* sermon thesis statement *directs that meaning to your audience today.*

[2]Keith Willhite, "A Bullet versus Buckshot: What Makes the Big Idea Work?" in *The Big Idea of Biblical Preaching*, ed. Keith Willhite and Scott M. Gibson (Grand Rapids: Baker, 1998), 14.

be using terms that relate to "them" and "their town," such as: "Moses instructed the Israelites to . . . "; "David demonstrated that a faithful Hebrew should . . . "; "Paul exhorted the Colossians to . . . "; or "Jesus instructed his disciples to. . . ."

You should develop your sermon thesis statement out of your text thesis statement. The sermon thesis statement carries the same idea as the text thesis statement, but you should write it directly to your audience, for you have now crossed "the principlizing bridge." Your sermon thesis statement indicates the direction your sermon will take; it says clearly and concisely what the sermon is about. It uses present-tense verbs and audience-focused words, such as "us" or "you." It provides a synthesis of the scope of the sermon.

Let's look at some examples.

Text: Luke 15:11–32 (the parable of the prodigal son)

Text thesis statement: The text thesis statement might read as follows: *Jesus told the Pharisees and teachers of the law that God loves sinners so much that even though he allows them freedom to reject him, his love and mercy toward them never ceases, and he rejoices over them whenever they return to him.* That statement sums up the parable without mentioning subthemes, such as the anger of the elder son. It is the central meaning of the story in their time.

Sermon thesis statement: As you develop a sermon thesis statement from this text thesis statement, cross over the principlizing bridge, change the past tense verbs to present tense, and change past audience references to present audience references, all the while never losing the central universal theology of the parable. Thus your sermon thesis statement might read: *God loves us so much that while he allows us to reject him, his love and mercy toward us will never cease, and he will rejoice over us when we return to him.* The resulting sermon focuses on God's immense, ever-patient love and his desire that all who are "lost" come into relationship with him.

Text: John 17:1–23

Text thesis statement: Just prior to Jesus' arrest, he offered a prayer to God the Father. The text thesis statement might read as follows: *Jesus prayed for God's plan to be fulfilled first in himself, then in his disciples, and then in all those who would believe in him* *in the future.* Of course, you derive this statement from your careful and complete exegesis of the text. It is the summary statement of what that text said to those people in "their town."

Sermon thesis statement: Moving into "our town," the sermon thesis statement would say: *As we pray for the church, we should ask that God's plan will be fulfilled in all believers, including ourselves, fellow believers, and all those who will become Christians in the future.* The sermon explains exactly what we should pray about concerning ourselves, other believers, and those who are yet to believe. Jesus modeled a wonderful prayer for us in this text.

Sermon Points

Now that we know the main idea of the sermon, we must develop the sermon. Every sermon needs a central idea (the *sermon thesis statement*), supported by main points that develop this central idea. These supporting points we refer to as *sermon points*. As mentioned earlier, you have several options as to how these points are presented in the sermon, but recognize that the sermon needs to be constructed around these points.

How do you find the points for a sermon? How do you write them or present them in a way that communicates with your audience? How many points should your sermon have? How does the text relate to your sermon points?

First of all, if you are a beginning preacher, don't try to be too creative with your basic sermon structure at first. Granted, there are numerous ways to structure sermons, but for simplicity's sake let's begin with the traditional sermon structure. As you become more experienced in preaching, you can experiment with innovative sermon structural forms.

In order to model going from the text thesis statement to the sermon points, we will use Luke 5:36–39 as our text. Based on the synthesis of your exegesis, you first develop a *text thesis statement* that summarizes what the passage meant in "their town." Note that in this passage, Jesus used the idea of new wine and old wineskins and old cloth and new cloth patches to teach the Pharisees a lesson about relating to him. Thus, the text thesis statement reads: *Jesus informed the Pharisees that he represents the new, true, unique, and better way to God and that even though it will be difficult for them, the truth he represents cannot be put into their old system but must replace the old way.*

As part of this synthesis procedure, we revisited all of the details and observations that were uncovered in the study and determined from them the main idea that moves through the passage. We synthesized several verses together to summarize the thought in the passage. The text thesis statement is a summary statement that includes all of the major elements in your passage; it includes several truths about the new way Jesus offered the Pharisees. Those major elements that build into the text thesis statement become the text points from which you can develop a text outline. It makes little difference whether you find the text points first or write the text thesis statement first; just make sure the text thesis statement summarizes the text points.

At this point you are still in "their town" understanding. Now take the text thesis statement across the principlizing bridge, converting it from a specific truth for a specific historical biblical audience into a universal biblical truth for all audiences. Then take that universal biblical truth and express it in terms that apply directly to your audience. That one universal theme becomes your sermon thesis statement: *What Jesus offers people cannot be added onto their previous beliefs about spiritual reality because his truth is unique and better, and even though it will not be easy, it must replace their old ways.* This statement incorporates all the truth of our text thesis statement but is directed to our audience. This is the main idea of the sermon.

You can now develop your main sermon points. Take your main text points (things the text says about the main idea) across the principlizing bridge, convert them to universal biblical truth, and then express them in contemporary terms that connect and relate to your audience. You may need to be selective and discerning in this step. Sometimes two text points can be merged together into one sermon point. Occasionally you will have text points that you cannot readily bring across the principlizing bridge and convert into universal biblical truth. Don't panic or despair. It is alright to have more text points than sermon points, so long as the crucial ideas are carried over across the bridge and into the sermon. Keep in mind that it is the main sermon idea (sermon thesis statement) that is critical. The important role of the sermon points is to build and support the main idea.

I can find at least three points derived from Luke 5:36–39. (1) Christianity is not an add-on religion. (2) It may be difficult for people to give up old beliefs for Christ. (3) People must replace their old ways to God with his new wine. Can you see each of these ideas in both the text thesis statement and the sermon thesis statement? Out of both comes our development of an outline style sermon.

After you have developed your sermon thesis statement and your sermon points, submit your results to a vigorous self-scrutiny. Ask yourself some honest questions about your statement and points.

- Does my statement really reflect what this passage is all about?
- Do my sermon thesis statement and my sermon points truly capture the intent of the biblical author?
- Do they fit the context of the passage?
- Are they oriented to my audience?
- Have I truly phrased the biblical truth in words that will connect to my audience?
- Is it in line with the audience's level of understanding and needs?

This stage is critical to your sermon effectiveness, so don't just assume the answers to these questions. Most effective preachers spend a lot of time on this process, rewording points and thesis statements, returning to the text to verify the validity of the revision, followed by more revising, followed by reflection on the audience, followed by more revision, and so on. We know this appears difficult, but if you keep working on the process, it will become more comfortable and you will start developing sermons that are on target with both the text and the audience.

We realize, of course, it is more difficult for beginning preachers, but even the most experienced biblical preachers struggle with this part of their sermon development. If you find yourself stumped with a passage or if you just can't get the right words for your sermon thesis statement, we encourage you to stop, take a break, spend some time in prayer, and then tackle it again. Work hard! Don't give up easily! Good sermon thesis statements and good sermon points result from a lot of faithful, hard work.

The number of theological principles you derive from your passage normally determines how many points you have in your sermon. Don't try to force your text into an artificial number of points, but try to match the structure and theology of the passage. In most cases you will find two or three main points in your passage, but occasionally you will uncover four or even five (especially when preaching Psalms). If there are more than five, think about preaching more than one sermon on that text. It is difficult to explain, illustrate, and apply more than five points in the time frame available for a normal sermon, and even five points require that you cover some of the points briefly. Two to four points represent the optimum size, and most of your sermons should fall into this range.

It is critical to bring the theology from "their town" into "our town," so your points must be oriented to your people, their needs, and their situation. Keep in mind all of the information you discovered while exegeting your audience (ch. 4). This knowledge will enable you to write relevant points that meet your people's needs in their present circumstances.

First, write your sermon points directly to your audience with words and terminology that will communicate with them. In G. Robert Jacks' fascinating book *Just Say the Word: Writing for the Ear*, the author argues that in sermon-writing preachers often try to obey the rules of writing formal term papers. The tragic (and boring) result is a sermon that sounds like a term paper. All of us regularly break the rules of formal grammar when we speak because we speak for people to hear and not to read, and the rules for speaking are somewhat different from the rules for writing. Sermons are delivered orally; they are not essays to be read.

Thus, be sure to write your sermons with the oral presentation in mind. Jacks suggests you ask yourself how you would say something verbally before you write it in the sermon.[3] This is true for all aspects of

[3]G. Robert Jacks, *Just Say the Word: Writing for the Ear* (Grand Rapids: Eerdmans, 1996), 18–19.

the sermon, but it is especially true for the sermon points, because it is in the sermon points that you designate what is especially important.

Text: Psalm 23

In this psalm David praises God because of what God has meant to him in his life. God has been his strength and protection throughout his life, even in dark and difficult times. A weak sermon outline of Psalm 23 might look like this:

David's Praise of God

1. God is the protector
2. God is the guide
3. God is the restorer

This outline brings out the main theological truths David learned, but in this particular form it falls well short of communicating this truth effectively. The goal of your sermon goes beyond just informing the audience of biblical material. You desire as well to bring the biblical truth discovered in the passage directly to bear on your audience. David's life was filled with warfare and political intrigue, difficulties that would certainly create fear and anxiety in most people. Yet David claimed he did not fear, for he knew that God was his help. A sermon on this passage should focus on God's ability to be there for all believers when they face difficult and frightening situations. Thus, a better outline is as follows:

How Can We Deal with Fear?

1. When we are afraid of those things that can harm us, God is our protector. (Ps. 23:1, 4–5)
2. When we are afraid because we don't know which way to go, God is our guide. (Ps. 23:2–3)
3. When we are afraid because we are tired, weary, and ready to quit, God is our restorer. (Ps. 23:2–3, 6)

This outline connects the timeless theological principles that David discovered to our lives today. Notice the sermon points also speak to issues that most people today encounter. Sidney Greidanus tells us that sermons should be directed to "specific needs in the congregation, by addressing the sermon" to those needs.[4] Write your points out as if they were personal truth statements written to your people in their situation. As mentioned above, the sermon points use present tense and relate to people where they live.

[4]Sidney Greidanus, *The Modern Preacher and the Ancient Text* (Grand Rapids: Eerdmans, 1988), 184.

107

Text: Colossians 3:12–17

A Bible study approach outline might look like this:

Paul's Call for Unity

1. Peace of Christ ruling
2. Word of Christ dwelling
3. Glory of Christ in all activity

In this example neither the thesis statement nor the points are directed toward the audience. Taking the same basic main ideas from the exegesis we can transform this outline into an effective sermon outline by directing the thesis and the points toward today's situation (and still stay faithful to the text), producing a much more effective sermon outline:

Things That Bring Unity to the Church

1. If we want to be unified, we must allow the peace of Christ to rule in our hearts. (Col. 3:15)
2. If we want to be unified, we must allow the Word of Christ to dwell in our hearts. (Col. 3:16)
3. If we want to be unified, we must all have as our goal the glory of God in all that we do. (Col. 3:17)

Other Options

Some preachers don't use a traditional outline approach. Does that mean they have no points for the audience? Certainly not. They just deliver them in a different way. Eugene Lowery, for example, suggests developing the sermon as if it were a "narrative art form." Such a sermon would have a narrative plot like a television series or a movie. Each plot would include a felt discrepancy and then move the viewers to an unknown solution. Moving from problem to solution shapes the sermon.

Lowery sees five steps in this process: upsetting the equilibrium, analyzing the discrepancy, disclosing the clue to resolution, experiencing the gospel (where the biblical story or passage interacts), and anticipating the consequence.[5] With this approach the distinct points we noted in our traditional examples are not clearly stated but they are integrated through clues or statements into the story or narrative.

[5]Eugene Lowery, *The Homiletical Plot* (Louisville: Westminster John Knox, 2001), 12, 23–26.

The audience discovers them along the way as the preacher gives these clues throughout the sermon.

For an example, let's return to Luke 5:36–39. You might begin with a story about a person who feels that all belief systems are equal and tries to incorporate parts of all of them into his belief system. Later he discovers the singular truth of the Christian gospel and is compelled to give up the old beliefs for the new, unique, and true way. You have introduced a discrepancy found in the world and in the text. Does the Christian faith stand alone as the way to God, or are there other ways that can be incorporated? Now continue your story with the Pharisees, who believed that their old ways were best and refused to replace them with Christ's way.

In the process of weaving such stories, you give clues to the fact that Christianity is not an add-on religion and that even though it is difficult to do, we must allow the new wine Jesus offers to supersede all other ways to God. You never have to say these points outright but you hint, give clues, and indicate with the stories that this is what the passage is relaying to us. If you weave the story well, the congregation will discover it along the way. Note that the same points are central to the narrative sermon because you still seek to allow the passage to speak its message in your sermon. The narrative sermon still has one main idea (sermon thesis) and revolves around that idea, incorporating the truths of the text, but it presents the sermon thesis and the main points to the audience in a very creative way.

Keep It Connected

Now that you know how to discover and write sermon points, we must consider the important issue of the unity and connectedness of the points. Their order is usually driven by their connection to the text or your narrative. Most sermon points move sequentially through the verses of a passage, although this is not a universal guideline. Yet it is critical that the sermon points fit together logically and theologically and relate clearly to the sermon thesis statement.

The clothesline: The sermon thesis statement is the line and the sermon points are the clothes hanging on the line.

⁶James Braga, *How to Prepare Bible Messages* (Portland: Multnomah, 1981), 139–40.

⁷Terry Carter, "Preaching for Clarity," *Proclaim* 26 (October–December 1995): 47–49.

Many preaching textbooks on expository or biblical preaching offer guidelines on how to develop sermon points. James Braga, for example, suggests that the "main divisions" (his phrase for the main sermon points) must grow out of the main sermon idea and be arranged in some progression.⁶ Others argue for logical order of the points. To these suggestions, we would add that since all the points grow out of the sermon thesis (or vice versa), you should state them in a way that shows the connection to each other and to the sermon thesis.

A good way to think of this is using the *clothesline concept.*⁷ The main thesis statement of the sermon is like a clothesline and the sermon points are the clothes hanging on the line, all connected together and attached to the line. Thus, when writing points, be careful to use words that show the close connection between the points and the thesis statement.

Text: Psalm 91

How Does God Care for Us?

1. *God cares for us by giving us* relief when life becomes too hot to bear. (Ps. 91:1, 12–13)
2. *God cares for us by giving us* warmth and comfort when life becomes too cold. (Ps. 91:4)
3. *God cares for us by giving us* refuge when life turns on us. (Ps. 91:1–2, 9)
4. *God cares for us by giving us* his angels to protect and watch over us when we feel all alone. (Ps. 91:11–12, 15)
5. *God cares for us by giving us* salvation when we are lost and dying. (Ps. 91:5–7, 14–16)

Note that each sermon point is directly connected to the main idea of God's care. The repetition of the phrase "God cares for us by giving us" stresses the main point of the sermon and indicates the relationship between each point. In addition, this parallel and repeated construction helps people remember the main idea of the sermon.

Some may perhaps argue that there is too much repetition of the main phrase in this outline. However, in a twenty- to thirty-minute sermon, the thesis is only repeated three to five times, depending on the number of points. This is not overkill, but rather a good way to remind your people of what the sermon is about and to help them remember the main point from this scripture passage. Connections and transition hold equally true for the narrative sermon. Keep the main idea or flow of the sermon at the center and then weave your clues or points in appropriately along the way.

Explain Yourself

There are several reasons for explaining the sermon points with details from the text.

1. Explanation shows that the sermon and its points are derived from Scripture.
2. The authority and power of the sermon is grounded in the Word of God, and the explanation assures the audience that what you are preaching is indeed a biblical sermon and not merely your opinion.
3. Explanation keeps you within the parameters of the text. If you cannot demonstrate that the text teaches a point, then that point does not belong in the sermon.
4. Explanation represents the real meat of the sermon, for it is part of the "thus says the Lord" portion of the message.

Your goal is not to preach a clever sermon but rather to proclaim to your audience what God has to say to them from the particular text you are working with. Therefore, do not fabricate points based on your own opinion or on predetermined pet subjects of yours that are unconnected to the text, even if you feel the audience ought to hear them. To preach a biblical sermon means that you present to your audience the principles or points that God has revealed in the biblical text. With that as your goal, you must demonstrate the validity of your points by giving an explanation of each point from the text. Show the audience how each point is evident in the passage. This applies to both outline and narrative sermons.

Your explanation of each point should cover the pertinent details in the text that combine together to establish a sermon point.

The explanation of sermon points should keep the sermon grounded in the biblical text.

These details include word meanings, grammatical issues, literary context, cultural and theological background, and other things gleaned from your exegetical work. Make explanations clear and concise and on a level readily understood by the audience. Don't get bogged down with trying to explain every single detail. Focus on the major details to provide the audience with understanding of the point you are making.

In a sermon on Hebrews 12:1–4 entitled "How Believers Can Keep the Faith," for example, one sermon point could be: "We can keep the faith if we rid ourselves of all the things that hinder us." In the explanation, explain the nuances of the Greek words that have been translated "hinder," "throw off," and "entangles." Since this text revolves around the analogy of comparing the faithful Christian life to running a distance race, take a minute to explain the track races of the first century. Most people at that time normally wore long robes, an attire extremely unsuitable for running because the robe would "entangle" one's legs and would trip them. Runners had to "throw off" such robes in order to run. Likewise, deal with the word "sin," because it is part of what needs to be shed (thrown off) by the believer in order to keep the faith. Through this information you clarify to your audience how this point truly derives from the text, and in the process you teach them some important biblical information.

Good Form

Once the theological principles (your sermon points) have been determined and the biblical material supporting them is identified, you must decide on the form in which you are going to package them. Some of you will prefer to read the text, introduce the sermon thesis statement, and then present the sermon points in an outline form. However, do not just list the points, as if you are giving the audience a list of things to do. Rather, introduce each point with a transitional statement.

A *transition* is a sentence that connects the idea just shared with the idea about to be stated. Without such a sentence there is an abruptness that hurts the ear. A transition can be as simple as: "What else can we learn about faith from this passage"; or, "In verse 2 we saw that God has blessed us with fantastic blessings. Now in verse 3 we discover. . . ." Avoid introducing points by saying, "first," "second," "third," and so on. Opt for logical connections rather than numerical connections.

Try to find ways to present points from your outline without making it sound like an outline. In the traditional sermon form the points are stated rather clearly and the textual explanation of each point normally follows immediately. If you prefer a more narrative method, include truth statements from the text in ways that force the audience to discover them on their own. The type of sermon packaging is a choice and depends on the personality of the preacher, the nature of the audience, the text being preached, and the context in which the sermon is preached. Regardless of the form, transitions are still important to move from one sermon segment to another.

The traditional style is easier, and we recommend it for beginning preachers. However, either style can be used effectively. As you get more comfortable with preaching, go ahead and vary your style. Preachers using both styles (along with variations) find themselves able to hold their audience's attention week after week and to communicate God's Word effectively. The key in both is to preach a biblical sermon in which your thesis statement and all your points come from the text, and in which you present sufficient biblical information to communicate the message as the inspired biblical author intended it. Form serves to enhance communication. Use whichever you feel most comfortable with, but never develop a sermon that ignores the key truths of the text you selected.

Transitions connect the ideas in a sermon in a smooth way and help move the sermon along to its intended end.

Summary

We dealt with three critical issues for biblical sermons in this chapter. All three—sermon thesis statement, sermon points, and explanation—combine to demonstrate to your listeners how the sermon is connected closely to the text and to reveal to them what God has to say today from that text.

1. The *sermon thesis statement* grows directly out of the text thesis statement. It is what the sermon is about and should be written in present tense and directed to the audience. Often the sermon thesis statement appears in some form in the introduction to indicate what the sermon is about.

2. The *main points* of the sermon come from the timeless, universal theological principles discovered in the hermeneutical journey (crossing the principlizing bridge). They are present tense, complete sentences that speak personally to the audience. The wording makes it clear that they are connected to the sermon thesis statement (clothesline principle). The points are usually clearly delineated in the sermon, but they may be woven into the narrative sermon in creative ways. That decision is an issue of sermon style, but every biblical sermon needs to have sermon points.

3. The *explanation* brings out what the text says about the theological principle underlying the sermon points. It includes word meanings, context, grammar details, theological and cultural background, and other significant exegetical insights. Make it only as long as it needs to be to explicate the sermon point and to reveal what God has to say about it. Keep it in simple and clear language, appropriate to your audience. In the narrative forms, incorporate this data into the storyline.

4. One last guideline: Sermons come in various forms and styles (see ch. 1, "Preaching a Biblical Sermon"). But regardless of how they are packaged, they must include a sermon thesis, some point or points, and a clear explanation of how the thesis and points derive from the biblical text.

Review Questions and Assignments

1. Write a text thesis statement and outline of the text, followed by a sermon thesis statement and an outline of the sermon points for the following texts: Deuteronomy 6:1–9; Psalm 1; Matthew 7:1–6; Acts 5:21–32; James 3:1–12.

2. Watch the sermons on video assigned in class (see the preface to this book) and write what you think the sermon thesis and points are for each one.

6

Applying the Message

Importance of Application
A Reluctant Applier
Application and the Interpretive Journey
Watch Out!
Summary Guidelines
Review Questions and Assignments

THE FOCUS OF CHAPTER 6:

Step 1	Grasp the Meaning of the Text in Their Town
Step 2	Measure the Width of the Interpretive River
Step 3	Cross the Principlizing Bridge
Step 4	Grasp the Text in Our Town
Step 5	Exegete Your Congregation
Step 6	Determine How Much Background Material to Include
Step 7	Determine the Sermon Thesis and Main Points
Step 8	Develop Text-Centered Applications
Step 9	Find Illustrations
Step 10	Write Out the Sermon and Practice Delivery

Recently I presented a pregame devotional to a university football squad. I talked for ten minutes, trying to challenge them spiritually. Then it was the coach's turn to talk football. First, he gave them the grades from the last game (I never knew there was such a thing as grades for a football game), based on how well they performed last week. He then challenged the players concerning the game at hand. He reminded them of the game plan they learned earlier in the week and of what they needed to do to win. Finally, he assured them if they did what they knew to do, they could win the game.

As I listened to the coach, it occurred to me that what he was really talking about was application (although he used the word "execution"). They had learned, listened, and practiced all week, going over plays, repeating them, and memorizing their individual assignments. Now it was game time. They knew what to do, and the coach challenged them to do it. The work of training would be useless unless they applied it to the real game.

In some ways the preacher takes on the role of a head coach. He leads the congregation to discover God's truth and expectations. If he preaches well, they grasp it. But his job remains incomplete until he challenges them to apply that truth in real life—in the big game. We call that part of the sermon *application*; this chapter focuses on how to get your team to live out the Word of God in real life.

Preach to change people!

Importance of Application

Can't you just give the audience the biblical information and then allow them and the Holy Spirit to work out the rest? Most effective preachers as well as teachers of preaching will answer an emphatic "no" to that question. The application portion of a sermon is critical to its effectiveness. Preaching involves more than just giving out biblical information. Preaching connects biblical truth to people's lives in a way that changes them. Joseph Stowell argues that "an effective sermon is measured not by its polished technique but by the ability of the preacher to connect the Word to the reality of the listener's life."[1]

Part of your task is to preach for change. The proclamation of God's Word should make a difference in the life of every individual in the church. In your sermons always strive to show the biblical connections to life today and to explain how applications of biblical truth can be incorporated into the lives of your people. Haddon Robinson emphasizes that "application is not incidental to effective expository preaching; it is crucial." He points out that preachers must relate biblical truth to people's lives. But, Robinson continues, the lives of people also "must be changed to be relevant to biblical faith."[2] Application truly is an integral part of the preaching task for each and every preacher.

[1] Joseph Stowell, "Preaching for Change," in *The Big Idea of Biblical Preaching*, ed. Keith Willhite and Scott M. Gibson (Grand Rapids: Baker, 1998), 125.

[2] Haddon Robinson, as quoted by Stephen Olford, *Anointed Expository Preaching* (Nashville: Broadman & Holman, 1998), 252.

First, apply the sermon to your own life.

A Reluctant Applier

Through years of teaching homiletics, we have discovered that students of preaching struggle with the application stage more than any other area. They work through the exegesis process and find all kinds of information to share. They usually find reasonably good stories (mostly personal) to illustrate the ideas of the sermon, but they struggle with helping people put the truth into action. Often they seem reluctant to take the final step and drive the application of the text home. Why is that?

First, some students struggle because they have difficulty identifying spiritual principles from the Bible and integrating them into their own life experience. Thus, it is difficult for them to apply the Bible to others. Effective preaching must begin with the preacher's walk with Christ. You must be a good follower to teach others how to follow. You must constantly be about the business of applying God's Word to your own life if you are to lead others in applying it to theirs. A good way to work on this is to take the biblical truths learned in your own Bible study or sermons and list practical ways you personally can make that truth active in your life. Intentionally work on some of the ideas you come up with. Exercises like this develop your own applicational aptitude, which in turn will improve your sermons.

Second, some of our students assume that application is the sole responsibility of the Holy Spirit. The preacher's role, they believe, is just to share the truth. While the Holy Spirit is indeed the key mover in the lives of your listeners, that does not mean he doesn't use you as a prompter for application. After all, the Spirit chose to use you as the medium for sharing the rest of the sermon, which he could have handled himself as well. You act as a partner with the Holy Spirit in the process of preaching and prompting applications. The Holy Spirit informs and guides your sermon preparation (if you involve the Spirit through prayer and dependence), allowing you to communicate the truth clearly. Then, as you challenge the audience to act on the spiritual principles discovered in the text, the Spirit aids you and urges the listener to action. The Spirit continues to lead and empower the listener as he or she attempts to apply the message.

The Holy Spirit often chooses to work through human preaching.

Finally, some beginning preachers want to avoid sounding legalistic. They think that giving the congregation a list of things to do is legalism. They miss the concept of application. Sermon application simply means showing your people ways they can incorporate the truths of the text into their lives. Admittedly, you do want to avoid legalistic formulas for Christian living, but there are numerous effective, nonlegalistic ways of applying God's Word.

Avoid legalism!

Application and the Interpretive Journey

Let's refresh our memories concerning the journey you have followed up to this point. We started with the biblical text. At the beginning of the Interpretive Journey, you determined what the text meant to the original audience. You then studied your audience (audience exegesis) to determine what issues they are faced with—spiritual, financial, physical, intellectual, and emotional. You also determined the width of the interpretive river, probing into the similarities and differences between the original audience and your contemporary one. Next, you crossed the river over the principlizing bridge, determining what universal, timeless, theological principles were in the text that were relevant to all audiences in all places and in all times. After going to all that trouble, surely you need to take some time in the sermon to show your audience how the text relates specifically to their lives. To borrow a slogan from an old tire commercial, application is "where the rubber meets the road" in the sermon.

James Earl Massey provides a somewhat academic definition of application: "Application involves the work of linking the import of the truth stated in the text and sermon with a hearer's situation and need."[3] David Mains calls for preaching "to communicate specific responses to genuine needs felt by people."[4] Application has to do with expected responses of the listeners. During the application, the preacher explains to them what they should do with the message and challenges them to actively engage the message by letting it change their lives. Until your people have been challenged to change something in their lives—a behavior, a belief, an attitude, an insecurity, a fear—you have not successfully completed your sermon.

[3]James Earl Massey, "Application in the Sermon," in *Handbook of Contemporary Preaching*, ed. Michael Duduit (Nashville: Broadman & Holman, 1992), 209.

[4]David Mains, "Working from Application to Action," in *Leadership Handbook of Preaching and Worship*, ed. James D. Berkley (Grand Rapids: Baker, 1992), 114.

119

*Correct applica-
tion flows out of
good exegesis.*

[5]Stowell, "Preaching for a Change," 127.

[6]C. H. Spurgeon, *Lectures to My Students* (Grand Rapids: Baker, 1977), 12–13.

Where to Start

Application begins with you, the preacher. Stowell reminds us that "personhood precedes proclamation." If you are going to apply the biblical message to your people, it is imperative that you yourself live a life "exemplary in speech, conduct, love, faith, and purity" in order to "capture the attention of listeners and open the door of their desire to change."[5] One thing is certain: If you live a bad example of applying biblical truth, your listeners will not allow you to direct them or give advice on how to apply Scripture.

Spurgeon described a preacher who was so good in the pulpit that the audience did not want him to leave it, but yet he lived so badly out of the pulpit that no one wanted him to return to it.[6] This preacher struggled with personal application of biblical truth. No preachers are perfect, of course, but certainly all should be striving openly to live the truth. Walking with Christ in obedience is what sets the stage for effective application in your sermon. If your congregation cannot see you living out the application of biblical truth in your life, there is little chance that they will listen to your advice on how to apply it to their lives.

As to the next step, it is important to understand that effective application always grows directly out of the main points of your sermon. If you have done your exegetical work correctly, applying God's truth correctly comes naturally. If you miss the meaning of the text, most likely you will not come up with a valid, biblically-based application. You may be able to present suggested behavior changes for your audience and you may be able to exhort them to change their lives, but if such presentations and exhortations are not connected clearly to the biblical text of the sermon, they lose their biblical authority.

In the previous chapter, you learned that the main idea of your sermon (sermon thesis statement) and the main points of your sermon (sermon points) should come out of your exegesis and your determination of the universal principles in the text. You also learned to phrase the main points of your sermon with present-tense verbs and to direct those points to your specific audience. This process sets up the proper biblical foundation for good application. You must now underscore the connection between the main principles of your text and your audience by urging them to change their lives as a result of those principles.

Let's look at an example. In chapter 5, we presented a sermon thesis statement from Colossians 3:12–17: "Things That Bring Unity to the Church." One of the sermon points was, "If we want to be unified, we must allow the Word of Christ to dwell in our hearts." There are numerous ways to apply this point, such as:

- We must know the Word of Christ if it is to dwell in us. We must spend time studying, meditating on, and memorizing God's Word.
- We must develop an attitude that allows Christ's Word to preside in our hearts in power.
- We must be witnesses of the truth and share the good news. Are we doing that?
- The Word of Christ also instructs us to be people of integrity and honesty. Are we living that way, or are there times when we are less than truthful and honest?

Thus, you can see how the sermon point itself guides you into the application process, at least in general terms.

Getting Specific

Next, you want to move beyond general applications to develop *specific* audience-directed applications that are faithful to the sermon point. Maintaining that balance is not always easy. Haddon Robinson describes the difficulty in this way: "In application we attempt to take what we believe is the truth of the eternal God, which was given in a particular time and place and situation, and apply it to people in the modern world who live in another time, another place, and a very different situation."[7] An ancient but eternal message must be adapted to our modern audience in ways that challenge them to utilize the truth in their own lives. When you have accomplished that, you have truly preached.

[7]See Ed Rowell, "The Heresy of Application: It's When We're Applying Scripture That Error Is Most Likely to Creep in—An Interview with Haddon Robinson," *Leadership* 18 (Fall 1997): 20.

There are a number of different approaches to developing specific applications. We suggest you try each of them and see which ones work best for you.

First, Duvall and Hays suggest three steps for developing a *personal* application of a text. These steps are helpful for developing valid *sermon* applications as well. With slight modification, they are as follows:

1. Observe how the principles in the text address the original situation.
2. Discover a parallel situation in your audience's contemporary context.
3. Make applications specific to your audience's situation, based on the same principles.[8]

Perhaps a little more explanation of these steps will clarify the process. By observing how the universal principles address the original audience, you catch the meaning and the expected response of the original audience. In this step you seek to find the intersection between the text and the situation of the original audience. Then you try to determine similar or parallel situations between the original audience and your audience today. Take the universal principle across the principlizing bridge and apply it to the parallel situation.

Grasping God's Word discusses Philippians 4:13 as an example, one that has relevance for you in preaching as well. In that text Paul writes, "I can do everything through him [Christ] who gives me strength." First, determine the original situation. Paul was a Christian who was experiencing a variety of difficult and trying circumstances because of his faithfulness to the gospel. A parallel situation for today would involve Christians who are experiencing trying and difficult situations because of their faithfulness to the gospel. Thus, as you direct this to your audience, you should say, "When you as a believer experience difficulty for the sake of the gospel, you can expect that God will strengthen you in order for you to endure that difficulty."[9] In simple terms, look for what it meant to Paul and the Philippians (the original context), what is common between your audience and the original one, and consequently how the truth practically affects

[8]Duvall and Hays, *Grasping God's Word*, 216–23.

[9]Ibid., 216.

the life of a listener in your congregation today in a parallel situation. This process can be effective for every sermon and with every text.

Duvall and Hays caution you to include all the elements in order to assure an application that is connected to the original meaning of the text. In the Philippians 4:13 example, it is important not to overlook one of the crucial points—Paul was strengthened when he endured persecution while trying to carry out his calling from God. Some people have used this passage to say that God will strengthen them in any difficult situation regardless of the cause. For example, Christian athletes have used this verse to claim strength from God in athletic competition. This "sports" application misses the message of this text because it overlooks one of the critical components of the original situation—Paul's persecution for faithfully trying to follow Christ. His difficult situation arose because of his faithfulness to God's calling. Your listeners may find themselves in difficult situations because they lied or made decisions out of selfish motives. This passage does not directly relate to their situation since the third element is not present in that situation.

In the third step of application, *Grasping God's Word* reminds you to make your applications as specific as possible. Failure to be specific in application is a common weakness for beginning preachers. They tend to make their applications too broad and generic. For example, a student preacher might preach a message on love and then suggest that the audience go out and love everyone. The audience nods with agreement, for no one will argue against the need to love everyone. However, those listeners leave the preaching event feeling they have been reminded to love but with no specific ideas on *how* to love, or even *whom* to love.

Although you cannot cover every possible situation that requires a loving action, you will help your audience by offering a few specific examples to jump-start the application of the truth process in their minds. You should be specific enough to get your people thinking about other examples, especially ones that relate to them. They should feel challenged to take your specific examples and modify them as needed so that the examples fit them as well.

Make your applications specific!

For example, a sermon on Matthew 5:43–48 will emphasize that Jesus commands us to love our enemies. If you leave that in a general sense, your people will walk away agreeing, but they do not really know where to start. As a result, many will do nothing. It would be much better if you narrowed the focus by asking them to think of someone specifically (by name) that they do not like or who does not like them. Remind them that regardless of the cause for the animosity, they are called to love their enemies. Then lay out some suggestions for how they can express love to those people this week in active, practical ways—a note, an apology, an invitation to lunch. Or perhaps they could mow their grass, bake a cake for them, offer to pick up their children at school, and the like.

These specific ideas might not fit the circumstances of every listener, but at least you start the thinking process and lead them down the correct path to developing a proper application. Make clear that the universal, timeless principle requires them to love their enemies in practical ways, and then prompt them to think of genuine, realistic ways of carrying out those principles.

Another way to take the message of your biblical sermon and hit your people where they live is to use what *Grasping God's Word* refers to as *real-world scenarios.* These scenarios act as examples of how the truth can be put into real life. They show the contemporary audience that God's Word is relevant in all ages and for all people.[10] In this way you can show how the truth comes alive in practical ways for the audience.

When you develop these scenarios, you must always remember the "audience exegesis" information we discussed in chapter 4. In order to be specific with your application, focus it on the audience at hand and their unique situation. What are they dealing with? In what kind of setting would this text come to bear on this audience? To which segment of the audience would these scriptural principles most likely apply and how? What unique issues does your audience deal with and how would the text speak to them? There is risk here because some scenarios might be a bit uncomfortable for the audience since a scenario might actually hit too close to home. But the

[10]Ibid., 218.

risk is worth it, because as your specific application scenario zeroes in on them, they will feel convicted, motivated, or determined to change, all of which are good responses.

Here is a scenario based on the example from Matthew about loving your enemy.

Create applicational real-world scenarios.

Text: Matthew 5:43–48

Scenario: Bill was an up-and-coming young executive in a large investment banking firm in a large city. The atmosphere in the office bordered on a dog-eat-dog mentality—everyone for himself. This tension troubled Bill at first because as a Christian he was uncomfortable with some of the confrontations that occurred, but he eventually got caught up in it himself. Sam, a rival in the business, especially irritated Bill, and they had developed not only a competitive relationship but one quite hateful and vindictive. They truly were enemies.

As passionate as Bill was concerning his job, he was equally so regarding his spiritual walk. One morning during his regular devotional time, he read in the Sermon on the Mount where Jesus called his disciples to love their enemies as well as their friends. Bill felt the sting of conviction. He had only one enemy he could name—and he hated Sam. But this injunction haunted him. He decided it was time to act on this truth of Scripture. So the next day Bill dropped by Sam's office and invited him to lunch. Shocked and a bit suspicious, Sam consented. At lunch Bill simply apologized for things he had said and done to Sam and for his attitudes and feelings toward him.

Bill didn't expect a miracle. He could not control Sam's actions, but he knew he could control his own responses. He made a new effort to fulfill Jesus' command to love our enemies.

David Mains offers additional helpful advice for making effective sermon application through a concept he calls *bridges to behavior*. Mains argues that most listeners concede that the sermon (when based on Scripture) is relevant to them and they want to apply it. They simply don't know how to put it into action. Mains encourages you to "build practical bridges" for your audience by outlining specific steps (bridges) in their response and then even walking them over these bridges step by step. Churches that have invitations at the end of the service regularly do this. For example, during the invitation, pastors

Build bridges for behavioral change.

[11]Mains, "Working from Application to Action," 114–16.

[12]Greidanus, *The Modern Preacher and the Ancient Text*, 184–85.

call for a response, but then they tell the respondents *exactly* what to do: walk down the aisle, share your need, pray with the pastor, and so on. Building a good practical bridge to application is similar in that you tell your audience the exact specific steps they should take in order to apply the point you are stressing.

To determine the nature of your bridge in a sermon, Mains suggests that you ask the following question: "What response does the text demand and how can I best move the people toward that response?"[11] In the sermon share some practical suggestions on how your listeners can carry out the proper response to the truth.

For example, Matthew 7:1–6 deals with judging others. To apply this in your sermon, you might ask your people to take a piece of paper and write on it all the faults they personally possess that they often criticize others for. This step may help them see how the "log" needs to come out of their eye before worrying about someone else's splinters. In this way you provide a practical bridge to begin application, and this beginning point often moves the listener to other specific action.

Note too that effective application should relate to the whole person. By this we mean that God's Word speaks to the entire life of a believer, and not just one aspect or component. Sidney Greidanus warns us about this by pointing out that in the past, many sermons have all too often focused application only on the audience's intellect or will. He recommends that other areas of human life, such as emotions and feelings, get equal consideration. He suggests that you be emotionally involved in your sermon and that you encourage your congregation to engage emotionally as well.[12]

Likewise, consider the whole person in terms of types of needs that you identify and address. A single working mother with two small children faces many unique emotional, physical, and spiritual challenges. Sometimes target your sermon application directly to her needs. In the same manner, working-class men who work seventy hours a week trying to provide for a large family deal with stresses, anxieties, and work issues that you also need to have in mind when you craft your applications. Even the wealthy business person faces ethical and personal struggles and temptations that biblical texts

"What response does the text demand and how can I best move the people toward that response?"
—MAINS

address. It is your task to consider how the biblical truth of your sermon intersects the lives of your people in their unique situations.

As we saw in chapter 4, audience exegesis provides critical information for developing "whole-person" application. Some preachers accomplish this by considering specific components of the audience. In the application part of sermon preparation, they make a list of the various types of people represented in the audience—single mother, divorced middle-aged man, business executive, teenager in a public school, young married couple, retired couple on a fixed income, father without a job, and the like. This list may be long. Use it to think about how the truth at hand applies practically to each person in their situation.

Of course, this introduces multiple variables in the application process. The more homogeneous a congregation is, the more focused application can be. But if a congregation consists of a conglomeration of various types of people in various situations, which is indeed true of most congregations, you should provide various options for application within a sermon. Some of your applications apply to everybody, but frequently you may want to zero in on an application that addresses the need of a special group in your church that you know is struggling. You cannot address every group in every sermon, but be cognizant of the different groups and try to reach each group with some regularity. Obviously, this requires hard and creative work, but it is important to good biblical preaching.

Develop applications to meet the needs of the whole person.

Examples

To illustrate some of the issues discussed above, let's consider two examples. Each example refers to a biblical text and a suggested sermon title. Then one sermon point from that sermon is cited, followed by an application.

Text: Hebrews 12:1–4

Title: How to Keep the Faith

Sermon Point: You can keep the faith if you rid yourself of anything that hinders your walk with Christ.

Application: Evaluate your life (home, work, leisure life) and identify specifically any unconfessed sins, attitudes, relationships,

Avoid oversimplifying!

or anything else that is hurting your Christian walk. If you find a hindrance, make a plan to rid yourself of it—such as confessing it and asking for forgiveness, changing the attitude, changing or stopping a relationship, ceasing an activity, and so on. Even consider finding some help with a few of the hindrances you uncovered. Your plan may include working with a counselor or enlisting a mentor or accountability partner. Make a plan that seriously deals with the problem with the goal of getting rid of it.

Text: Philippians 1:19–26

Sermon Title: Recognizing a Christian

Sermon Point: If people are going to recognize you as a Christian, you must live a life that is not controlled by earthly circumstances.

Application: Are there some situations or circumstances that have you paralyzed with fear, anxiety, anger, or despair? Remind yourself today that God is capable of delivering you from the circumstance and carrying you through it as he did for Paul in prison. In this week's prayer time begin with, "God, here is my circumstance and today I will trust and depend on you in it." Also place on your mirror this week a reminder note stating: "I do not control the circumstances but I do control my response. I can let them get the best of me or I can trust God and react accordingly."

Watch Out!

There are at least three major mistakes to avoid when applying your sermon message to your audience.

First, although you do want to be as specific as possible, avoid oversimplification. For example, one of the things our students often do when applying points (regardless of the spiritual principle) is exhort the audience to have a more consistent quiet time. While this exhortation may truly speak to a portion of the audience, it misses some of the real issues that many believers face; in reality, this advice often ignores the spiritual truth being preached by redirecting the audience in a tangential direction. Listeners desire more direct attention given to their situation, and they desire to hear some solutions (if there are solutions) in the sermon application.

Praying more, going to church more, and giving more are all important applications, but they sound a little simplistic to listeners who are struggling with such difficult problems as uncontrolled anger, addictions, or immorality. Such stock applications cause your listeners to think that you really didn't think through the application of the biblical principle. If you do refer them to spiritual disciplines, explain exactly how those disciplines address their problem. Even give an example or illustration of someone who applied the truth by working through spiritual disciplines of prayer, meditation, or Bible study. Application should never smack of pat answers to difficult issues.

Second, Haddon Robinson warns preachers to avoid legalism in their application process. He defines the "essence of legalism" as "giving to a specific application the force of the principle."[13] That is, if you make the application of a spiritual principle assume the force of the principle itself, you are in danger of laying down laws for your people rather than offering suggested applications. Likewise, although you do want to exhort your audience to respond, you do not want to leave your audience with the implication that they must go out immediately and carry out your application exactly as you stated it or else they will find themselves in sin. Most preachers would never say this explicitly, but the way they word the application or the tone they use could communicate that to the listeners. In such application you merely succeed in giving the congregation a "to do list" of spiritual activities that they interpret as making God happy or making the preacher happy. Both fall short of good application by compromising the biblical principle of grace.

Third, avoid what might be called an "unbalanced" concept of application. As mentioned earlier, some preachers assume that the Holy Spirit does the work of application once the truth has been presented. They tend to minimize application in the sermon, primarily giving just biblical information and usually leaving the challenge of putting it into action with the Holy Spirit and the listener. But note how often God chooses to use people as prompters for application. Look at the messages of the prophets in the Old Testament. They presented God's Word

[13]Haddon Robinson, *Making a Difference in Preaching* (Grand Rapids: Baker, 1999), 90–91.

and then called for specific action as response to that word. That is your task as well.

Conversely, a few preachers forget the Holy Spirit's role and believe they must give all the rules for living through their sermons. This tends toward legalism. Trust that God will use your specific applications in the lives of your listeners, and likewise trust that the Holy Spirit will help your listeners with their specific needs as they relate to the preached Word. Balance is the key here. Faithfully present and offer suggestions of specific relevant application and then let the Holy Spirit guide the believers to act.

Finally, another balance issue concerns pragmatism versus application of biblical truth. Be specific, but don't fall into the trap of just listing ten items that can be done with the truth. Often application means suggesting ways to adjust our thinking or attitudes, which in turn leads to transforming our minds. For instance, when speaking of loving enemies, ask your audience to think about why they don't like a certain person and to work on thinking only good thoughts about that person. This takes time, but then changing hearts takes time.

Summary Guidelines

1. Application finishes the sermon. It calls for response and action after the truth of God's Word has been presented. Without application the sermon is incomplete, so don't ignore this important facet of the preaching task.

2. Application begins with a proper understanding of the meaning of the text. If you miss this during the exegesis, you miss the proper application. Application grows directly out of the main sermon idea and out of the points of the sermon. Craft the points of your sermon in a way that speaks directly to the audience.

3. The makeup and character of the audience determine the specifics of your application. Use the audience exegesis to target application from the text that answers their questions and their needs. What are they dealing with spiritually, physically, emotionally, intellectually, and socially? Is there an application from this principle to answer those concerns?

4. Remember the steps to application. How did the spiritual principle address the original audience? Find the parallels between their time and ours and make sure the contemporary application parallels the original one. Avoid tangents that ignore the context and the original authorial intent. Make the application specific by developing some scenarios specifically written to your audience's situation.

5. Remember to apply the biblical message to the whole person and not just to the intellectual or volitional realms. God's Word speaks to all areas of human life.

6. Try building practical "bridges" that move your audience toward application in realistic step-by-step increments. Give some simple action steps to start them on the road to applying the text. Even though you cannot cover all possible applications for a principle, you can give simple ideas that function as "starters," helping the audience to begin their own thinking process about applying this text.

7. Watch out for legalism and trite simplicity in applications. Good application deals with the genuine needs of the audience.

Now go, preach biblical truth, and lead your people into a meaningful and life-changing response.

Review Questions and Assignments

For the following principles write out (1) how it addressed the original audience, (2) a parallel situation today, and (3) some specific applications for your home church audience.

1. A new life means that we make a commitment to live that new life in Jesus. (Rom. 6:4, 8)

2. God gives each of us a gift that should be used for the church. (Rom. 12:6–8)

3. Pride negates the effectiveness of our prayer. (Luke 18:11–14)

4. When we find ourselves surrounded by spiritual enemies, God is our protector. (Ps. 23:4–5)

5. When we encounter the living God, we are confronted with our own sin and shortcomings. (Isa. 6:5)

Illustrating Biblical Truth 7

THE FOCUS OF CHAPTER 7:	
Step 1	Grasp the Meaning of the Text in Their Town
Step 2	Measure the Width of the Interpretive River
Step 3	Cross the Principlizing Bridge
Step 4	Grasp the Text in Our Town
Step 5	Exegete Your Congregation
Step 6	Determine How Much Background Material to Include
Step 7	Determine the Sermon Thesis and Main Points
Step 8	Develop Text-Centered Applications
Step 9	Find Illustrations
Step 10	Write Out the Sermon and Practice Delivery

Have you ever experienced a preaching event that so impacted your mind and heart that it still floods your memory? Let me share an experience of mine. Rob Bell spoke—or should I say truly communicated—at a gathering of pastors in San Diego a few years ago. He began rather normally by reading about the Day of Atonement from Leviticus in the Old Testament. As he described the high priest adorned with elaborate ritual garb, out walked the high priest—or at least a great portrayal of him. Rob described and shared the significance of each part of the attire as he pointed to the man standing in front of us. He transitioned to the work of the high priest on the

A good illustration will imbed the message into the minds and hearts of your audience.

Day of Atonement by speaking of the sacrifice and the blood atonement. Rob elaborated on the movement of the high priest into the Most Holy Place, where he would sprinkle the blood of a sacrificed goat over the mercy seat of the ark of the covenant. This ritual covered the sins of the people of Israel.

But, Rob continued, the work of the high priest was not yet complete. Keep in mind I am still looking at this man in all his priestly robes standing before me. Rob explained that now another animal—a second goat—would be brought in for the priest. Guess what? In came a goat—a real, live goat. As this gifted preacher wove the story of how the high priest placed his hands on the goat, the visible priest moved to the goat and placed his hands on him, signifying that the sins of Israel had now been transferred to the scapegoat, who would carry the sins away. Rob narrowed to the main point. This goat was to be taken away, and then the priest's task was complete. Jesus came to be the sacrifice for us. He takes away our sins.

The goat was then led off the stage. Rob continued by explaining that when Israel's high priest was done and the sins of Israel were taken away, he would sit down in front of the people, and at that moment the people of Israel would erupt into praise and celebration. Rob assured us the priest was about to sit. The goat had left the building. When he did sit, Rob told us we were to burst into praise and celebration. That is exactly what happened: When the high priest walked to the chair and sat down, we—all 2,000 of us—went crazy with praise, dancing, and all other sorts of excitement. Why? We had just heard a great sermon communicating that our sins had been taken away.

How can I remember that sermon in such detail after two years? One reason—the sermon illustration drove the message home and imbedded it into my mind and heart. I will never forget that sermon. But I guarantee if Rob had just stood up and talked about the Day of Atonement for thirty minutes, I might not even remember what he preached about.

Now you may be thinking: "I certainly cannot bring actors and animals into my sermons every week." True, but you probably could on occasion. In any case, the point we are trying to make with this elaborate example is that all sermons need elements that carry a similar impact. You may use a goat, share a story, use a prop or object lesson, or show a movie clip to move the message along and aid in the communication of your sermon. In this chapter we will spend some time thinking about how we can give our sermons more punch to ensure greater impact on people.

Reasons to Illustrate

All of us preach to audiences who are accustomed to reality TV and unaccustomed to listening to a long lecture with lists of points. Rob Harley claims that the culture of the Western world has developed a people who "are no longer disposed to getting their information and their values by sitting in orderly rows listening to someone stand behind a lectern for 30 to 45 minutes at a time." Television has exacerbated this situation. "Add to this trend, the effect of television on people's attention spans—about six seconds before a child's mind will wander, for adults about eight seconds—and you see the potential for boring messages and distractions to derail listeners' thought processes away from what you are saying."[1] Contemporary audiences are just not wired for long, information-bearing discourses. They need stories, examples, or imaginative pictures to help convey the message.

John Killinger provides us a second reason for using illustrations. A good sermon is one that "achieves a healthy balance between abstraction and imagery." Killinger bases his argument on the fact that different people tend to think differently. Some are "right-brained," meaning they are more imaginative and creative. Others are "left-brained," tending more to pragmatism and analytical thinking. Even preachers tend to one category or the other. That is why some preachers prefer practical, outline sermons while others preach more imaginatively. Certainly the competent preacher tests the sermon for logic and theological meaning, but then "consults the right side of the brain for ways of illustrating the thoughts, of turning them into images or pictures that will give them life and specificity."[2] In other

[1]Rob Harley, *The Power of the Story* (Auckland, New Zealand: End Results, 2001), 13.

[2]John Killinger, *The Fundamentals of Preaching* (Minneapolis: Augsburg Fortress, 1996), 105–6.

words, illustrations speak to people who learn better through visual or imaginative styles.

Illustrations are capable of infusing the sermon with an emotional charge that connects the message, the audience, and their culture. David Buttrick in *Homiletic: Moves and Structures* describes this connection in these words: "Illustrations have enormous power: One fourteen-sentence illustration has more potential force than twenty sentences of content."[3] Certainly sermons without content are empty, but sermons without illustrations often fail to connect with the audience. Some preachers just move through the verses of the text, giving us ample data on the meaning but never helping us see it with our imagination. Words are not always sufficient to engage our senses, our imagination, and our dreams. To be honest, illustrations make sermons more interesting, and people pay attention to what interests them.

A final reason for illustrations is that some spiritual truths are complex and difficult for people to understand. Instead of just adding more words to the mix, offer pictures, stories, or examples to unpack that truth for the audience.

[3]David Buttrick, *Homiletic: Moves and Structures* (Philadelphia: Fortress, 1987), 138.

Reasons for Using Illustrations

- Audiences today are not wired for lectures.
- Some people need pictures in order to learn.
- Illustrations infuse emotional charge into the sermon.
- Illustrations help clarify difficult concepts.

Defining Illustrations

According to *Webster's New Word Dictionary*, the term "illustrate" means "to explain or make clear by examples." Based on that definition, an illustration clarifies the spiritual principle at hand. I recall taking geometry in high school and finding it difficult to grasp concepts until the teacher used the blackboard to illustrate. Sermon illustrations serve as pictures designed to help the audience grasp the spiritual concept. Pictures come in various forms—stories, object lessons, quotes, personal observations, or a variety of other forms. But they always fulfill one goal—to clarify the point or concept. Thus, if a spiritual truth is the least bit complex or if one person in the audience could be helped by an example or a picture, then illustrate. Jesus himself taught by example that people need stories, examples, and analogies to clarify truth in their minds.

Finding Illustrations

The secret to finding great illustrations: Read! Read! Read!

While we cannot give all the ins and outs of finding illustrations, we can get you started. As you get more experience, you will begin to find illustrations in all kinds of places.

Personal Stories

Personal stories are effective illustrations when used in moderation and when they fit the point being illustrated. They remind the congregation that you have a life outside the pulpit. They reveal your humanity and show a willingness to be open and vulnerable to the audience. They present you as a genuine struggler along with the congregation (i.e., if you don't always portray yourself as the hero in personal stories). They show the personal side of truth.

But be careful. When used too often personal stories tend to grow stale and even repulsive. We probably all know people who repeat the same story or talk only about themselves. You get the picture. Some of your listeners only see you on Sunday at the sermon hour. If every example of spiritual truth comes from your experience, they think one of several things: You are the best example in the world of spiritual truth, both negative and positive; or you are egotistical; or you don't have any other illustration sources (which doesn't speak well of your imagination or intelligence). When used wisely and sparingly, personal stories effectively clarify the text. Remember that the goal of an illustration is to illuminate God's truth. If you use personal stories with that in mind, they produce good results.

Have You Read Any Good Books Lately?

Are you ready for the secret to finding good illustrations? Get your pen and paper ready. Here it is. Read! Read! Read! Preachers who repeatedly come up with insightful, thought-provoking, and enlightening illustrations are those who read regularly. Well-read preachers generally illustrate well. Others may search constantly for that perfect illustration, but readers come across them daily.

You as a preacher should read everything fit to read. Broad reading is the key to good illustrations. Many of you spend all your time reading good theology books. That works fine for boosting your personal understanding, but it doesn't provide many illustrations for your sermons. Read magazines, biographies, fiction, and maybe even some of the material your audience reads.

Read classics because the stories are timeless. Some of the best and most interesting illustrations, for example, are found in some of Mark Twain's writings. Read some of the latest Christian works because the more serious believers in the congregation read them. The newspaper also provides a good source for human interest stories and other issues that relate to your audience. If you spend just thirty minutes a day reading something of value, you will be helped tremendously with illustration material.

Let Them See It

People are immersed today in visual media, and its influence appears to be growing stronger. Most people watch several hours of television per day and more than a few movies per month. This medium shapes our lives, beliefs, values, and opinions—for good or for bad. Regardless of what preachers think of visual media, you need to acknowledge its power to influence your listeners and its potential for enhancing your sermons. We encourage you to use the visual media as a tool for communicating. Stories from television, news, or movies can serve as powerful illustrations, though you must keep a few things in mind.

Many preachers in contemporary churches, equipped with screens and the most up-to-date audiovisual gadgets, use movie and television clips regularly to illustrate points in the sermon. Some utilize them effectively while others use them without much discernment just because they are interesting and innovative. Like all illustrations, the way you use these media tools is what makes them effective or ineffective.

Movie clips are so popular as illustrations that entire books compiling clips from movies are being published. Craig Larson and Andrew Zahn have edited the book *Movie-Based Illustrations for Preaching and Teaching*, which includes over a hundred clips for use as sermon illustrations. They address issues related to these illustrations, such as how to determine what is objectionable and should not be used in a sermon. They insist that you should "not illustrate from any movie regarded as having no redeeming value." They also refuse to use scenes that "contain(s) objectionable elements."[4]

We tend to agree with Larson and Zahn but would go one step further. Some movies or television programs watched regularly by your audience should not be highlighted in a sermon setting. Even though you intend the selected clip to illustrate a spiritual truth, it still advertises a portion of a program that in its entirety may be unacceptable or offensive. In 1 Corinthians 8 Paul warns believers not to do anything to offend weaker Christian friends or harm their spiritual growth. That principle applies here. Some movies or television programs (even if you use only a brief clip that actually does illustrate your point) have little redeeming moral or social value, and using them in a sermon may do more harm than good.

Another consideration is how advertising the program will reflect on you as the preacher. For the listeners to realize you watch a program or movie that promotes unchristian values could hinder your leadership. We do not want to encourage legalism by making this argument, but you still must consider audience response when using media clips as illustrations. In making judgments about which clips are acceptable, keep your audience exegesis in mind. What would offend in one congregation may present no problem for another.

Be sure that the visual media illustrations you select relate directly to your sermon points. In addition, even when you can find great clips that touch on the topic of the sermon, you must still prepare the audience for the clip, transition to the clip, and connect the clip to the biblical point at hand. For more on this, see "Connections and Transitions," below.

Be sure that the visual media illustrations you select relate directly to your sermon points.

[4]Craig Brian Larson and Andrew Zahn, *Movie-Based Illustrations for Preaching and Teaching* (Grand Rapids: Zondervan, 2003), 10. See also Craig Brian Larson and Lori Quicke, *More Movie-Based Illustrations for Preaching and Teaching* (Grand Rapids: Zondervan, 2004); Doug Fields and Eddie James, *Videos That Teach* (Grand Rapids: Zondervan, 1999); idem, *Videos That Teach 2* (Grand Rapids: Zondervan, 2002); idem, *Videos That Teach 3* (Grand Rapids: Zondervan, 2004); Bryan Belknap, *Group's Blockbuster Movie Illustrations* (Loveland, CO: Group Publishing, 2001); idem, *Group's Blockbuster Movie Illustrations: The Sequel* (Loveland, CO: Group Publishing, 2003).

One last thing. Larson and Zahn remind us that churches need permission to show movie clips in worship services, although if you verbally relate the scene from the movie without actually showing the clip, no permission is necessary. Churches may purchase yearly licenses that "cover clips in sermons, plus videos shown in classes and youth groups and at events such as family film nights—as long as no admission fee is charged and the title is not advertised to the general public."[5]

[5]Ibid. Prices, addresses, and phone numbers for these licenses can be found in this source.

Life Illustrates Well

Life illustrations include things that happen to those you know or hear about. You obtain these stories by observation or conversation. You see or hear of some event that sheds light on biblical truth. These stories are effective because they allow the audience to relate to real people who have experienced real situations.

We offer two cautions for using real-life illustrations, however. First, never use another person's story unless you have permission to do so. Even if that person is not in the audience, he or she might resent the broadcasting of that incident from the pulpit. Likewise, get permission before telling stories about your own family. My family has a standing rule that because being part of a pastor's family involves so much public scrutiny, no family stories are allowed in sermons. This personal policy preserves a bit of privacy for us. You can never be certain what will embarrass people. The rule of thumb is to always get permission before sharing a personal story.

Second, be careful about sharing any stories from counseling or ministry situations. Many pastors believe they can share life stories if no names are mentioned. Even if the rest of the audience cannot recognize the main characters of the story, the counselee might and become reluctant to share with you ever again. Some preachers believe counseling and ministry stories are acceptable as long as the stories do not relate to the current church. But be careful. Potential counselees might conclude that if you share another's story, you will eventually share their stories. Always get permission before sharing stories from counseling situations and let the congregation know you have gotten such permission.

You Can Borrow One

Sometimes you hear great illustrations from wonderful preachers at conferences or on the radio or television. These illustrations seem good enough to be recycled, and this is normally acceptable if certain guidelines are followed. Always give credit for the source of the illustration: "In a sermon by Joe Preacher he tells the story about…." If Joe mentioned his source, you can refer to it as the source of the illustration. Never use a story told by another preacher about his life and tell it as your own. We shouldn't have to mention this caution in a preaching textbook, but regrettably we know this happens, and the consequences can be disastrous. Christian ethics includes the use of sermon illustrations.

> *Your imagination is one of your best sources for good illustrations.*

Use Your Imagination

The human imagination is often a forgotten resource for sermon illustrations. Some preachers possess a talent for writing fictional stories that powerfully illustrate truth. Created stories are advantageous because they can be written to illustrate virtually every spiritual principle. We know a missionary who writes a new storybook every Christmas for his daughters. There is little doubt that if he needs an illustration, he can create it.

I have dabbled in creative writing myself. One Easter I collaborated with the choir to create a monologue that would be interspersed with music. Based on Peter's recollections of Jesus and the text relating to those, I freely imagined Peter's thoughts and emotions as I recounted the resurrection story. The audience talked about it for weeks, and they experienced Easter in a new way.

Some Hard Work

You will find some illustrations as a result of old-fashioned hard work and research. For example, if you are preaching on how Christians should respond to the problem of world hunger, search for statistics related to the needs of the world as a means of persuading your audience to get involved. The field of science offers plenty of illustrative material. Make sure you keep your language nontechnical so that everyone can follow you.

For example, I once preached a sermon on the Holy Spirit as the unifying force in the church. I illustrated this unity and connection using an article from *Reader's Digest* about the great forests of the Western United States being connected by root systems. This phenomenon results from a certain fungus that reduces competition between trees and promotes cooperation. We could use a fungus like that in the church, and I pointed out that it is the Holy Spirit that unifies us. Science, sociology, psychology, history, political science, art, literature, and many other disciplines provide useful and interesting illustrations that can strengthen your sermon.

Surf the Web

We live in a technological and computer-oriented world, and all of us are becoming more dependent on internet sources for our information. This is true in our search for illustrative material. The web offers numerous avenues for discovering data helpful to sermons. Some websites even promote preaching instruction while providing resources for everything from whole sermons to outlines to illustrations. We suggest, of course, that you develop your own sermons, but the internet does provide yet another option for illustrations.

However, we offer a note of caution related to material found in the preaching-related websites. If a story or quote or other type of illustration is found on the internet, it may indicate that it has been around and has probably surfaced in sermons on numerous occasions. This would also be true with sermon illustration books. The fact that they have been collected usually indicates they have been used. However, compared to the illustration book, the web may be fresher since it can be updated daily. Don't shun these sources, but still try to keep illustrations as original as possible. Christianity Today is one organization that consistently provides up-to-date, reliable information on the web. Start by visiting *ChristianityToday.com* where you can survey the many resources available for preachers. We especially recommend "Christianity Today Library" for access to high-quality, well-researched material in a searchable format.

Using Illustrations

Connections and Transitions

Connecting your illustrations to the sermon point is the key consideration. On their own most illustrations are interesting, but they should never be used merely to build interest. Their primary role is to clarify, illuminate, or simplify a point, principle, or truth. Students will sometimes discover a great story and feel compelled to include it even if it does not clarify or illustrate anything related to the heart of the sermon. Some will even shape the entire sermon around a captivating story. Remember the sermon should always be driven by the biblical text, not by a gripping illustration. The tail should not be allowed to wag the dog. Illustrations are not ends in themselves, but tools to make sermon points more understandable and inspiring.

Another aspect in connecting an illustration to a sermon is the concept of movement. Some preachers use illustrations to move the sermon forward or to create a certain mood in the audience. By doing so they advance the plot and set up the listener to grasp the truth better. In this case the illustration doesn't clarify just one point but becomes a component of the whole idea. The illustration may itself serve as the transition or connection within the sermon.

Transitions often determine the effectiveness of a sermon. A *transition* is the logical, natural movement from one concept or idea within the sermon to another. Illustrations crave transitions because transitions provide the lead-in and pave the way for the illustration to accomplish its goal of clarifying biblical truth. You can introduce an illustration with something as simple as "in a similar way" or "this idea might best be seen in a story about...."

Avoid abrupt, rough transitions where the sermon shifts harshly from the biblical discussion to some random story. At least give your audience a clue that you are about to move into a story. Usually after giving your illustration, you should insert a sentence or two showing how the illustration opens a window to the sermon point. This transition following the illustration is crucial, since it allows you to explain why this illustration fits the spiritual truth and makes it clearer. Use transitions such as, "Just as the father in the story struggled with guilt because of the way he treated people, the Bible reminds us that we will have similar guilt," or "Jason would not give up his old life in order to follow Jesus and the rich young ruler felt the same way. It was too much of a sacrifice."

When you omit transition sentences in and out of your illustrations (or, for that matter, in and out of any sermon segment), you leave the sermon sounding wooden and clumsy, forcing the audience to find their own connections. Buttrick says that in the transitions we are "initiating a thoughtful connection between the content and illustration in the consciousness of a congregation."[6] Transitions are like the threads that tie together the sermon point and the illustration so that the two function as one.

Evaluating Illustrations

Some illustrations simply don't belong in sermons. Braga suggests that "the bizarre, the coarse, and the grotesque have no place in preaching. Their use by the preacher may lay him open for the charge of frivolity, vulgarity, or irreverence."[7] Braga is rightly concerned with the reputation of the preacher. A preacher's character is foundational to persuasive communication. When a preacher tells an off-color joke or uses an offensive or distasteful illustration, the audience will begin to question his character. Once again, your audience exegesis offers insight concerning congregational tolerance.

Evaluate an illustration carefully before using it because stories have the power to stimulate the imagination to envision what is being described. For instance, a good novel will captivate your imagination by building certain images and pictures in your mind about a character or a scene. You see with your mind's eye the people, the setting, and the chain of events. This is part of the fun of getting lost in a good book. Your imagination is engaged. (This is probably the main reason why we sometimes don't like the movie after we have read the book. The movie doesn't match the visions we have already created in our minds.) Similarly, sermon illustrations unleash the audience's imagination. The listeners use your spoken words to draw pictures in their

[6]Buttrick, *Homiletic: Moves and Structures*, 149.

[7]James Braga, *How to Prepare Bible Messages* (Portland: Multnomah, 1981), 198.

minds. Because of the power of the human imagination, you need to ask, "What specifically do I want them thinking about and imagining as I present the truth about God?"

When preachers share detailed stories about people having affairs or about a person's addiction to pornography, they should be aware of the potential effect on their listeners. What may at first seem like a fitting illustration for a sermon addressing adultery or immorality may cause your listeners to fantasize about sexual scenarios. Are those the images you want in the minds of your people during a worship experience? We don't think so. Could one inappropriate illustration derail an entire sermon? Certainly. In other words, illustrations should be avoided when they trigger images in the imagination that overpower the worship experience. We don't wish to be puritanical here, but having heard many inappropriate illustrations, we feel obligated to remind you of the power and unpredictability of the imagination.

You should also avoid insensitive illustrations—stories that cause pain or unintentionally hurt some members of the audience. Without thinking, we have used illustrations and halfway through the story realized that someone in the audience just lost a loved one to suicide or drug abuse or some other issue related to the story. As you choose your illustrations, be sensitive to the feelings and circumstances of the audience.

What do I want my audience thinking about as I present the truth about God?

Length

Illustrations clarify sermon points, but they do not constitute *the point* of the sermon. Therefore, avoid illustrations that consume vast amounts of sermon time. Almost all preaching professors agree that good illustrations should be brief and to the point. Most sermon material focuses on biblical truth, and the illustration merely enhances that truth. When the illustration is too lengthy, balance is lost and the illustration overshadows the message.

Keep your illustrations brief and tie them closely to the biblical point. If they ramble on, the audience may forget what you were seeking to illustrate. No illustration is worth five minutes of a twenty-minute

Good stories are memorable.

sermon. If a long story cannot be edited into a shorter version, find another illustration.

Number

There is no hard and fast rule about the correct number of illustrations, though many experts argue that one illustration per main idea or point in the sermon is sufficient. Buttrick speaks in terms of moves rather than points, but he still cautions preachers to use only one illustration per move.[8]

In our preaching classes we limit students to one illustration per point plus one for the introduction and conclusion, respectively. In a narrative sermon, we teach them to keep a good balance between biblical truth, which should be prominent, and illustrative material. They need to learn to find and use illustrations without allowing them to take over the sermon. Too few illustrations make for a bland sermon without much relevance to real life. Too many illustrations can blur the biblical message and confuse the audience about the nature of spiritual truth.

Storytelling

As you may have noticed, we mention "stories" often when discussing illustrations. Many illustrations take the form of a story. Thus, this question is appropriate: Can you tell a story? Some preachers can and some can't. For those who struggle here, we think improvement is possible. You can become a better storyteller if you work at it. Growing in this area will improve your preaching. Bruce Salmon insists that "stories are a great way of getting people to understand the point you are making, by the sheer power of illustration."[9] Stories connect the biblical truth to an illustration form that is more memorable. But the value of a story is in the telling. So let's work on it.

Salmon lists several characteristics of a good story:[10]

- single, clearly defined theme
- single perspective from which the story develops

[8]Buttrick, *Homiletic: Moves and Structures*, 135.

[9]Bruce C. Salmon, *Storytelling in Preaching: A Guide to the Theory and Practice* (Nashville: Broadman, 1988), 8.

[10]Ibid., 39–40.

- a well-formed plot that moves from calm to conflict to resolution
- realistic, graphic detail
- appeal to the senses
- only a few major characters
- reliance on direct speech
- judicious use of repetition with the most important thing being mentioned last

If you're not a natural storyteller, become a student of story-telling and strive to improve your skill. Listen to great storytellers like Garrison Keillor. Learn from good books, such as Bruce Salmon's *Storytelling in Preaching*, Rob Harley's *The Power of Story*, and John Walsh's *The Art of Storytelling*. The Bible itself presents a grand story, and learning how to tell stories well can only improve your biblical preaching.

Saving Illustrations

What should you do when you begin to accumulate a large collection of illustrative material? How can you keep up with it? We have discovered that if you randomly select fifteen preachers, you will get fifteen different ideas for organizing sermons and illustrations. Some use the simple method of throwing them all into a desk drawer and then shuffling through them as needed. This fits some personalities. More organized preachers use folders and card files, cataloging each illustration with a note on which file to search. The folders are often labeled with topics like faith, hope, and love, or catalogued under specific Scripture texts.

These methods may appear old-fashioned to you, and you may opt for computer-based data storage. The same principles apply with folders and easy retrieval. Organization style—complex or simple—remains your own personal choice, and you will no doubt find one that fits you best. For those who need help, books such as Michael Green, *Green's Filing Systems for Pastors and Christian Workers*, can be helpful.

Things to Avoid

1. Never include an illustration unless it either clarifies or moves the audience toward biblical truth.
2. Never allow an illustration to ramble on and on so that the audience forgets the spiritual principle.
3. Never use an illustration that needs explanation since that defeats the purpose of using an illustration.
4. Don't use inappropriate illustrations that carry the audience's imagination away from God.

Summary

1. Select illustrations that clearly connect to the point you are trying to make.
2. Be creative and vary your illustrations. Use numerous sources. Read, read, read!
3. Give credit where credit is due.
4. Use as many illustrations as you need, but usually only one per point, principle, or movement in the sermon.
5. Make sure your transition into and out of the illustration solidifies the connection to the point. Don't leave the audience guessing.

Now write a sermon filled with interesting life illustrations that make the truth clear, understandable, and interesting.

Review Questions and Assignments

Here is a list of possible sermon issues that you might include in a message:

- Faith in times of fear
- Need for witnessing to the lost world
- Dealing with depression
- God's guidance in times of confusion
- Need for strong marriages

For each issue:

1. Find an interesting story or article from print media.
2. Find a movie clip.
3. Find a personal story.
4. Write a story.

8

Delivering a Biblical Sermon

Stand and Deliver
Keep It Natural
A Matter of Style
You're in Good Voice Today
Body Language
Other Issues
Getting Better and Better
Review Questions and Assignments

As he approaches the podium, the crowd already senses his contagious energy. He begins to speak, immediately capturing the crowd. His booming voice fills the auditorium, but it is not so loud that he can't raise it when he wants to really emphasize a point. Weaving humor and seriousness together throughout, inflecting his voice and changing his demeanor, he holds the crowd in his hand. The power of his delivery is enhanced by animated expression of his hands, face, and body. The crowd is entranced by his whir of activity. In fact, his movements on stage give the impression of perpetual motion although he never really leaves the podium. What makes this biblical message so enthralling and powerful? Is it just what he has to say? Certainly the content of the sermon is engaging, but it is his delivery that captivates the crowd.

As I write this, I have been watching one of the preachers highlighted on the video series, *Great Preachers*. I know at least one of the reasons why this man is included in the category of "great preachers." It is his delivery—full of animation, voice control, and movement choreographed to the message. His name is Tony Campolo, and I have often marveled at his expertise at delivering a sermon.

Campolo is master at an oft-neglected part of the preaching experience—the delivery. His delivery carries the sermon and places it in our hearts and minds. Although the sermon he preaches is solid, I cannot help but think that if another person took the exact same words and preached them, the effect would not be the same. His ability to deliver with passion and energy makes the difference.

What about you? Does your delivery enhance your message or detract from it? Do you spend an appropriate amount of time developing your delivery? Can you stand and deliver?

> To be an effective and powerful preacher, you must spend time working on your delivery.

Stand and Deliver

In a typical homiletics class many students often work hard at exegesis and try carefully to develop a quality sermon. In fact, they often work on the sermon right up to their assigned time to preach. Then they just do the best they can, often having given little time to prepare for communicating the message verbally. Unfortunately, this usually results in extremely poor sermon deliveries.

The tendency for students to procrastinate has forced us to require that they finish their sermons and turn them in a few days before their scheduled delivery. This forced schedule provides time for them to work on their presentation. Students must realize that the delivery of the sermon is just as crucial as its development. Unfortunately, our students are not alone in their neglect of sermon delivery preparation. Ralph Lewis comments that during his fifty years of preaching and instructing preachers, he has noticed that sermon delivery has nearly become "a forgotten factor in ministerial training."[1]

[1]Ralph Lewis. "Sermon Delivery," in *Leadership Handbook of Preaching and Worship* (Grand Rapids: Baker, 1992), 119.

Thomas Long argues that written sermons are "a contradiction in terms." Although we encourage you to write out your sermons, we concur with Long that as long as it remains only in written form, it is not really a sermon. Sermons are meant to be delivered. They are "spoken event(s)."[2] Brown, Clinard, and Northcutt state: "The delivery of the sermon is the most dynamic moment of the preaching experience." It is more dynamic than the preparation and development because it is the point of communication. They conclude that a "sermon is never a sermon until it is delivered."[3] Your sermon may look good and communicate well on paper, but it must be delivered orally in person to an audience. Few people will read your sermons. They come to hear and experience them and be changed by them. Delivery matters.

Keep It Natural

We begin with you, the preacher. Above all, your delivery needs to be natural—that is, consistent with your personality and the normal ways you express yourself, with some practiced refinement. Your sermon delivery style should enhance communication rather than detract from it. Any time your delivery itself becomes the focal point for the audience, you risk damaging your message. Strive for a delivery that seems natural so that the audience focuses on the truth of your message rather than on distractions in your delivery.

I had a friend in seminary whom I knew quite well. I knew his voice, his mannerisms, and his usual ways of communicating. So the first time I heard him preach, I was shocked. Was this the same guy? I hardly recognized his voice (it had changed to a preacherly tone), his gestures (they appeared contrived and wooden), or his general demeanor. I found it all but impossible to focus on the message because I could not get past my friend's strange personality transformation. Bryan Chapell rightly emphasizes that "the goal of the preacher is to get out of the way of the message."[4]

How can you learn to communicate in a way that is natural and consistent with your personality, yet still powerful? In what follows we will consider several important dimensions of sermon delivery, including style, voice, and body language.

[2]Thomas G. Long. *The Witness of Preaching* (Louisville: Westminster John Knox, 1989), 181.

[3]H. C. Brown, H. Gordon Clinard, and Jesse J. Northcutt. *Steps to the Sermon* (Nashville: Broadman, 1963), 164.

[4]Bryan Chapell. *Redeeming the Expository Sermon: Christ-Centered Preaching* (Grand Rapids: Baker, 1994), 315.

A Matter of Style

Every preacher has his own way of doing things—his style. McDill claims that style is the normal manner in which a preacher expresses his thoughts and ideas in both speech and writing.[5] This definition suggests that each preacher has his or her own way of using vocabulary, speech patterns, and body language, based largely on one's personality, education, experience, and comfort level.

Some argue that your delivery style is shaped by your personality and cannot be changed, even if there are aspects of your style that hinder communication. But behavioral change is indeed possible, and so is a change in sermon-delivery style. While we all have a natural style, sometimes adjustment becomes necessary in order to communicate better. For example, we often encounter students who have little facial expression, body movement, or variation in voice tone. While they may have grown comfortable with this particular style, they must do some adjusting to communicate effectively with most audiences. Even a comfortable style can be changed while still maintaining a natural quality.

Others connect style to the actual mechanics of the presentation. Brown, Clinard, and Northcutt, for example, suggest that "style" is what the preacher chooses to take into the pulpit with him in the form of notes, that is, in his manner of presentation.[6] In this sense, there are three basic stylistic methods of preaching.

Manuscript Preaching Style

In this style, the preacher writes a complete manuscript and carries it into the pulpit. Some read word for word while others read the more familiar parts of the manuscript with some variation or freestyle delivery. It requires a great deal of talent to be able to read and maintain eye contact and still make it sound like something other than a formal document.

Some students and preachers possess a natural talent for manuscript preaching, but this approach is perhaps the most difficult style to develop. However, Scott Duvall enjoys this style of preaching. He

Your preaching style should be natural and comfortable, both to you and to your audience.

[5]Wayne McDill, *The Moment of Truth* (Nashville: Broadman & Holman, 1999), 114.

[6]Brown, Clinard, and Northcutt, *Steps to the Sermon*, 185.

carries a full manuscript into the pulpit with the key ideas highlighted. He has learned to carry off this type of presentation in a way that appears extemporaneous. If you want to develop this style, plan to devote a lot of time to becoming familiar with your manuscript through repeated reading.

Memorization Style

In this style the preacher memorizes the entire sermon manuscript and delivers it from memory. Normally no notes are taken into the pulpit. This requires tremendous effort, a great deal of time, and a talent for memorization. Some preachers love this unencumbered delivery experience because it allows for maximum eye contact with the audience. This method, however, carries risks since most of us can get rattled and forget portions of the sermon. Although some preachers enjoy this style of preaching, especially when the situation allows them ample time for preparation, most will need to carry a key-idea outline into the pulpit as a safety net.

Extemporaneous Style

This style also starts with a full manuscript or an extensive outline of the sermon. The written work is studied and then reduced to notes—sometimes brief, at other times quite extensive. I (Terry) prefer this style, and I usually make notes on a three-by-five card, outlining the main sermon points and illustrations. I carry this card into the pulpit with me, and this outline keeps me on track, protecting me from forgetting the sermon's flow of thought. The extemporaneous style still allows me freedom to speak without being tied to set words, phrases, or sentences.

Even if you choose this style, it is still smart to write and file a complete manuscript for future use along with the abbreviated pulpit notes. The brief notes by themselves don't always make sense three years later. Let's face it. After a few years, we may forget what "the story about a boy with a fishing lure" is exactly. The manuscript contains the full story, but the pulpit notes allow for a free and natural presentation.

Believe it or not, some even recommend a completely impromptu style, where the preacher goes to the pulpit with no prior preparation, opens the Bible, and speaks anything that comes to mind. This style is not an option for developing and delivering a meaningful sermon based on Scripture. Avoid it!

All three styles can be used to preach inductive, deductive, or narrative sermons. Whatever style works best depends completely on you—your comfort zone, talents, and personality. We encourage you to experiment and find the style of delivery that best fits you, remembering that it never hurts to vary your style occasionally.

Preach within the normal pitch range of your voice.

You're in Good Voice Today

Have you ever said something and then been told that even though you used the right words, your tone of voice conveyed another message? Maybe you sounded a bit irritated or angry or just impatient. We all suffer from this mistake. It's not always the words; sometimes it is just the way we say it. Your voice is a big part of the delivery of your message. Several important elements are related to the voice in the delivery.

Pitch

Phonation is the production of sound as the air passes through the vocal chords. The sound produced always has a tonal quality called pitch, which is either high or low (like notes on a piano). Some people are naturally high-pitched while others are on the low end of the scale. Neither is necessarily better than the other for preaching. You should try to preach within the normal pitch range of your voice to maintain throat health and comfort.

When a preacher at one end of the pitch scale preaches an entire sermon at the other end, it can result in a fatigued voice, or worse, a damaged voice. Have you ever heard someone trying to sing an old Beach Boys' song with a falsetto voice? It hurts. Too much of that kind of voice stress over a period of time will harm the vocal chords. The key is to stay in your personal pitch range and vary only for emphasis.

Vary your volume for emphasis.

Nervousness tends to raise the voice pitch to higher levels, but you can learn to speak within the normal ranges even when you are nervous.

Pace

Pace is the rate at which you speak words. Variety in pace helps create interest, though anxious speakers tend to increase pace and maintain a fast pace throughout the sermon. Some beginning preachers preach twenty-five-minute sermons in fifteen minutes simply because they get nervous and speak too fast. A pace that is too quick exceeds the audience's level of comprehension. A rushed message also conveys nervousness to the audience, detracting from the message.

Other beginners, however, suffer the other extreme, preaching at a slow pace, often because of their cultural background or personality. This too presents problems for communication because the average listener hears and comprehends faster than slow-paced speaking. The audience grows bored, loses interest, or falls asleep.

According to Joel Gregory, the normal pace for preaching is 125 to 190 words per minute. Experts say that 200 words or more per minute will result in a loss of comprehension for the listener.[7] Your goal is to keep the speaking pace at levels that aid comprehension and then vary from time to time for emphasis.

Problems related to vocal pacing can be corrected with time and effort. By the way, as you preach, pause occasionally and take a breath. Pauses or moments of silence provide powerful breaks in sermon delivery that allow the audience time to mull over what you just said. Pauses also can communicate emphasis and focus.

Volume

Volume refers to how loud you speak. Some preachers continuously raise their voices while preaching, so that it often sounds like yelling. Raising the voice creates emphasis, but when every word is spoken loudly, volume loses its power to attract attention and bring emphasis.

The key to volume is adequacy and variety. Always speak loudly enough so everyone can hear you, but vary the volume to bring attention and emphasis to certain parts of the sermon. You can accomplish

[7]Joel Gregory, "The Voice in Preaching," in *Handbook of Contemporary Preaching*, ed. Michael Duduit (Nashville: Broadman & Holman, 1992), 394.

this by raising and lowering your voice. For instance, when describing Elijah's encounter with God on the mountain, use a raised voice when speaking of the wind and earthquake, but a softer voice when describing God's "gentle whisper" (1 Kings 19:12).

Learn to project your voice so that people sitting on the back row can hear you clearly. Obviously microphones enhance our ability here, but if you learn to project properly without one, you will have fewer problems with a microphone (assuming the sound system is reliable). Remember too that if you live by technology, you sometimes die by it. That is, the electricity occasionally goes out, and then your voice stands alone. Be prepared with good voice habits.

Another issue related to volume is known as the "trail-off syndrome." Chapell describes this annoying habit: "Beginning preachers unaccustomed to speaking with power consistently drop their volume at the end of sentences to express seriousness or fervor."[8] They speak loud enough for most of the sentence, but toward the end their voice trails off and the sound grows so soft the words are barely audible. Listeners often catch the meaning, but after a while they grow weary of making the effort. Work on finishing out every sentence to the end. Keep volume at audible levels at all times even when going low for emphasis.

Articulation

Articulation is how you shape sounds into letters and words that communicate.[9] Pronunciation and diction are part of this process. Pronunciation is the correct sounding of a word, and diction consists of using the proper sounds for letters and words. Some people possess physiological problems that hinder their ability to articulate properly, but most have just been trained by culture, laziness, or example to slur words or to use slang terms and colloquialisms.

Some language patterns do indeed interfere with effective communication of the gospel message. Poor articulation frequently causes miscommunication (the audience does not understand what you are saying) or irritation (mispronunciation or poor diction gets on their nerves). The solution is simple. Make a decision to improve

[8]Chapell, *Redeeming the Expository Sermon*, 317.

[9]Al Fasol, *A Complete Guide to Sermon Delivery* (Nashville: Broadman & Holman, 1996), 29.

your pronunciation and diction so that you can communicate the message more effectively. Work on making proper letter sounds and pronouncing the entire word. Practice the pronunciation of words, especially biblical names. Your audience will understand what you are saying and appreciate your effort to communicate clearly. The goal is not to get rid of all traces of cultural heritage but to make sure none of that baggage hinders the message.

You may struggle with some of the voice issues mentioned above. Several years ago I fought a problem with raised pitch during preaching because I was nervous. By Sunday evening my voice was stressed and I was experiencing a great deal of physical discomfort. Since preaching and teaching is my calling, I sought professional help. Through working with a speech therapist and a throat specialist, I learned to speak more naturally, using proper breathing methods. I also realized that part of the problem was a result of caffeine consumption. I had to ease up on the coffee. Medical doctors, therapists, voice coaches, and speech teachers stand ready to help you with voice issues. Take advantage of them. They may be God's way of helping you.

Body Language

You have a great sermon prepared and the hard part is done. It would be great if all you had to do was to stand up and speak the words for maximum effectiveness. But it takes more than just words to deliver the message. Experts tell us that a major part of sermon delivery is body language. Roy DeBrand suggests that the "visual in preaching is vitally important to communication."[10] By "visual" DeBrand means things related to your body, such as dress, posture, gestures, facial expressions, and eye contact. The "visual" has the potential to enhance or harm your message. Haddon Robinson reminds us that mannerisms, unnoticed in normal conversation, can "become distressingly obvious in public speaking":

> Mannerisms and repetitive behavior peculiar to you may go unnoticed by your friends and be tolerated by your associates, but in the pulpit, they scream for attention and divert your listeners

[10]Roy DeBrand. "The Visual in Preaching," in *Handbook of Contemporary Preaching*, ed. Michael Duduit (Nashville: Broadman & Holman, 1992), 398.

from what you are saying. In the pulpit, therefore, the movement of the body must be disciplined to be effective.[11]

In other words, pay attention to your physical mannerisms in the pulpit. Listeners are annoyed by the physical habits of some preachers (rattling keys in their pocket, focusing their eyes above the audience, scratching their nose, or worse). While annoying habits hurt sermon communication, body movements such as appropriate gestures, good eye contact, or animation assist communication. Your goal is to eliminate any annoying or distracting habits and improve helpful practices.

Hands and Feet

DeBrand defines a gesture as "any movement of the head, body, or limbs to emphasize something we are saying."[12] Some use gestures quite naturally as they speak. They are alive with movement even when reporting what they just bought at WalMart. Others hardly exhibit any expression or movement when speaking. Which of the two would you rather see in the pulpit? The more active preacher gets our vote. Audiences are accustomed to that kind of action from television and movies. Gestures relate to movement of the hands and arms, but also the legs, torso, and head.

We agree with Robinson that the sermon content should prompt appropriate body movement.[13] Body movement should correspond to the message and its meaning. If, for example, you use an illustration where a batter hits a home run, you may want to actually take a batter's stance and take a swing. The words and the movement are congruent. When preaching about David slaying Goliath with a slingshot, swing your hands above your head in the same fashion that David might have done as he prepared to slay Goliath.

Be sure to keep movement natural, matching what is being said. If you speak about the top of the mountain, signify it with a raised hand showing how high. When speaking about the valley, go low with your hand to show how deep. Support your message by gestures.

Those who move a great deal may need to work on keeping the movement connected to the content and occasionally tone it down. Those who never move must work intentionally on becoming more

> *Your body movement should correspond to your message.*

[11]Haddon Robinson, *Biblical Preaching: The Development and Delivery of Expository Messages*, 2nd ed. (Grand Rapids: Baker, 2001), 205.

[12]DeBrand, "The Visual in Preaching," 401.

[13]Robinson, *Biblical Preaching*, 208.

animated in order to enhance communication. You could speak in front of a mirror or ask a friend to give you honest feedback as you seek to improve your gestures.

Your Face Talks

In normal conversation with friends, many students have little problem smiling when something is humorous or frowning when the subject is repulsive, but when delivering their sermons, they keep a stone face throughout. Facial expression is perhaps the most important of all the body language. Albert Mehravian has provided a formula for the effective nature of various components of speaking and communication. Seven percent of the message comes through the words, thirty-eight percent from the voice, and fifty-five percent from facial expressions.[14] Your face communicates anger, joy, disgust, irritation, excitement, sadness, discomfort, pain, ecstasy, contentment, love, hate, stress, relaxation, and many other human emotions and attitudes.

Watch some actors closely. They know the power of facial expression. The goal in preaching is for facial expressions to be congruent with the spoken message, just like the gestures. To preach on love while expressing disgust or irritation or anger with your face confuses your audience. Unfortunately, your face often speaks louder than your words; a contradictory facial expression will cause your listeners to miss the spoken message.

Occasionally we encounter students who preach with stern, harsh looks regardless of the topic of the sermon. Perhaps that stern facial expression is a result of nervousness or an attempt to imitate other preachers. But when they watch the replay of their sermon, they see the mixed message. In any case, a good mirror and some practice works wonders. Also ask a trusted friend to evaluate you regularly.

Look at Me When You Talk

When you talk with someone who refuses to look at you, doesn't it drive you crazy? Lack of eye contact causes distrust and disconnection in the communication process. DeBrand argues that eye contact is

[14]As noted in ibid., 203.

the most natural and important visual tool in the sermon process. Proper eye contact says you care about your audience and have something important to say to them.[15]

[15]DeBrand, "The Visual in Preaching," 404.

Be sure to look at the entire audience. Preach to everyone and let your eye confirm your message. My wife reminds me regularly that my eyes tend to focus on certain segments of the audience to the neglect of others. Some speakers are more one-sided in vision. Students who are either right-eyed or left-eyed struggle to keep from automatically setting their eyes in only one direction. When listeners feel neglected, their attention is diverted and their interest wanes. Work hard to consciously look at the entire audience, including people in the balcony (if there is one). There is no excuse for neglecting anyone in the audience.

In addition, look straight at your audience—not over them, at the ceiling, at their feet, or anywhere else. Look into their eyes. You may think audiences don't notice when you look above their heads at some imaginary point but they do. In fact, every listener needs to feel you are personally speaking to them. You are preaching to people, and they need to experience that connection by direct eye contact.

Finally, find people across the congregation who exude energy, and focus on them during the sermon. Some listeners are attentive and truly interested. Others are sleeping, talking, or just not interested. Look at everyone but focus on those scattered around the room who seem captured by your sermon. You will draw energy from these listeners and that, in turn, will energize your sermon. But don't stare or give too much attention to one person in the audience. That could break your own train of thought, send the wrong message to others in the room, and make one person feel uncomfortable, believing the entire sermon is directed at him or her.

An Animated Delivery

Animation is an important element in making cartoons work on the screen. Cartoonists learn to exaggerate all the features of the cartoon character, including actions to grab audience attention. They produce "animated" characters. A little of that belongs in sermon delivery.

> *Look into the eyes of your audience.*

According to Webster, animation means "to give life or motion to, to make spirited, to inspire." The word is derived from the Latin word meaning "soul." In other words, to preach with animation means to "preach with soul." "Preach as though you were alive, as though you yourself were responsive to the word you have to give to the congregation."[16]

Be animated in the pulpit not in the sense of a cartoon character but by being alive and spirited. In a sense this concept includes much of what we have said thus far in this chapter, but it goes beyond that. Sermon deliveries need energy and liveliness. Tony Campolo does not struggle here. People should sense that you genuinely care about what you are communicating. Your passion and energy will be transmitted to the audience through your face, body language, and attitude. Craddock argues for a genuine, natural energy that comes from knowing the importance of your message and interacting with it. "People cannot live by ideas alone; the whole being has to register the value of those ideas. We call this passion."[17]

Some of you struggle here because your personality does not exude passion or energy. You are physically understated in normal conversation and animation comes hard for you in communication. Nevertheless, your audience needs to know that you believe deeply in what you are saying. Therefore, muster some energy in the pulpit— movement, facial expression, and at least a trace of excitement over the message. Sometimes good facial expressions and a small amount of movement can suffice. Pray for God to give you an authentic excitement about your sermon. Practice appropriate animation in front of a mirror. Be yourself, however, since you should not try to transform yourself into a cheerleader for God when your personality does not lend itself to such. When your passion for the sermon is natural and driven by your heart, you will usually generate an energized response from your audience.

[16]John Killinger, *Fundamentals of Preaching* (Philadelphia: Fortress, 1985), 158.

[17]Fred Craddock, *Preaching* (Nashville: Abingdon, 1985), 221.

Things to Avoid

1. A monotone, expressionless, drawn-out delivery style will hurt communication.
2. Don't imitate other preachers. Find your own style.
3. Avoid anything in the delivery that distracts from the message. That includes voice, style, gestures, habits, and facial expressions.

Other Issues

Monotony is a sermon killer.

Keep It Conversational

The days of speakers using loud, booming, "preacher" voices are over. The postmodern audience responds better to natural, more personal preaching styles that are relational and conversational. Today's audiences generally prefer a more casual approach to preaching that does not sound like the preaching their grandparents heard. Your audience probably prefers something more akin to a conversation about God's truth. Calvin Miller says that this conversational approach is like saying to the audience, "Draw up your pew and let's have a coffee-and-doughnuts communication."[18]

Some preaching students struggle with this because they imitate preachers from earlier generations who did use a preacherly tone, vocabulary, and volume. They should know that the conversational style (used when talking with their friends) works effectively in the pulpit. Chapell calls this "heightened conversation," by which he means the "heightening (not changing) of your normal speech" in order to communicate important matters like the biblical message. The conversation is heightened by intensifying your facial expressions and body language so that you become more animated without losing the conversational tone.

[18]Calvin Miller, as quoted in Johnston, *Preaching to a Postmodern World*, 129.

Change It Up

People tend to get bored easily. We must make sure that our sermon delivery doesn't help them with that tendency. Variety can help us here. Monotony kills speeches of any kind, including sermons. Vary your voice pitch and volume, your gestures and movement, and your facial expressions. Audiences have been well-trained by television and movies to expect variation of all sorts. Watching tapes of your sermons will give you a clear picture of what holds the audience's attention and what does not. Viewing yourself develops in you the ability to detect patterns of monotony that kill communication.

The Way You Talk

Does your mother still correct your grammar? Does grammar even matter? Those preachers who think that grammar doesn't matter and that people will get the message even if they use poor grammar or slang need to preach to an audience that includes an English teacher. Most audiences have people who are knowledgeable about language usage, and at least one of them will enjoy correcting you following your sermon. Almost every preacher has experienced the "grammatical moment" just after the close of the service.

Incorrect grammar and "bubba" language doesn't honor the pulpit if it hinders communication. James Cox argues that many congregants are troubled by hearing messages filled with poor grammar. Consequently, preachers should "aim at correctness, availing themselves of reliable English grammars and of the regular services of friendly critics who will help them clean up their mistakes."[19] If you have developed poor grammatical habits, commit to improving your communication skills. Unpolished speech may work fine in informal settings, but the Lord may choose to use you with a different audience. Will you be ready to communicate effectively with this new audience?

Put It to Memory

You should work hard to know at least some parts of your sermon well—to memorize these parts. Memorization is hard work and takes time, but every sermon is made better by at least some memorization. Introductions and conclusions should never be read or delivered while depending on copious notes. These two elements of the sermon are critical and need special attention. In the introduction, you are seeking to grab the attention of your audience, so eye contact and natural animation are critical. Dependence on notes can kill the moment. Likewise, in the conclusion you are bringing the heart of the sermon to bear on the audience. Eye contact and animation are just as critical at this phase. You want your first impression (introduction) and your last word (conclusion) to anchor your sermon and highlight your message. Memorization enables you to move away

[19]James W. Cox, *Preaching: A Comprehensive Approach to the Design and Delivery of Sermons* (San Francisco: Harper & Row, 1993), 242.

from an overdependence on notes and to connect in a powerful and genuine way with your audience.

> *Overdependence on notes can kill your sermon.*

You may wish to memorize the biblical text as well. It is an effective way to convince your audience that you have invested time studying the passage. If you choose to read the passage, make sure you have read it several times before and practiced pronouncing the words aloud and placing emphases where needed. Nothing gets a sermon off to a worse start than a poorly read text. Sloppy reading leaves the impression that this is the first time you have read your text.

When using stories as illustrations, we encourage you to memorize them. Delivering a powerful illustration or story by reading it can prove to be counterproductive. Know the story by heart so that you can tell it and retain eye contact, which makes a powerful impression on your listeners. We also urge you to memorize the main points of your sermon and transition statements between main points. These are critical junctures, and memorization can prevent you from stumbling at precisely the wrong moment.

PowerPoint, Screens, and My Delivery

For many upcoming preachers, the computer is a second home for everything from writing to shopping to sermon preparation and delivery. More and more churches are equipped with computer projection technology, providing preachers with options for how to present a sermon. PowerPoint and other presentation software are being used in sermons more and more frequently.

Today, as I write this chapter, I am also preparing to preach in the morning service at a church equipped with all the whistles and bells needed for a PowerPoint presentation. I emailed my points and text to the church earlier in the week, and when I stand and deliver, the text and points will appear on monitors located around the room. The audience will see and hear me, but they will also read portions of my message. This technology allows us to incorporate new and creative illustrations, such as video and music clips, into the message. Even if you are technologically challenged, someone in your church

Don't become too predictable in your delivery style.

can probably help you. We encourage you to use this technology to enhance your preaching of God's Word.

There are cautions, however, with using technology in a sermon. Audience tolerance comes into play here. Some more traditional churches find it hard to change worship practice, including sermon delivery. Knowledge of your audience will inform you of their tolerance level. Even if they are traditional, you may be able to introduce them to a little technology at a time. Most young and new churches, however, begin with computers and screens as a normal part of the worship practice.

Moreover, as teachers we have discovered that students think PowerPoint presentations in the classroom can be helpful, but only to a point. When the teacher depends only on PowerPoint, the students grow tired of it. It becomes too routine. They prefer variety and often a more personal touch to the delivery. Don't become so predictable in your sermon delivery that the people know exactly how everything will go every week. Use technology effectively, but don't overuse it.

Leave Your Audience Wanting More

Recently I sat beside a friend, a retired pastor, while both of us listened to a very long sermon. My friend had carried on a preaching ministry during a time when long sermons were the norm, but he had learned a few things by experience. When the sermon finally ended, I asked him what he thought of it. Being very kind, he replied that it was a good sermon except that the preacher passed by many good stopping places without stopping.

[20]Ibid., 251.

James Cox describes an effective delivery style as "economical" because "it does not waste words."[20] Effective sermons make every word count. Wordiness in preaching is more of a curse than a blessing. We go one step further than Cox and argue simply that a sermon should not have too many words. Never forget that postmodern listeners, conditioned by television and media, have a short attention span. Long, drawn-out sermons overextend the listener's capacity and do not communicate as well as shorter, more concise sermons. Few

Don't keep your audience beyond their limit to listen and understand.

contemporary American audiences possess the capacity to sit still and follow closely a forty-five minute sermon.

Shorter sermons are probably more difficult to craft than longer ones, but they are also more effective. By avoiding long sermons, your audience will be more inclined to listen to you while you speak. Leave them wanting to hear more rather than wishing they had heard less. If you prepare solid, biblically-based sermons with interesting illustrations and challenging application that can be delivered in under twenty-five minutes, you will capture your audience.

Getting Better and Better

At this point you may be thinking, "Wow! There's too much to work on. I'll never become an accomplished preacher." We admit there are many points to remember related to the delivery of sermons. How can you possibly do all that we've talked about?

Perhaps an analogy from the world's greatest game will help. I am an avid golfer with a great love for the game. To improve my ability, I have taken several lessons and have read numerous books and magazines, filling my mind with all the swing details. When I stand over the ball preparing to swing the club, I am often overcome with all I am supposed to remember about a good golf swing. The experts, however, advise golfers like me not to think about the details as we are hitting the ball. Instead, they recommend just hitting the ball.

This is true of preaching delivery too. Work on it, practice it, and then just get up and swing.[21] Read good books, ask your friends for feedback, tape your sermons, and view the tapes. Improving your sermon delivery is a process of learning, failing, relearning, practicing, and then practicing some more. Don't expect instant miracles, but devote yourself to improving little by little over time. You want to be your best in order to honor God's timeless and precious message to his people.

Summary Guidelines for Sermon Delivery

1. Develop a natural, animated, conversational style that fits your personality.
2. Let the content of the message control body language.
3. Eye contact is critical, so find a style that heightens a connection to your audience.
4. Practice in front of a mirror, get input from others, watch yourself on video, and read materials designed to improve delivery.
5. Admit your delivery struggles, recognize that improvement is a process, and begin making progress little by little.

[21] For those who need more help, there are some excellent books dealing with the technical side of sermon delivery. One of the best is Fasol's *A Complete Guide to Sermon Delivery*. The cover alone reveals the book's broad concern, which includes vocal production, facial expression, eye contact, posture, articulation, and gestures.

Review Questions and Assignments

1. Which mechanical style of delivery is best for you and why?
2. When thinking of your voice in delivery, in which area are you strongest and in which are you weakest?
3. Why is body language so important? Which aspect of body language is most important? Where could you use some improvement?
4. Watch two different preachers from the *Great Preachers* series (Gateway Films). Compare and contrast their delivery styles, paying particular attention to voice pitch, pace, volume, articulation, body language, gestures, facial expressions, eye contact, animation, and use of variety. Which has the most effective delivery? Why?

Part 2
Preaching the New Testament

Preaching Letters

> Stand firm and hold to the teachings we passed on to
> you, whether by word of mouth or by letter.
> **2 Thessalonians 2:15**

Even with email, instant messaging, cell phones, text messaging, web cams, and whatever else may be just around the corner, we all still enjoy receiving an old-fashioned, pen-and-ink letter. Whether formal business correspondence or a personal note from a friend or relative, letters continue to play an important role in our society. In the ancient world, letters played an even more significant role. Much of the New Testament is comprised of letters that capture in a unique way the growth, successes, problems, and challenges of the early church. They serve as windows into the life of these particular congregations. You preach these letters because contemporary churches need the divine wisdom found within their pages.

In this chapter we will summarize the nature of New Testament letters and look briefly at how to read them properly. We will highlight several "sermon keys" or guidelines for preaching the letters and mention a few "things to avoid" (e.g., common word-study fallacies). The chapter concludes with two sample sermon outlines from New Testament letters.

Interpretive Keys

There are several characteristics of New Testament letters that serve as keys for their interpretation. *First, letters were considered to be substitutes for the personal presence of the author.* The original audience would have viewed a New Testament letter as a substitute for the apostles themselves. The letters of Peter and John and Paul carry authority because they wrote as Christ's authentic apostles or representatives (i.e., as witnesses to the resurrected Christ). They were viewed as God-appointed leaders of the congregations to whom they wrote.

Because of travel limitations, early Christian leaders were often unable to address an issue or deal with a situation in person. Their only option was to write a letter, but their letter functioned as an extension of their authoritative presence. Letters provided a way for these leaders to minister from a distance. This explains why New Testament letters are generally longer than their ancient counterparts. The biblical authors needed space to send appropriate greetings, update readers about their current situation, instruct, encourage, deal with difficult issues, counter false teaching, and much more.

Second, New Testament letters were occasional or situational. The New Testament letters were not written to contemplate pie-in-the-sky theological issues. Rather, they were written to address specific situations faced by real churches. These letters are examples of theology being applied to practical, real-life situations. The topics covered in the various letters are usually dictated by the issues challenging the community receiving the letter (e.g., the Colossians facing a threat from false teaching or the Corinthians wrestling with what it meant to be truly spiritual). Consequently, when interpreting New Testament letters you must be careful not to conclude too much from one letter. When you look to certain letters for advice or instruction about topics they do not touch upon, you run the risk of making one particular letter bear too much weight.

For example, the Galatians were struggling with legalism and needed to hear a word from Paul about freedom in Christ. James, by contrast, was writing to people who had grown comfortable with their religious surroundings and needed to be reminded that genuine faith must indeed produce good works. Both letters offer a corrective message tailored to the circumstances of those specific churches. If you fail to see the letters as occasional or situational, you will be tempted to conclude too much from one letter (e.g., that Paul does not believe in good works as the product of true faith or that James has no concept of freedom in Christ) and thereby misinterpret the letter. Since the letters are situational, you must make yourself aware of the situation that called for the letter in the first place. Knowing the original situation will help you identify theological principles within the letter and put you on solid ground when it comes to preaching its message.

Third, New Testament letters were meant to be read aloud over and over to specific congregations. In contrast to the normal way of reading a letter today (privately and silently), people in the first century preferred to hear their letters read aloud. Since it was too expensive and time-consuming to make a copy of each letter for every individual (and not everyone could read), most Christians heard the letters read during their weekly worship gatherings (see, e.g., Col. 4:16; 1 Thess. 5:27; 2 Thess. 2:15). Paul's more personal letter to Philemon was addressed not only to the slave owner himself but also to the church that gathered in his house (Philem. 1–2).

The Christian community benefited from hearing the letters read aloud over and over. When interpreting the letters, you should remember that they lend themselves to oral presentation, even repeated oral presentation. The letters were not merely thrown together at the last minute like people today compose emails. Instead, the ancient authors took time and gave careful thought to crafting a literary work designed to maximize the impact on the listener.

Fourth, the letter's opening often includes clues to interpreting the whole letter. Most New Testament letters utilized a standard form that consisted of an opening, a body, and a conclusion. Although there was some variation, the letter opening normally included the name of the writer, the name of the recipients, a greeting, and an introductory prayer or statement.

You should pay attention to how the writer and recipients are described. For example, in Galatia where Paul's apostleship was being questioned, he begins the letter with an emphasis on the divine origin of his apostleship. The tone of Galatians is also set when Paul omits any customary expressions of affection for his readers, such as "saints" or "beloved." You should also look to the opening statement or prayer for topics and themes that will be developed more in the body of the letter. In 1 Corinthians, for instance, where Paul writes extensively about what it means to be truly spiritual, he opens with these words:

> I always thank God for you because of his grace given you in Christ Jesus. For in him you have been enriched in every way—in all your speaking and in all your knowledge—because our testimony about Christ was confirmed in you. Therefore you do not lack any spiritual gift as you eagerly wait for our Lord Jesus Christ to be revealed. (1 Cor. 1:4–7)

Likewise, in 1 Timothy, where Paul instructs Timothy about wrestling with false teaching, he opens the letter with the following command:

> As I urged you when I went into Macedonia, stay there in Ephesus so that you may command certain men not to teach false doctrines any longer nor to devote themselves to myths and endless genealogies. These promote controversies rather than God's work—which is by faith. The goal of this command is love, which comes from a pure heart and a good conscience and a sincere faith. (1 Tim. 1:3–5)

New Testament letter writers often send strong signals about their purposes in the opening section of the letter, and you should pay extra attention to that section.

The Interpretive Journey

With these specific interpretive keys in mind, you should look to the Interpretive Journey as a way to develop biblical sermons based on New Testament letters. *First, determine the meaning of the text in their town.* Since letters were meant to be read aloud from beginning to end, start your sermon preparation by reading the whole letter. This may take some time, but it will keep you from separating a small portion of the letter from its larger context and purpose. You would never read a love letter from your spouse or friend by skipping to the second paragraph on page three while ignoring all that surrounds that paragraph. You should resist the temptation to do the same with God's love letter, the Bible.

Since letters are situational, part of understanding what the passage meant for the original audience is reconstructing the original occasion (i.e., the historical-cultural context) for the letter. Use study tools like Bible dictionaries and commentaries to reconstruct the original situation of the biblical writer and his audience. Knowing that Paul wants Philemon not only to withhold punishment of Onesimus (a runaway Christian slave) but also to set him free helps you understand the persuasive power of Paul's suggestive language:

> So if you [Philemon] consider me [Paul] a partner, welcome him [Onesimus] as you would welcome me. If he has done you any wrong or owes you anything, charge it to me. I, Paul, am writing this with my own hand. I will pay it back—not to mention that you owe me your very self. I do wish, brother, that I may have some benefit from you in the Lord; refresh my heart in Christ. Confident of your obedience, I write to you, knowing that you will do even more than I ask.
>
> And one thing more: Prepare a guest room for me, because I hope to be restored to you in answer to your prayers. (Philem. 17–22)

This section is loaded with power language as a means of persuading Philemon. Paul puts himself and Onesimus on the same level (an apostle and a runaway slave). He reminds Philemon that he has some indebtedness of his own to deal with—"not to mention that you owe me your very self." He assumes Philemon's future obedience in a strong but subtle command, and he promises a personal visit, a challenge for Philemon to act accordingly before Paul arrives in person to check out his response.

After you have a good grasp of the occasion of the letter, you need to identify the literary context of the passage you are studying.

How does what comes before and what comes after your passage help you understand your passage? Try to get a sense of the author's argument or flow of thought as it runs through your passage.

Finally, use your observation skills to read the passage carefully. Look for details. Notice important connections. Study significant words. To make sure you understand what the passage meant to the biblical audience, write a past-tense statement that summarizes the meaning of your passage for the original audience (i.e., a text thesis statement).

Second, measure the width of the river to cross. Here you ask about the differences and similarities between the biblical audience and your audience. In New Testament letters, the river is not usually very wide, since the letters were written to Christians on this side of the death and resurrection of Jesus Christ. Nevertheless, the river can sometimes present a challenge even in the letters when they deal with ancient issues that are unusual to today. When Paul deals with the issue of eating meat that had been offered to idols (1 Cor. 8), the issue of praying or prophesying with your head covered (1 Cor. 11), or the issue of ritual circumcision (Galatians), the water gets a bit deep. Normally, however, the river is narrow and shallow and your audience can readily identify with the issue in question.

Third, cross the river by determining the theological principles in this passage. In light of how today's situation compares to and differs from the situation of the biblical audience, try to identify the universal principles that are reflected in the text. Theological principles provide a bridge across the river of historical and cultural barriers that separate the ancient text and the contemporary audience. Often in New Testament letters, the author communicates his message in the form of a theological principle. Here are some examples:

Romans 12:17: "Do not repay anyone evil for evil."
Galatians 5:16: "Live by the Spirit, and you will not gratify the desires of the sinful nature."
Ephesians 5:21: "Submit to one another out of reverence for Christ."
1 John 4:19: "We love because he first loved us."

At those times when the author doesn't state a theological principle directly, look for the underlying reason for the instruction or command that results in the specific advice contained in the letter. Why does Paul prefer prophecy over speaking in tongues? Why does he tell the Corinthians to wait on each other before they take the Lord's Supper? Why does he warn the Galatians against being circumcised? Normally when you find the underlying reason (the "why" behind the "what"), you have found the theological principle. Look to the surrounding context to discover the underlying reason.

> *We cross the bridge between their world and ours by means of theological principles.*

After you have written out your principle or principles in one or two sentences using present tense verbs, test them against the following criteria:

- Is the principle strongly tied to and reflected in the biblical text?
- Is the principle timeless and universal or is it attached to a particular situation?
- Is the principle transcultural or is it bound to only one specific culture?
- Is the principle harmonious with teachings of the rest of Scripture?
- Is the principle congruent with the similarities and differences between the two audiences?
- Is the principle relevant to both the biblical and contemporary audience?

These criteria should help you determine whether you have truly discovered a theological principle.

Fourth, apply the theological principle to individual Christians today. This application to Christians today represents the last phase of interpreting a New Testament letter. While theological principles are determined by the meaning of the text and are the same for all Christians, they may be applied to individual believers in a variety of ways. The process of applying a biblical text involves three phases:

1. Identify the key elements that emerge from the intersection between the theological principles in the text and the original historical-cultural situation.

Use your imagination to recreate the original situation.

2. Think of a parallel situation in a contemporary context that includes all the key elements.

3. Make the application specific in the lives of your listeners in a way that is both faithful to the meaning of the text and relevant to the contemporary audience.

Sermon Keys

When preaching New Testament letters you need to re-create the historical situation of the letter for the contemporary audience so that your listeners think and feel what the biblical audience must have been experiencing. You will find it difficult (and sometimes impossible) to re-create the historical circumstances exactly, but it is important to try. Use your imagination to get inside the situation yourself so that you can communicate effectively with your audience. Think about how the individual characters must have felt. Consider their physical surroundings. Reflect a bit on the relational dynamics involved in the circumstances. When listeners experience the "questions" or "problems" posed by the original situation, the answer supplied by the biblical text will arrive with enormous power.[1] This calls for a disciplined imagination at its creative best.

Another key to preaching the letters is to clarify the thought flow of the biblical author. You don't have to drone on and on about how the letter unfolds or attempt to include everything, but you should honor the author's train of thought. Your sermon should clarify rather than confuse the line of thinking presented in the letter. This sermon key is essential to preaching New Testament letters properly. We strongly suggest that you preach paragraphs of the letter as opposed to isolated verses. It is simply too tempting to extract a single verse and use it to prove your point. Preaching paragraphs will help you focus on the thought flow of the original author. And often in letters when you grasp the main points of a paragraph, you discover your basic sermon outline.

Although you will be focusing on paragraphs as the basic unit for the sermon, you will also profit from analyzing and even highlighting smaller

[1] See Duvall and Hays, *Grasping God's Word*, ch. 6, for more information about identifying a letter's historical-cultural context.

sections of text in the process. New Testament letters lend themselves to a sermon series on the letter itself (e.g., preaching through Ephesians). As you expound on the details of a paragraph, word studies are especially useful (see below). Often the argument of an author hangs on a particular word or phrase so that exploring the meaning of that word in your sermon pays rich dividends. Just make sure that you model for your listeners how to study words properly (context, context, context).

Remember that as contemporary preachers you stand with your listeners as recipients of the letters more than you stand with the apostles as the authors, although you are responsible for communicating the apostle's message. This sermon key serves as a reminder to take your preaching responsibility seriously, but not to take yourselves too seriously. Take on an attitude of humility lest you begin to think you have been added to the apostolic circle alongside Peter and Paul.

A final sermon key is to remember that the letters exemplify applied theology at its best. In the letters you have examples of how theology should be made specific in the lives of individual Christians and their communities. In your preaching you too should make your applications of scriptural truth specific and practical. Don't leave people stranded on the bridge of theological principles.

Things to Avoid

Preaching New Testament letters has its challenges. *The major pitfall is ignoring or discarding either the historical or literary context.* Perhaps the greatest temptation you have as a preacher is to be relevant at the expense of being biblical. Yet today's listeners, and especially the younger ones, are put off by cute, alliterative sermon outlines that smack of a counterfeit, plastic theology. The Bible is relevant; your challenge as a preacher is to expose its relevance through a contextual communication and rigorous application of truth. As Ben Witherington says, "Good preaching should draw on the Word as its primary source (not on human need, experience, tradition, or rational considerations) and should be prepared to apply that Word vigorously to the congregation, even if it hurts."[2]

[2]Ben Witherington III, *Revelation* (NCBC; Cambridge: Cambridge Univ. Press, 2003), 124.

To be relevant at the expense of being biblical is, in the end, to be irrelevant.

[3]See Duvall and Hays, *Grasping God's Word*, ch. 8, for more detail.

You also need to avoid the expectation that your listeners must duplicate the unique experiences of the apostles (e.g., Paul's imprisonment, missionary journeys, or thorn in the flesh). Your audience shares a common humanity with the people of the first century and thus common needs, but they don't necessarily share a common role in redemptive history. This calls for wisdom when making application of the unique experiences of early church leaders. Focus on the underlying theological principle rather than the often unique ways that principle was applied in the lives of the apostles.

Word studies are very appropriate when studying and preaching New Testament letters. We encourage you to do word studies correctly by avoiding common fallacies.[3]

English-only fallacy. This means basing your word study on the English word (e.g., looking up the word in an English dictionary) rather than the underlying Greek word. For example, let's say you go to an English dictionary to find out more about the word "believe" and discover that it means "to have a firm conviction about the goodness of something" or "to hold an opinion." The Greek word *pisteuō*, often translated "believe," normally involves more than just holding an opinion or even having a firm conviction; it includes acting on that conviction. Our English dictionary dilutes the meaning of the Greek word.

Root fallacy. A common problem is thinking that the real meaning of the word must be found in its original root (the equivalent to saying that *butterfly* really means a fly coated with butter!). The Greek word *hypomenô* is sometimes thought to mean "remain (*menō*) under (*hypo*)" because the two different parts of the word seem to indicate its origins. But in Luke 2:43 the boy Jesus "stays behind" in Jerusalem as his parents journey home. The word can mean "stand firm," "stand your ground," and "endure." Even when it means "endure," we should be careful about saying that it really means "to remain under" since that could prove awkward (e.g., Paul says in 2 Tim. 2:10 that he "endures everything"). Studying the origins of words is important, especially in Old Testament studies, but we simply cannot assume that knowing the root of the word reveals its true meaning.

Time-frame fallacy. Sometimes preachers grab onto a late word meaning (usually today's meaning) and read it back into the Bible. D. A. Carson uses the English word "dynamite" and the Greek word *dynamis* (sometimes translated "power") to illustrate a particular form of the time-frame fallacy:

> I do not know how many times I have heard preachers offer some such rendering of Romans 1:16 as this: "I am not ashamed of the gospel, for it is the *dynamite* of God unto salvation for everyone who believes"—often with a knowing tilt of the head, as if something profound or even esoteric has been uttered.... Did Paul think of dynamite when he penned this word?[4]

Our answer to Carson's rhetorical question should certainly be "no," since the English word "dynamite" originated centuries later than the Greek word *dynamis*. Moreover, Paul's concept of power is an empty tomb, not a stick of dynamite.

Overload fallacy. You should not think that a single Greek word includes all of its meanings every time it is used (like thinking that *spring* refers to all its possible meanings—a metal coil, season of the year, jumping around, etc.—every time it is used). Take, for instance, the Greek word *paradidōmi*, which has a range of meaning including (a) to entrust, (b) to betray, (c) to commend, (d) to instruct, and (e) to allow or permit. Overload fallacy occurs when we assume that a word like *paradidōmi* carries not just one but all of those senses in every context, so that we can pick and choose which one(s) fit best with our sermon.

Word-count fallacy. This fallacy occurs when you insist that a word must have the same meaning every time it is used. For example, the word *paschō* is translated with something like "suffer" (i.e., to have negative experiences) six of the seven times it is used in Paul's letters. In Galatians 3:4, however, the word probably refers to the Galatians' positive spiritual experiences such as God's gift of his Spirit and miracles. Paul seems to be asking them if they really want to give up their past spiritual experiences (good ones) for the legalism of the Judaizers. Although the word often means negative experiences, ultimately the context (not word counts) must determine its meaning in a particular setting.

[4]D. A. Carson, *Exegetical Fallacies*, 2nd ed. (Grand Rapids: Baker, 1996), 34.

Word-concept fallacy. You can never assume that once you have studied a word, you have studied the entire concept. For example, to study the concept of the church, you have to do more than study the word "church" (*ekklēsia*). You need to study dozens of images of the church in the New Testament to study the concept of the church (e.g., body, bride, building). Studying a single word is not the same thing as studying a larger concept.

Selective-evidence fallacy. It is all too easy to pick the word meaning that favors your interpretation of the passage and ignore or reject the legitimate word meaning that goes against your view. You will often hear sermons on John 21:15–17 that specify that *agapaō* refers to God-like love, while *phileō* refers to brotherly love (i.e., like the city Philadelphia). This may indeed be what Jesus is saying in John 21, but that conclusion must be supported from the immediate context and not merely from a general definition of these two words. A study of *phileō* in the New Testament shows that the word can also be used of God-like love (see, e.g., John 5:20; 16:27; 20:2; Rev. 3:19).

Word studies are profitable because words are important, but they should be done properly. Often words simply mean what they appear to mean (e.g., the word "remain" or "abide"), and there is no secret meaning to be conjured up through a detailed word study or by appealing to the Greek. What is more profitable with a word like "abide" is to ask how it functions in its various contexts (e.g., What are the various objects of abiding?).

As has been demonstrated by other scholars, the New Testament letters assume a larger theological story or narrative thought world.[5] *Keep this larger biblical story in mind when preaching from the letters so that your sermon that is based on a very small section will not violate the larger picture.* William Willimon observes how Paul himself keeps the big story in mind when dealing with the most practical of church issues:

> Paul goes dramatically, sweepingly theological. A fight over who is in charge of the gospel at Corinth becomes an occasion for Paul to pull out his biggest theological affirmations.... God grant us contemporary preachers the grace to turn all our grubby congregational squabbles into high theology.[6]

[5]See Joel B. Green and Michael Pasquarello III, eds., *Narrative Reading, Narrative Preaching* (Grand Rapids: Baker, 2003), esp. chs. 4–5; Ben Witherington III, *Paul's Narrative Thought World* (Grand Rapids: Eerdmans, 1994). For an overview of the grand narrative or story of Israel, see C. Marvin Pate, et al., *The Story of Israel: A Biblical Theology* (Downers Grove, IL: InterVarsity Press, 2004).

[6]As quoted in Green and Pasquarello, *Narrative Reading, Narrative Preaching*, 108–9.

At the conclusion of your study and perhaps as you begin drafting a sermon outline, you need to ask how this thesis and outline relates to the overall biblical story. We merely caution you against missing the forest of the Bible by looking too closely at the trees of individual verses.

A final thing to avoid is the pressure to funnel all sermon application into the action category. Today's listeners live in an action-oriented world, and sometimes this cultural expectation will pressure you to come up with a behavioral "to do" for every application. Some passages, however, call for a change of thinking rather than a change of behavior. Remember that thinking differently is every bit as legitimate an application as acting differently. Don't be afraid to call for a thinking change in the application section of your sermon. Thinking differently certainly results in acting differently, but that may be for the next passage.

Examples

Text: 2 Timothy 3:16–17

Suggested title: God Has Something to Say

Context: In 2 Timothy 3:1–4:5 Paul spoke to Timothy (and by extension to the church) about the godlessness of the last days and the need to stay faithful to Scripture. In contrast to the long list of qualities defining the false teachers (3:1–9, 13; 4:3–5) stands the way of life and teaching of godly mentors, including their willingness to suffer. This faithful teaching is grounded in Scripture, and Paul uses the dark backdrop of godlessness and heresy to elaborate on the nature, benefits, and purpose of Scripture in 3:16–17.

Text thesis statement: Paul instructed Timothy that all Scripture was inspired by God and was useful for thoroughly preparing believers to do what God wants them to do.

Text outline:
1. Paul asserted that all Scripture was inspired by God. (2 Tim. 3:16a)
2. Paul stressed that Scripture was useful for teaching, rebuking, correcting, and training in righteousness. (2 Tim. 3:16b)

3. Paul emphasized that Scripture's purpose was to equip believers to do the good things that God wants them to do. (2 Tim. 3:17)

Crossing the bridge: In this particular case, crossing the bridge between the original situation to our day will not be difficult. You may or may not be serving as pastor or leader of a church, but you are a Christian trying to live faithfully in the midst of an abundance of false teaching. You too may be tempted to get caught up in the latest religious fad that could easily lead down the wrong road. You too may feel the weight of being responsible for what people are taught. Although the term "Scripture" here technically refers to the Old Testament, the words of Jesus and his apostles were already being assigned the same level of religious authority when 2 Timothy was written. The bridge of theological principles for 2 Timothy 3:16–17 on the nature, usefulness, and purpose of Scripture makes it easy to cross from the ancient to the contemporary audience.

Sermon thesis statement: God speaks to us through the Scriptures with the intent of shaping our character and preparing us to minister to others.

Sermon outline:
1. God is the source of all Scripture. (2 Tim. 3:16a)
2. God uses Scripture to shape our character. (2 Tim 3:16b)
3. God uses Scripture to prepare us to minister to others. (2 Tim. 3:17)

Text: 1 Peter 5:5–7

Suggested title: God's Surprising Solution to Anxiety

Context: In his first letter Peter encouraged Christians to stand firm in God's grace delivered and experienced through Jesus Christ (5:12). He began his letter by emphasizing the foundation of salvation in Christ before moving into the body of the letter, where he gave practical advice about how to live out that salvation in everyday life. In the paragraph that precedes our passage (5:1–4), Peter spoke to the leaders about how they were to exercise leadership. In the paragraph that follows (5:8–11), Peter urged his readers to be on the alert for spiritual opposition while relying on God's empowering grace.

In 5:5–7 Peter addressed the younger men about being good followers before directing his advice to everyone. His focus in this short section was on humility—God's command to humble ourselves, God's reward for humbling ourselves, and God's provision for living a humble life. In the command to "clothe" ourselves with humility are echoes of Jesus' taking up the towel when he washed the disciples' feet (John 13). The provision of God's inviting us to "cast our anxieties" on the Lord is reminiscent of the "do not worry" passage in the Sermon on the Mount (Matt. 6:25–34).

Text thesis statement: God commanded believers to humble themselves, promised to exalt the humble, and promised to bear the burdens of those who chose to live in humility.

Text outline:

1. God commanded believers to clothe themselves with humility. (1 Peter 5:5)
2. God rewarded those who humbled themselves. (1 Peter 5:6)
3. God provided for those who humbled themselves. (1 Peter 5:7)

Crossing the bridge: As in the first example, crossing the bridge of theological principles in New Testament letters is normally not difficult. This holds true for this passage in 1 Peter. The advice is directed toward Christians and pertains to areas of life (pride and humility) that are just as relevant now as they were in the first century. As Christians live together, they battle pride and seek to live in humility. The advice from 1 Peter 5:5–7 hits home.

Sermon thesis statement: God commands us to put on humility rather than pride, promises to reward us in his own time and way, and offers to accept our anxieties as we live in humility.

Sermon outline:

1. God has a command for us: "Clothe yourselves with humility." (1 Peter 5:5)
2. God has a reward for us: "[I will] lift you up." (1 Peter 5:6)
3. God has a provision for us: "Cast all your anxiety on him." (1 Peter 5:7)

Review Questions and Assignments

1. Develop a text thesis statement, a text outline, a sermon thesis statement, and a sermon outline for Romans 12:1–2.
2. Develop a text thesis statement, a text outline, a sermon thesis statement, and a sermon outline for James 3:1–12.

3. Develop a text thesis statement, a text outline, a sermon thesis statement, and a sermon outline for 1 Corinthians 13:1–13.

4. Develop a text thesis statement, a text outline, a sermon thesis statement, and a sermon outline for Ephesians 4:11–16.

Preaching the Gospels and Acts   10

> Jesus went into Galilee, proclaiming the good news of
> God. "The time has come," he said. "The kingdom of
> God is near. Repent and believe the good news!"
> **Mark 1:14–15**

Everybody loves a good story. Stories capture our attention like nothing else because we find ourselves "entering" the story and identifying with the characters in a personal way. When Jesus heals the broken person, we feel his compassion. When he rebukes the Pharisees, we think about the hypocrisy in our own hearts. When Paul travels across Asia Minor planting churches, we get excited about how God might want to use us. There is nothing as powerful as a good story.

Most of the narrative material in the New Testament is found in the Gospels and Acts. While Jesus himself never published an autobiography, we do have four versions of the one story of Jesus—Matthew, Mark, Luke, and John. The four canonical Gospels comprise almost half of the New Testament in terms of size. They are technically known as *Christological biographies* or historical stories about Jesus told for particular theological purposes.

Although we have four versions of the life and ministry of Jesus, we only have one account of the birth and growth of the early church—Acts. Using narrative material interlaced with speeches from the main characters, Acts shows how the gospel of Jesus Christ progressed triumphantly from its birthplace of Jerusalem to the leading city of the empire, Rome. We refer to Acts as *theological history—*

Avoid making powerful, interesting stories anemic and boring.

accurate, reliable history, but history reported in a way that advances the Christian faith.

When you preach from the Gospels or Acts, you begin with textual material that is engaging by nature. As preachers, we pray that we don't get in the way by making powerful, interesting stories anemic and boring. In order for your sermons to reflect the power and depth of the stories themselves, you need a closer look at how to cultivate the rich ground known as New Testament narrative.

Interpretive Keys

First, interpret the Gospels and Acts in a manner consistent with their intended purposes. The Gospel writers (like any reporter or historian) could not tell all that there was to tell about Jesus. John admits as much in the final sentence of his gospel (John 21:25): "Jesus did many other things as well. If every one of them were written down, I suppose that even the whole world would not have room for the books that would be written." You can read Jesus' longest speeches (e.g., the Sermon on the Mount) in a matter of minutes, yet he often spoke to the crowds for hours at a time. The same is true about many of the speeches in Acts. There was simply not enough space to tell the whole story. As a result, under the direction of the Spirit, the biblical authors chose what to include (and omit) as well as how to arrange the material in a way that effectively communicated the good news to their contemporaries.

The Gospels were written with two primary purposes in mind. They tell us the story of Jesus, the Christ (or Messiah), and through those stories the gospel writers are sending a theological message to the first readers (and to today's Christians). In both the Gospels and Acts the material has been selected and arranged in order to communicate theological truth to the audience. All storytelling is storytelling for a particular purpose and from a particular point of view, and New Testament narrative is no exception. Since the Holy Spirit saw fit to inspire New Testament narrative in this way, we need to adopt a way of reading it that matches the method used to create it.

These twin purposes can be transformed into two interpretive questions that form the foundation for reading New Testament narrative. First, what do the smaller stories tell us about Jesus (or in the case of Acts, what do they tell us about the central characters or the church)? Second, what is the biblical writer trying to say to his readers by the way that he links together the smaller stories into the larger narrative? The chart below depicts the two central interpretive questions for reading the Gospels and Acts.

Episode 1	Episode 2	Episode 3	Episode 4
What is this episode telling us about the main character?	What is this episode telling us about the main character?	What is this episode telling us about the main character?	What is this episode telling us about the main character?

Episodes 1, 2, 3, and 4

What is the biblical author trying to communicate to his readers by the way he connects these stories together?

We can illustrate this interpretive approach using Mark 4:35–5:43.

Mark 4:35–41	Mark 5:1–20	Mark 5:24b–34	Mark 5:21–24a; 5:35–43
Jesus exerts his power over the sea and responds with faith during a very difficult circumstance.	Jesus casts out a legion of demons, restores the man to his right mind, and sends him out as a faithful follower.	Jesus heals the woman with the hemorrhage who, because of faith, touched him, then confessed him publicly.	Jesus raises the daughter of Jairus from the dead in the presence of Peter, James, John, and the girl's parents.

Through his mighty works Jesus shows himself sovereign over the forces hostile to God. Demons, disease, and death strike fear and hopelessness into the hearts of people. Mark's first-century readers were facing persecution and hostility. Through this series of stories, Mark assures them that Jesus has power over everything they fear! He can calm the sea, cast out demons, heal diseases, and raise the dead. They should trust him in the midst of the desperate situations of life.

Second, as you read the individual stories, ask the standard "story questions" that you would ask of any story: Who? What? When? Where? Why? and How? By asking these simple questions you will put yourself in a position to make significant discoveries about the passage. Who are the characters? What is the storyline? When and where does the action occur? Specifically, how does the action take place? Why do things happen the way they do?

For example, as you ask the standard story questions of the Mark passage above, you will notice that there are several key questions asked by the main characters. The disciples question Jesus' indifference (Mark 4:38). Jesus questions the disciples' lack of faith (4:40). This causes the disciples in turn to question Jesus' identity: "Who is this guy that can control the sea?" (4:41). Observing these three questions is crucial for understanding how the entire passage comes together. There is no substitute for careful observation of the details of a passage.

Third, pay close attention to what is emphasized within the text itself. Reading the text closely may seem like an obvious key, but it is often overlooked. Does the story include direct discourse (places where the character's speech is placed in quotation marks in the biblical text)? Direct discourse (e.g., Jesus' conversation with the woman at the well in John 4 or Philip's talk with the Ethiopian in Acts 8) offers an exceptionally clear window through which to see the theological message of the story. Also look for words or themes that are repeated in the story. Authors use repetition to signal important truths. In addition, look for specific clues or instructions about the author's meaning. Often you will find such information in the introduction or conclusion to a story or in the author's parenthetical comments.

Fourth, read individual stories within the larger context of a series of stories. Since the biblical writer is trying to communicate a message by the way he puts together the smaller stories, you need to look at the surrounding stories to get a feel for the overarching meaning. The most important thing to do when reading a series of stories is to look for connections. Look for common themes or patterns in the smaller stories. Search for logical connections like cause-and-effect. Pay attention to the author's use of transition statements or conjunctions to join together the smaller stories. Notice how the stories differ at key points. Notice what the smaller stories add to the central theme of the larger section. Compare the characters, paying close attention to Jesus, the main character of the Gospels. Focus on his identity, his mission, his teaching, and responses to him. Seeing connections used by the author will help you discern the intended message in the series of stories. For an example of reading a series of stories, look again at the summary statement in the chart on Mark 4–5 (page 189).

Fifth, be alert for special literary forms and interpret them appropriately. One reason why Jesus was such an engaging teacher was that he conveyed his message through a wide array of literary forms and techniques. When you encounter *exaggeration*, ask the simple question: "What's the real point here?" Never try to force a literal interpretation on figurative language (e.g., suggesting that gouging out your right eye will actually prevent you from lusting). When interpreting *metaphor* and *simile*, find the point of comparison intended by the author. Try to visualize the figure of speech since the visual image usually carries the emotional impact. Be careful not to press the details of the comparison too far (e.g., you are the salt of the earth).

When interpreting *irony*, find the point of contrast between what is expected and what actually happens. There you will find the unexpected twist to the story (e.g., Jesus commends "idle" Mary while he corrects "helpful" Martha). When interpreting *rhetorical questions*, rephrase them as statements in order to see the main point (e.g., you can't add a single minute to your life by worrying). When interpreting *parallelism*, don't isolate one line of text from the parallel lines. The lines work together to communicate meaning (e.g., ask, seek, and knock). When interpreting Jesus' *parables*, look for one main point per main character or group of characters in each story.[1]

Finally, regarding the book of Acts, look at how its major themes run through individual stories and speeches. Luke's overarching purpose in

[1]Since parables play such a major role in Jesus' teaching, we recommend further study in Craig L. Blomberg, *Preaching the Parables: From Responsible Interpretation to Powerful Proclamation* (Grand Rapids: Baker, 2004).

Acts surfaces in a number of theological themes. Just as the gospel of Luke emphasizes what Jesus began to do during his earthly ministry, Jesus now continues to work through the *Holy Spirit*. Closely related to the Spirit's role in guiding the church is the theme of *God's sovereignty*. The Spirit works chiefly through the *church* (the people of God) to accomplish his will. The early Christians were marked as people of *prayer*, and you will find them praying in almost every chapter of Acts.

Luke's message in Acts is clear: To be a follower of Jesus Christ means to be a faithful *witness* to the gospel. Such faithfulness was not without cost, however, when you notice that the early Christians often *suffered* because of their faith commitments. In spite of such hardships, the gospel advanced beyond the Jewish household to the *Gentile* nations. You get the clear impression that God is serious about a mission that includes the Gentiles. As you interpret Acts, always ask how the passage contributes to the central themes that run through the book—Holy Spirit, God's sovereignty, church, prayer, witness, suffering, and Gentile mission.

Keep in mind the major themes of Acts:

1. Holy Spirit
2. God's sovereignty
3. The church
4. Prayer
5. Witness
6. Suffering
7. Gospel to the Gentiles

Sermon Keys

The starting place when preaching New Testament narrative is to *root your sermon in the historical-cultural context in such a way that your audience can connect personally with the biblical story.* Your audience needs to experience by imagination the situation faced by the biblical audience. Consider the following example. After a full day of teaching the crowds and as the sun was setting, Jesus said to his disciples, "Let us go over to the other side" (Mark 4:35). This simple phrase could easily be passed over, but it reveals much about the original situation. By taking just a few moments in your sermon to unpack this statement, you will enliven your audience's imagination and usher them into a personal experience of the story. "Let's go over to the other side" would involve the following for the original disciples:

- They must travel across the sea at night (consider the symbols of darkness and the "evil" sea in biblical history).

- They face the frightening possibility of being on the sea at night during a storm (something professional fishermen would have been mindful of).
- The trip goes from the safety of the western shore to the eastern side. You could emphasize the sociological implications of leaving the safety of the Jewish surroundings and going to pagan country. The disciples knew the danger of going to unfamiliar, unsafe, unclean, "Gentile country."
- Shortly after they land on the other side, their worst fears come true as they are met by the demon-possessed man who lived among the tombs. Most people can identify with Jesus leading them into situations where they are afraid, inadequate, and uncomfortable. They will also be struck by Jesus' motivation for leading us to such places—the priority of people in his ministry.

Perhaps even more lies behind this seemingly shallow expression, "Let's go over to the other side," but you can see why it is not something you should skip over. New Testament stories are connected to real places, real people, and real experiences. If you give time during your sermon (usually at the beginning) to helping your audience walk in the shoes of the biblical audience, the story will come alive for your hearers. A sermon is more than historical-cultural information, however, and this leads us to our second sermon key.

You must ground the sermon in its literary context. Look at how the passage in question fits into the larger narrative context (cf. the interpretive keys above). Watch especially for contrasting stories placed side by side. In Mark 4–5 after Jesus had demonstrated his power by calming the storm, casting out the demons, healing the sick woman, and raising the dead girl, he went back to his hometown of Nazareth, where their lack of faith severely limited his ministry (Mark 6:1–6).

Sometimes the biblical author forces us to notice the contrast using a technique known as interchange. The author switches back and forth between two stories to contrast (or sometimes compare) the main characters or central themes. Luke does this in the middle section of

Your sermon will be successful to the extent that you enable your audience to identify with the characters of the story.

Acts to present the transition from Peter as the lead character in the first half of the book to Paul as the lead character in the second half.

Mark 5 also illustrates the use of interchange. At the end of Mark 5 the story begins with Jairus approaching Jesus with the news that his twelve-year-old daughter was dying. While Jesus is on his way to see the little girl, he is touched by a woman who has been sick for twelve years. After healing the woman, he continues on to Jairus's home where the daughter has now died, and Jesus proceeds to raise her to life. By interchanging these two stories (starting with one, moving to the second, then returning to the first), Mark wants his readers to compare and contrast the characters in each story and Jesus' actions in both situations.

By crafting a sermon that takes advantage of the literary context, you can make the biblical story come alive for your audience. Imagine a line in your sermon that would go something like this: "If the public figure Jairus could care for his twelve-year-old daughter, how much more could Jesus have compassion on his 'daughter' who had suffered a painful illness for twelve years." There are many more points of comparison and contrast between these two stories that you could use to drive home your sermon points.

Third, take time in your sermon to develop the main characters. People identify with biblical characters—with their flaws, hopes, and struggles. The colorful characters of the Bible are one reason why people are attracted to the Bible. We don't exaggerate when we say your sermon will be successful to the extent that you enable your audience to identify with the characters of the story. This calls for a "sanctified imagination" on your part as you study the context carefully and think through each of the standard story questions. Ask yourself how these people felt, what they thought, and so on. For instance, consider the story of Jesus healing the ten lepers in Luke 17:11–19:

> Now on his way to Jerusalem, Jesus traveled along the border between Samaria and Galilee. As he was going into a village, ten men who had leprosy met him. They stood at a distance and called out in a loud voice, "Jesus, Master, have pity on us!"

When he saw them, he said, "Go, show yourselves to the priests." And as they went, they were cleansed.

One of them, when he saw he was healed, came back, praising God in a loud voice. He threw himself at Jesus' feet and thanked him—and he was a Samaritan.

Jesus asked, "Were not all ten cleansed? Where are the other nine? Was no one found to return and give praise to God except this foreigner?" Then he said to him, "Rise and go; your faith has made you well."

Jesus and the "foreign" leper are the central characters in the story. As you enable your listeners to identify with the Gentile leper, help them to consider life from the leper's perspective:

- Help them identify with the social, religious, emotional, and physical dimensions of this man's lonely state of affairs. A leper in the ancient world lived in exile, and your audience needs to feel his pain.
- His hopelessness had driven him to Jesus. Help your audience relate to his weak, desperate faith.
- The tension this leper must have felt once healed was undoubtedly great. All ten are healed as they journey to meet the priests. Once healed, this one would have been tempted to run home and see his family again. His longing for a normal life likely stood in tension with his desire to return to Jesus and give thanks.
- Mention the physical manifestations of his faith: He comes back, praises God loudly, and falls at Jesus' feet. Confront your audience with the inevitable results of genuine faith.
- Explore the Jew-Gentile elements in the relationship between these main characters. Did this foreigner know that he would not be permitted to meet with the priests? Is that why he returned to Jesus? Why did he return to Jesus since Jesus was a Jewish healer?
- Imagine how the man must have contemplated for some time Jesus' final words: "Rise and go; your faith has made you well."

A fourth sermon key relates to how we treat Jesus as a main character. When Jesus is central to the story (often the case in the Gospels),

Don't shy away from proclaiming the full humanity and full divinity of Jesus wherever each is revealed in the Gospels.

make sure to consider both his divine and human qualities. Remember that the first disciples assumed that Jesus was a human being because of his physical presence with them; they only came to recognize his deity over time. Contemporary Christians tend to affirm first that Jesus is God and sometimes struggle to acknowledge that he was a real human being.

Don't shy away from proclaiming the full humanity and full divinity of Jesus wherever each is revealed in the Gospels. Jesus not only healed people, cast out demons, and performed miracles (evidence of deity), but he also experienced the limitations, pressures, and pain of a human being. It does not honor Jesus to focus on his deity to the exclusion of his humanity or to focus on his humanity in a way that denies his deity. The Gospels teach what people need to hear: Jesus was fully human and fully divine, not merely that he appeared to be one or the other.

Fifth, you must preserve the narrative heart of the passage, although your style of presentation may vary. When preaching a story, you can pause periodically to apply a theological principle to your audience, or you can tell the story and make application at the end of the sermon. You can use movie clips, skits, dramatic readings, testimony, and other creative means of communication. You can retell the story, explain the story, or reenact the story. Regardless of your communication approach and style, focus on preserving what we call the narrative heart of the passage.

The narrative heart is the theological essence of the story as revealed through the main characters and the plotline.

The narrative heart is the theological essence of the story as revealed through the main characters and the plotline (often starting with a problem, growing into conflict, climaxing in a solution, and concluding with a life lesson). For example, you could dream up many approaches to a sermon on the shocking death of Ananias and his wife Sapphira in Acts 5, but while the specific sermon outline and style of communication could vary, you would want to confront your audience with the heart of the matter—God will judge premeditated hypocrisy that seeks to destroy the fellowship that the Spirit of God has created in the body of Christ.

One great danger in contemporary preaching is the temptation to perform a (narrative) heart transplant on the text. Sometimes preachers fail to do the work necessary to discover the theological core of the story, conclude (from their superficial reading) that the text is boring and irrelevant, substitute a different narrative core from the contemporary world of athletics, nature, entertainment, and so on, and then give the sermon a light coat of biblical jargon. In the case of Acts 5, for example, the story is no longer about God judging hypocrisy with all seriousness but about the need for Christians to make wise financial investments (or something of the sort).

Sixth, help your audience experience the story by engaging their senses. To get your message across, you need to appeal to sight, smell, sound, and touch as well as hearing. When preaching a sermon on Jesus' temptation to use his power selfishly and turn the stones into bread, have the smell of freshly-baked bread drift through the worship center. Lower the lights to portray darkness when preaching on an imprisonment passage in Acts. When preaching about Jesus using the coin as an object lesson of "giving to Caesar what is Ceasar's, and to God what is God's" (Matt. 22:15–22), ask people to keep a coin in their hands during the sermon. At the end of the sermon invite them to place the coin in one location of the worship center and then walk to a different location, representing their giving themselves to God. Appealing to the senses of your audience through the sermon can be a bit risky, but when done appropriately, it drives home your point in powerful and lasting ways.

Things to Avoid

We encourage you to *avoid flattening the story into a series of descriptive, instructional points.* Telling stories is more powerful than telling about stories. Not even a clever series of alliterative sermon points will be as engaging as the biblical story itself. Since narrative is one of the most powerful forms of communication, why rob yourself of the opportunity to capture your audience by reducing the story to descriptive statements? Even more captivating than a good movie is

Don't rush to resolve conflict in a story.

a good book because not even Hollywood can compete with the human imagination. Let the story carry the sermon. Study the historical and literary contexts thoroughly and practice the art of retelling the biblical story with enthusiasm and creativity.[2]

A second thing to avoid is focusing on details of the story to the extent that your audience misses the main point. You might be surprised how tempting it is once you get into a story to focus on minute details at the expense of the central idea. We think it is appropriate to develop the details of a passage, but not to the extent that they take over the sermon and overshadow the main point. Curiosity can be your friend if you use it to raise questions about and uncover insights into the text. Curiosity, however, must be contained or it will lead to some worthless (and even dangerous) detours. Highlight details that contribute to your audience's grasp of the main point of the story.

We also caution against moving too quickly to resolve the conflict in the story and, as a result, killing the suspense for your audience. Conflict in the story is what sparks interest. When you grow impatient and rush to solve the problem or answer the question too early in the sermon, you leave your listeners with little reason to keep on listening. In order to create and retain interest, you need to pace your sermon by balancing slow- and fast-paced elements in the sermon. Galli and Larson write:

> Sermons also have slow- and fast-paced elements. To listeners a five-minute story runs, while a five-minute definition crawls. Slow-paced material addresses the intellect. It is abstract, generalized, factual, analytical. Definitions, principles, Hebrew and Greek word studies, analysis, deductive reasoning, exegesis, explanation, and description are generally slower paced. Fast-paced elements address the heart. They appeal to emotions, personal interest, the will, the imagination. They are specific, concrete, visual, personal. In general, rapid-paced elements include stories, illustrations, exhortation, challenge, application, and humor.[3]

As you vary the pace of the sermon by balancing matters of the head and the heart, your audience will experience a deliberate movement toward resolution of conflict. Since listeners crave answers, res-

[2]For help on crafting a story sermon, see Mark Miller, *Experiential Storytelling: (Re)Discovering Narrative to Communicate God's Message* (Grand Rapids: Zondervan, 2003); John Walsh, *The Art of Storytelling: Easy Steps to Presenting an Unforgettable Story* (Chicago: Moody, 2003).

[3]Mark Galli and Craig Brian Larson, *Preaching That Connects: Using the Techniques of Journalists to Add Impact to Your Sermons* (Grand Rapids: Zondervan, 1994), 118.

olution, and the "rest of the story," you will have no problem holding their attention.

Finally, avoid automatically equating the ancient audience with the modern audience. This calls for an awareness of our place in redemptive history. Contemporary Christians compare well to the ancient readers/hearers of New Testament letters, but they are a step removed from some of the characters within New Testament narrative who play unique roles (e.g., Paul), and two steps or more away from Jesus and the original disciples. In other words, you have to be aware of the shift in biblical history from the period of Jesus' ministry on earth to the period of the Spirit's ministry through the apostles.

Moreover, as you read and preach the book of Acts, you have to wrestle with whether you should interpret and preach a specific passage as *normative* for the church of all times or merely *descriptive* of what was valuable and inspiring in the early church.[4] These interpretive issues are complex and should caution us against a routine, mechanical equating of your audience with the ancient audience. There may indeed be parallels, but you need to think through the issues before you proclaim particular assumptions.

[4]For a full discussion of whether we should read Acts as normative or descriptive, perhaps the most significant interpretive issue related to this biblical book, see Duvall and Hays, *Grasping God's Word*, ch. 16.

Examples

Text: Matthew 16:13–17:8; Acts 3

Suggested title: Listen to Jesus

Context: At Jesus' baptism, the Spirit descended and the Father spoke, quoting two Old Testament passages (see Matt. 3:17): "This is my Son" from Psalm 2:7 and "whom I love; with him I am well pleased" from Isaiah 42:1. We fast forward the ministry of Jesus several years to his withdrawal to the region of Caesarea Philippi, where he asked his disciples a crucial question: "Who do people say the Son of Man is?" What follows in Jesus' teaching and the transfiguration account is a complete transformation of the way the original disciples thought about Jesus' mission. The climactic verse for this sermon is the additional quote from the Father at Jesus' transfiguration: "Listen to him" (Deut. 18:15)—a text repeated by Peter in his sermon recorded in Acts 3. This intertextual connection between Matthew 17:5 and Acts 3:22–23 reveals the transformation that occurred in Peter's life when he stopped trying to create Jesus the Messiah in his own image and began listening to Jesus define who he was and what he came to do.

Text thesis statement: Confessing Jesus as "the Christ" meant changing Peter's preconceived notions to match Jesus' definition of his messiahship and the demands of discipleship.

Text outline:
1. Peter confessed Jesus as the Christ. (Matt. 16:13–20)
2. Peter corrected Jesus for insisting that he was a suffering-and-dying messiah. (Matt. 16:21–22)
3. Jesus rebuked Peter for failing to grasp the true nature of his messiahship, a rebuke that is confirmed at the transfiguration. (Matt. 16:23–17:8)
4. After his transformation, the Lord used Peter to proclaim the good news of Christ in a powerful way. (Acts 3)

Crossing the bridge: There are several dynamics at work in this story of the transformation of Peter. He confesses Jesus prior to Jesus' resurrection, a perspective that we don't share. We do, however, sometimes hold distorted views of Jesus, a condition we share with Peter. For instance, we too battle the temptation to create a Jesus that is user-friendly, comfortable, and convenient rather than one who demands that we deny ourselves, take up our cross, and follow him. We will not witness the transfiguration where we hear the Father's voice instructing us to "listen to" the Son. Nevertheless, we are instructed through the story to stop trying to tame Jesus and instead to "listen to him."

When it comes to being used by God, Peter played a unique role in the early days of the church. We shouldn't leave people with the expectation that if they listen to Jesus, they will see thousands saved as a result of their next sermon, Sunday school lesson, or testimony. We should have the liberty to draw a parallel between God using Peter and God using us in a general way as a result of listening to Jesus.

Sermon thesis statement: As we listen to Jesus, God will transform our understanding of who he is and what he came to do and prepare us to be used by him in a powerful way.

Sermon outline:
1. We sometimes confess Christ with an untested boldness. (Matt. 16:13–20)

2. We sometimes rebuke Christ with a naive presumption. (Matt. 16:21–22)
3. We sometimes listen to Christ out of fearful desperation. (Matt. 16:23–17:8)
4. As we listen to Christ, God will use us as instruments of transformation. (Acts 3)

Text: Luke 18:1–8

Suggested title: Hanging in There over the Long Haul

Context: The context of this parable begins in Luke 17:20, when Jesus introduced the topic of the coming kingdom of God. At his first coming Jesus began the new age of God's rule. But God does not instantly remove kingdom citizens from this world. At his second coming, Jesus will bring the old age to a final end. Therefore, Christians are indeed citizens of one kingdom living in another kingdom. We live in the overlap between the ages— between the beginning of God's new age and the final end of the old age.

Against that backdrop Jesus tells the parable in Luke 18:1–8 for the purpose of showing his disciples "that they should always pray and not give up." The context of Jesus' second coming appears again at the end of the parable where Jesus asks, "However, when the Son of Man comes, will he find faith on the earth?" (18:8). Jesus uses the parable to encourage his disciples not to give up when they face injustice, but instead to persevere in prayer. Disciples will face injustice in this world prior to Christ's return. Prayer is the primary means of faithful persevering.

The judge-widow parable is followed by another parable, one comparing the faith of the Pharisee and the tax collector (Luke 18:9–14). Perhaps Jesus' use of the word "faith" in 18:8 triggered a question about the nature of genuine, enduring faith. Since the Pharisees would have assumed that they themselves were shining examples of persevering faith, Jesus uses this second parable to correct his disciples' understanding of faith. Or else, since both parables focus on prayer, perhaps Jesus uses the follow-up parable as a way of shedding more light on the topic of prayer. Of course, since prayer is a primary means of expressing our faith, the twin concerns of faith and prayer could very well go together, especially when facing injustice and suffering.

Text thesis statement: Through the story of an unjust judge and a persistent widow, Jesus taught that God would bring about justice for his chosen ones through the coming of the Son of Man and that their response should be one of enduring prayer.

Text outline:

1. There was a judge who neither feared God nor cared about people. (Luke 18:2)
2. There was a widow whose only hope was persistent pleading. (Luke 18:3)
3. The woman's pleading paid off as the judge reluctantly granted her justice. (Luke 18:4–5)
4. Jesus applies the parable to his disciples' life situation. (Luke 18:6–8)

Crossing the bridge: Readers are often confused by this parable because they mistakenly assume that we are exactly like the widow and God is exactly like the judge. If we draw that parallel too strictly, we will be forced to conclude that Christians have to harass and badger God before he will finally answer our prayers. God and the judge are alike only in that they are both authority figures and both reward persistence. The parable, however, is more about contrast than comparison. Jesus' point is that God is different from the judge and we are different from the widow. Unlike the unrighteous judge God does care about justice and about people. Unlike the widow, we are God's "chosen ones," his prized possession. Jesus uses a standard Jewish argument that moves from the lesser to the greater—if an unjust, power-hungry judge will respond to the pleas of a helpless widow, *how much more* will a righteous and loving Father respond to the cries of his beloved children!

It is tempting to ignore the surrounding context and assure people that praying for justice will yield an instant answer from God. While the parable teaches that God's justice is certain, it also teaches that the timing of his justice is only guaranteed at the return of Christ. God may grant justice in our lifetime, but he will most certainly grant justice when the Righteous Judge appears at the end of this age.

Jesus applies the parable to the original audience in 18:8 where he asks the concluding rhetorical question: "When the Son of Man comes, will he find faith on the earth?" Jesus will certainly bring justice when he returns, but will there be anybody still trusting in him at that point? As a point of application, our instant-gratification, fast-paced culture will struggle with the solution conveyed by this story (i.e., the delay of justice). People want justice and they want it now! Jesus is turning his audience toward a persevering trust in God and God's timing. This is reminiscent of the prayer of the godly echoed throughout Scripture, especially in the Psalms: "How long, O LORD."

Sermon thesis statement: When Christians face injustice in this world, they should always pray and never give up, believing that God will bring justice—sometimes in this life, but certainly when Jesus returns.

Sermon outline:
1. Unlike the judge, God will bring about justice for his people. (Luke 18:2, 4–8)
2. Like the widow, we must persevere through prayer. (Luke 18:1, 3–5, 7–8)

Review Questions and Assignments

1. Develop a text thesis statement, a text outline, a sermon thesis statement, and a sermon outline for Mark 10:35–45.

2. Develop a text thesis statement, a text outline, a sermon thesis statement, and a sermon outline for Luke 18:9–14.

3. Develop a text thesis statement, a text outline, a sermon thesis statement, and a sermon outline for Luke 15:11–32.

4. Develop a text thesis statement, a text outline, a sermon thesis statement, and a sermon outline for Acts 15:1–35.

11

Preaching Revelation

> They overcame him
>   by the blood of the Lamb
>   and by the word of their testimony;
> they did not love their lives so much
>   as to shrink from death.
>
> **Revelation 12:11**

To interpret and preach from Revelation is to begin a journey that is anything but boring. You can expect to wrestle with the meaning of bizarre images, struggle with communicating through words a text that is full of pictures, and face the temptation to water down the warnings when they hit close to home. Your reward will be the opportunity to bring perspective and hope to people who desperately need it.

The last book of the Bible describes itself in the first verse as a "revelation of Jesus Christ," an expression that functions as a title for the entire book. The term "revelation" (*apokalypsis*) suggests that something once hidden is now being unveiled or displayed openly. In this "final chapter" of the story of salvation, God pulls back the curtain to give his people a glimpse of his plans for human history, plans that center around Jesus Christ. Revelation is powerful, difficult, perplexing, colorful, suspenseful, tragic, and amazing. It is like a raging river, a bloody battle, an enticing mystery, and a breathtaking wedding all rolled into one. Anything but boring!

Interpretive Keys

With Revelation more than with any other book of the Bible, how you interpret a passage will determine how you craft the sermon. The interpretive approach we suggest makes context and the intent of the author primary factors in seeking to understand the message of this book. *The first interpretive key, therefore, is to become familiar with the historical context of the book.* Some sixty years after Christ's death, Christians living under Roman rule were feeling pressure to compromise with the powers that be or suffer the consequences. John himself has been banished to Patmos because of his commitment to Christ (1:9), and persecution appears to be increasing in intensity and scope (2:3, 9–10, 13; 3:8). You will find references to martyrs (e.g., 6:9) along with a number of places where we are told that pagan powers shed the blood of the saints (ch. 13; 16:5–6; 17:6; 18:24; 19:2; 20:4).

Most scholars favor a date for Revelation toward the end of the first century during the reign of the Roman ruler Domitian (A.D. 81– 96), the emperor who wanted his subjects to address him as *dominus et deus noster* ("Our Lord and God"). For Christians, the earliest and most basic confession was "Jesus is Lord." When Christians refused to confess "Caesar is Lord" in worship of the emperor, they were considered disloyal to the state and became subject to persecution.

Not every Christian in Asia Minor, however, was standing strong against persecution. The messages to the seven churches are filled with warnings for those tempted to turn away from Christ and compromise with the world system. Revelation 18:4 presents an explicit warning to God's people related to Rome (Babylon): "Come out of her, my people, so that you will not share in her sins, so that you will not receive any of her plagues."

Revelation is filled with comfort for those who are being persecuted and with warning for those who are trying to avoid it. As Craig Keener puts it, "Revelation speaks to churches both alive and dead, but more of the churches are in danger of compromising with the world than of dying from it."[1] The historical context is one in which false religion has formed a partnership with pagan political power,

> *Revelation is filled with comfort for those who are being persecuted and with warning for those who are trying to avoid it.*

---

[1]Craig S. Keener, *Revelation* (NIVAC; Grand Rapids: Zondervan, 2000), 39.

Revelation is also a prophetic-apocalyptic letter.

thereby putting pressure on those who claim to follow Christ. Will they compromise with the world to avoid persecution or will they openly confess Christ, knowing that it may cost them their lives? As you study and preach Revelation in its historical context, you will want to keep in mind the twin concerns of hope for the suffering and warning for the complacent.

The second interpretive key also relates to context—literary context. The reason why Revelation is such a strange book (especially after the first few chapters) is that it combines three different literary genres: letter, prophecy, and apocalyptic. As a *letter* (1:4–5; 22:21) the book is addressed to seven specific first-century churches and, because of the symbolism of the number seven, to the church in all times and places. Although many of the interpretive keys for reading New Testament letters apply to Revelation, its genre as prophecy and apocalyptic dominate the book.

Revelation claims to be a *prophetic* letter (1:3; 22:6–7, 10, 18–19). Biblical prophecy includes both *prediction* of the future and *proclamation* of God's truth for the present, with the emphasis falling on the latter. The readers of this prophecy are exhorted to do what God has said (i.e., to obey the prophecy or proclamation). The nature of Revelation as prophetic literature reminds us that the book is not just about the future but about how God wants his people to live in the present. As a prophetic letter Revelation stands in the tradition of the Old Testament prophets and draws much of its language and imagery from them. Review the interpretive keys for reading the prophets (ch. 14) as preparation to interpret Revelation responsibly.

Revelation is also a prophetic-*apocalyptic* letter. In the very first verse we are told that the book is a revelation or apocalypse (*apokalypsis*) that comes from God, through Jesus Christ, through an angel, through John, to the servants of God (1:1). Most scholars believe that apocalyptic grew out of Hebrew prophecy and actually represents an intensified form of prophecy written during a time of crisis. The hope delivered by apocalyptic literature is that God will soon intervene in human history to deliver his people and judge their enemies (cf. the Old Testament books of Daniel, Ezekiel, and Zechariah).

Apocalyptic literature often uses dramatic picture language to communicate its message. As Fee and Stuart point out, while we are familiar with picture language used in other parts of Scripture, apocalyptic literature uses images that are often forms of fantasy rather than reality—e.g., locusts with scorpion's tails and human heads (9:7–10), a woman clothed with the sun (12:1), and a beast with seven heads and ten horns (13:1).[2] Often what makes the image fantastically strange is how the items are combined to form the image. For example, we know about women and we know about the sun, but we don't know much about a woman clothed with the sun. As a prophetic-apocalyptic letter, Revelation is full of strange visions and bizarre images, and interpreting such picture language appropriately is crucial to correct interpretation.

The third interpretive key is to honor the larger story of Revelation. As you interpret and preach smaller sections of the book, you should do so in light of how the entire book unfolds. The following description of the narrative framework of Revelation will help you as you prepare to preach from particular sections. Remember, a sermon that dishonors or violates the larger story of Revelation is not a biblical sermon.

- *1:1–3:22—Introduction.* Chapter 1 introduces us to John and describes his vision of "one like a son of man" (Jesus) who walks among the seven golden lampstands (the churches). John has been selected to write the revelation of Jesus Christ on a scroll and send it to these churches. Chapters 2–3 contain the seven messages to the churches.
- *4:1–5:14—Vision of God and the Lamb.* The seven messages set the scene on earth and clarify the twin dangers that the church faces: persecution and compromise. In Chapters 4–5 the scene shifts to heaven, where God reigns in majestic power from his throne. All of heaven worships the Creator. Also worthy of ceaseless praise is the Lion-Lamb (Jesus), who alone is able to open the scroll. By his sacrificial death the Lamb has redeemed a people to serve God.

[2]Gordon Fee and Douglas Stuart, *How to Read the Bible for All Its Worth* (Grand Rapids: Zondervan, 1993), 233.

- *6:1–8:1—Opening of the seven seals.* The stage has been set and the unveiling of God's ultimate victory formally begins. This section marks the first of a series of three judgment visions, each with seven elements (seals, trumpets, bowls). Crucial to understanding the larger story is the question in the opening of the sixth seal: "Who can stand?" (as the Lamb pours out his wrath). The answer comes in Revelation 7 with two visions of God's people—the 144,000 on earth, sealed with divine protection, and the great multitude standing before God's throne.
- *8:2–11:19—Sounding of the seven trumpets.* The trumpets reveal God's judgment on a wicked world. They are patterned after the plagues of Egypt leading up to the Exodus. In spite of the ever-intensifying judgments, the "earth-dwellers" (a common term in Revelation for unbelievers) refuse to repent (9:20–21). As in 8:1, before the seventh element in the series, there is an interlude, this time consisting of two visions: the angel and the little scroll (10:1–11) and the two witnesses (11:1–14). These visions once again offer the saints encouragement and instruction about what they should do as God carries out his purposes in history.
- *12:1–14:20—The people of God versus the powers of evil.* Revelation 12 explains the real reason why God's people face hostility in this world. The root cause is the conflict between God and Satan (the dragon). Although Satan was decisively defeated by Christ's death and resurrection, he vents his rage for a limited time on God's people. Chapter 13 introduces Satan's two agents for waging war against them—the beast out of the sea and the beast out of the earth. The dragon and the two beasts constitute a satanic or unholy trinity resolute on seducing and destroying God's people. In chapter 14 we once again receive a glimpse of the final future that God has in store for his people. In spite of the persecution they now face in this world, the followers of the Lamb will one day stand with him on Mount Zion and sing a new song of redemption.

- *15:1–16:21—Pouring out of the seven bowls.* Chapter 15 features seven angels with seven golden bowls filled with God's wrath. The bowls follow the seals and trumpets as the final series of seven. Chapter 16 describes the pouring out of these seven bowls on the unrepentant world. The plagues are devastating, uninterrupted, universal manifestations of God's anger toward sin and evil. God will make Babylon the Great (the Roman empire in the first century) drink the "wine of the fury of his wrath" (16:19). In response the earth-dwellers not only refuse to repent, they go so far as to curse God (16:9, 11, 21).

- *17:1–19:5—The judgment of Babylon.* From this point on in Revelation, John sets before us a "tale of two cities"—the city of man (earthly Babylon destined for destruction) and the city of God (heavenly Jerusalem, where God will dwell among his people forever).[3] Chapters 17–18 depict the death of Babylon, a pagan power said to be "drunk with the blood of the saints, the blood of those who bore testimony to Jesus" (17:6). This world's funeral laments for the deceased Babylon (ch. 18) give way to the explosive celebration in heaven as God's people rejoice over Babylon's downfall (19:1–5).

- *19:6–22:5—God's ultimate victory.* This section of Revelation portrays God's ultimate victory over the forces of evil and the final reward for his people. The scene opens with the announcement of the wedding of the Lamb (19:6–10) and the return of Christ for his bride (19:11–16). The Warrior-Christ returns, captures the two beasts and their allies, and throws them into the fiery lake of burning sulfur (19:17–21). The dragon or Satan is bound (20:1–3), during which time Jesus' faithful followers reign with him (20:4–6). Satan is then released from his temporary prison, only to join the two beasts in eternal torment (20:7–10). The dead are judged by him who sits on the great white throne. Anyone whose name is not found written in the book of life is also thrown into the lake of fire (20:11–15). At this point death itself is judged.

[3]Robert H. Mounce, *The Book of Revelation*, rev. ed. (NICNT; Grand Rapids: Eerdmans, 1998), 306.

Having judged sin, Satan, and death, God ushers in the eternal state of glory. There is a general description of the "new heaven and a new earth" in 21:1–8, followed by a more detailed presentation in 21:9–22:5. The Old Testament promise that God would live among his people finds its ultimate fulfillment here (21:3). There is no temple in this city of God because God Almighty and the Lamb are its temple (21:22). God's victory is complete and the fellowship he desired with Adam and Eve is now recovered in a restored Garden of Eden, complete with a tree of life (22:1–2). The curse of sin is removed, and redeemed humanity is once again able to walk with God and see his face (22:4).

- *22:6–21 — Conclusion.* Revelation closes with a final blessing on those who keep "the words of the prophecy in this book" (22:7) and a warning for those who practice sexual immorality, idolatry, and the like (22:15). The book is an authentic revelation from God and should be read faithfully to the churches (22:6, 16). Jesus assures his people that his return is imminent (22:7, 12, 20). And John responds with a prayer-statement that Christians of all times can make their own: "Come, Lord Jesus." In the meantime, John writes, "the grace of the Lord Jesus be with God's people. Amen" (22:21).

You may find it helpful to return to this overview any time you are preaching from Revelation as a means of reminding yourself to honor its larger story in your preaching.

The fourth interpretive key is to look to the Old Testament and to the historical context when seeking to understand Revelation's symbols and images. One reason why Revelation is difficult is that while you may understand the words you are reading, you may not know what they are referring to. In other words, you usually know what Revelation is saying, but you're often not sure what it is talking about. For more insight into the images and symbols of Revelation, we point you to the first-century historical context and to the Old Testament. The book is addressed to Christians living in the first century, and it is filled with echoes and allusions to the Old Testament.

As a brief example of how the historical context and the Old Testament can clarify images and symbols, consider Revelation 5. You will have a much better understanding of the scroll (5:1) by reading more about scrolls in the first century.[4] Revelation 5 is also filled with Exodus imagery—the Passover Lamb, the Lamb's blood providing salvation from judgment, and the commemoration of the rescue event with a "new song" (just to name a few). Before you look at today's newspaper as a way of uncovering the meaning of the symbols of Revelation, look to the historical context and the Bible of the early church, the Old Testament.[5]

The fifth interpretive key, and perhaps the most important, is to focus on the main idea and not to press all details. With most literary genres in the Bible, you begin with the details and work your way toward an understanding of the whole. In New Testament letters, for instance, you observe details and study words in order to grasp the author's thought. With Revelation, however, things are turned upside down. Here you should start with the big picture and work toward an understanding of the details. Start by summarizing the main idea of a particular section and resist the temptation to chase the rabbit of apocalyptic details. Knowing the details of a passage might satisfy your curiosity and perhaps heighten the impact on the reader, but it will not change the main idea and could sidetrack you completely. Keep the main point of each scene or episode squarely in your sights.

Sermon Keys

First, preach Revelation with a great deal of humility. Revelation is not an easy book! Your audience may pressure you to be the "know-everything expert" who can finally answer all their questions. Preaching from Revelation presents an extraordinary opportunity to demonstrate to people the benefit of living with unanswered questions. When people are determined to satisfy their curiosity or refuse to live with any mystery, they often read into Revelation things that simply are not there. This is your chance to get them out of the habit of forcing an interpretation simply to relieve the tension of not

> *For the meaning of Revelation's images, look to the Old Testament rather than to today's newspapers.*

[4]See Ben Witherington III, "A Closer Look—On Ancient Scrolls," in *Revelation* (NCBC; Cambridge: Cambridge Univ. Press, 2003), 119.

[5]We suggest that the preacher consult the better evangelical commentaries on Revelation in order to unlock the Old Testament context. See G. K. Beale, *The Book of Revelation: A Commentary on the Greek Text* (NIGTC; Grand Rapids: Eerdmans, 1999); Keener, *Revelation*; Craig R. Koester, *Revelation and the End of All Things* (Grand Rapids: Eerdmans, 2001); Mounce, *The Book of Revelation*; Grant Osborne, *Revelation* (BECNT; Grand Rapids: Baker, 2001); and Witherington, *Revelation*.

Never lose sight of the main message: "God will win!"

[6]Richard Bauckham, *The Theology of the Book of Revelation* (Cambridge: Cambridge Univ. Press, 1993), 10.

[7]Ibid., 7.

[8]Ibid., 17.

[9]Beale, *The Book of Revelation*, 175.

knowing the answer to every question. Offer a disclaimer at the beginning of your sermon that you do not have all the answers.

Second, keep the larger purpose of Revelation in mind. That purpose is tied up with its powerful use of images that create a symbolic world in which the readers may live during the time they read (or hear) the book. When they enter this symbolic world, its message affects them and changes their entire perspective on the world in which they live.[6] They are able to see their own situation in this world from a heavenly vantage point as they are transported by visions to the place where they can see God's ultimate victory over the forces of evil.[7] In this way Revelation provides Christians with a set of "prophetic counter-images" to purge their imagination of the pagan view of the world and replace it with a view of what is real and how the world will be one day under God's rule.[8]

As Christians in hostile circumstances read the book again and again, they are continually reminded that "what they believe is not strange and odd, but truly normal from God's perspective."[9] Your sermons from Revelation should never lose sight of the main message: "God will win!" Often within a single passage you will see a dual message—comfort for the afflicted and affliction for the comfortable. As a faithful communicator of God's Word, you need to prepare yourself to address both groups within the same congregation.

A third sermon key is to preach episodes or scenes rather than specific verses or even individual images. The book is arranged according to visions or scenes, much like New Testament letters are organized by paragraphs. When selecting a text for a sermon from Revelation, ignore the verses and find the beginning and ending of a particular scene.

Fourth, Revelation is like Old Testament prophetic literature in that it is organized around themes or topics. Revelation does have more of a narrative or story structure than the prophets, but there remains a healthy dose of the topical. This affects sermon organization in at least two ways. First, you should feel free to preach sermons that emphasize one such topic or theological theme as it runs throughout the book. You could, for example, preach a series on the seven beatitudes in Revelation, or the songs in Revelation, or the women of Revelation.

To be sure, you still need to study the immediate context, but the context of the entire book plays a larger role than in most other literature.

In addition, if you are preaching from a single scene, don't be surprised if your sermon outline varies from your textual outline. In other words, even within a single episode you may see the need to group verses by theme rather than in linear order. For instance, in the second sample sermon outline at the end of this chapter, the textual outline is as follows:

1. The first heavenly sign—a woman (Rev. 12:1–2)
2. The second heavenly sign—a dragon (Rev. 12:3–4a)
3. The woman gives birth to a male child (Rev. 12:4b–6)
4. A war in heaven (Rev. 12:7–9)
5. The suffering saints on earth overcome Satan (Rev. 12:10–12)

But the corresponding sermon outline reflects the thematic way in which Revelation communicates its message:

1. We should expect to be attacked by God's archenemy, Satan. (Rev. 12:3–4, 9, 12)
2. We need to be reminded that Satan has already been defeated by Jesus Christ. (Rev. 12:1–2, 5–10)
3. We can overcome Satan now by trusting in Christ's work, being faithful in our confession, and being willing to suffer. (Rev. 12:11)

A fifth sermon key is to resist the temptation to outdo the book itself when it comes to images and symbols. Perhaps the most difficult thing about preaching from Revelation is that the text is already full of pictures. Normally we use word pictures or illustrations to make the text come alive, but in Revelation the text often consists of word pictures. You can either compete with the biblical images with a different set of images, or you can think of ways to help people see and imagine the symbols that are already there. We recommend the second approach. Introducing new images could confuse people and detract from the biblical message. We recommend, instead, that you find creative ways to help people get inside the situation and experience the biblical image as the original audience might have experienced it. Consider appealing to the different senses or using various media to accomplish your goal of engaging their imagination.

The final sermon key relates to application of sermons from Revelation. Keep in mind how the context of your audience parallels (or fails to parallel) the original context. Often Revelation will provide comfort for persecuted Christians. What do you do when no one in your congregation is facing persecution? You should avoid manufacturing artificial circumstances just to apply the text. Rather than pretending to be the persecuted church, perhaps your application should be to learn more about and pray for Christians around the world who are facing real persecution.

Things to Avoid

Perhaps the greatest temptation when interpreting and preaching Revelation is to ignore the first century and leapfrog into the twenty-first century. Using today's news headlines as the key to grasping Revelation completely ignores John's meaning for his original audience. As Keener notes, this "newspaper" approach does not fit well with a high view of Scripture since it implies that in Revelation God was not really speaking to the very first Christians.[10]

[10]Keener, *Revelation*, 21– 22.

Doesn't the newspaper approach seem arrogant? What if Christ does not return until A.D. 7000? Would Revelation still have a message for today's Christians since they would not be the last generation? Never forget that the very first Christians were blessed for obeying Revelation (1:3) and that the book is described as an unsealed (or open) book, even for people living in John's day (22:10). Discovering the message to the original audience is top priority with any book of the Bible, but especially with this one.

Avoid the expectation that Revelation should provide us with a strict chronological map of future events. The book certainly contains an overall chronological progression, but you can get into trouble if you attempt to arrange every detail on a single, clear-cut timeline. The book is filled with prophetic-apocalyptic visions that serve to make a dramatic impact on the reader rather than present a precise chronological sequence of future events. For example, the sixth seal (6:12–17) takes us to the end of the age, but when the seventh seal is opened, we are given a whole new set of judgments—the trumpets. The seventh trumpet (11:15–19) also takes us to the end of the age, yet with the first bowl in 16:1–2 we are given another series of judgments. Revelation 19–22 paints the most colorful and detailed picture of the end, but, as you can see, this is not the first time the readers have been transported to the very end. Instead of trying to find a neat, linear map of future events in Revelation, we encourage you to grasp the main message in each vision about living faithfully in the here and now.

You will also stumble when interpreting and preaching Revelation if you attempt to take everything literally. For example, Jesus is described in chapter 4 both as a lion and a lamb. It seems impossible to take either of these descriptions literally without completely destroying the other. Through these two images John is communicating that the powerful, mighty ruler has conquered through his sacrificial death.

In Revelation 4 God is on the throne, whereas in Revelation 5 Jesus is said to occupy the same throne. To begin to think spatially about how both could fit on one throne is the wrong approach to take. John is using the throne image to tell his readers that Jesus is divine. Picture language with its symbols, images, and figures is capable of conveying literal truth and describing literal events. Jesus does conquer through sacrifice (a literal cross), and he is literally divine. But while you should always take Revelation seriously, you should not always (or even normally) take it literally.

We are told in 1:1 that God "showed" or "signified" the book to John. When interpreting much of the Bible, the general rule is to interpret literally except where the context clearly calls for a symbolic reading. The word "signify" (NIV, "made it known") in verse 1 suggests that when we come to Revelation, the general rule is to interpret symbolically unless the context calls for a literal reading.[11]

Finally, when interpreting and preaching Revelation, avoid the pressure to superimpose on Revelation a prepackaged theological system without

Take Revelation seriously but not always literally.

[11]Beale, *Revelation*, 52.

215

letting the book speak for itself. Don't misunderstand, Revelation is one of the most powerful theological works in Scripture, but it should be approached on its own terms (not an easy task in itself). For example, to interpret 4:1–2 as the rapture of the church is an attempt to find in Revelation a reference to an event that exempts the church from facing tribulation. These verses, however, clearly refer to John's personal prophetic experience that occurs several times in Revelation (17:1; 21:9–10), rather than to the church collectively. There are many places where Revelation resists systematization, and the wise preacher will follow suit.

Examples

Text: Revelation 5

Suggested title: From Weeping to Worship

Context: In Revelation 4 God is seated firmly on his throne, a symbol of his complete sovereignty. This scene stands in contrast to the situation faced by the churches of chapters 2–3. They are having some success, but some are facing persecution from Rome, the religious-political-economic superpower of the first century, while others are compromising with the world system.

The central question at the end of Revelation 4 is how God's rule will move from heaven (where he is in control and worshiped enthusiastically) to earth (where the church struggles to stay faithful in the face of increasing pressure). The question itself is reminiscent of the prayer Jesus taught his disciples to pray: "Your kingdom come, Your will be done on earth as it is in heaven" (Matt. 6:10). Revelation 5 answers the question and serves as the foundation for the rest of the book.

Text thesis statement: God's work of conquering evil and redeeming a people centers in the sacrificial death of Jesus Christ, the Lion-Lamb—the One who is worthy of worship.

Text outline:
1. John sees the sealed scroll in God's hand, but weeps despairingly when no one is found worthy to open the scroll. (Rev. 5:1–4)
2. Jesus, the Lion-Lamb, is worthy to open the scroll because by his death on the cross he purchased a people for God. (Rev. 5:5–7, 10)

3. John sees how the unfolding of God's plan through Christ will result in unprecedented worship by all of creation. (Rev. 5:8–14)

Crossing the bridge: When we read Revelation 5 and try to determine its meaning and to communicate that meaning to our audience, we find ourselves identifying with John as he experiences the vision. We certainly are not apostles, nor are we having a heavenly prophetic vision, but as Christians we do share with John a common membership in God's people. In some ways John functions as our representative in witnessing and experiencing the heavenly vision. We can identify with his emotional despair when no one is found worthy to open the scroll. We can emphasize the limitations of his human perspective in grasping God's plan. We can relate to John's experience of hearing about a lion and turning to see a lamb.

As with John, our experience of this passage will quickly become Christocentric. Jesus now receives the scroll from and shares the throne with God, directly affirming his deity. Jesus conquers as a lion, but the manner of conquest is that of a sacrificial lamb, affirming the paradox of victory through suffering and sacrifice. Jesus has redeemed a multicultural people of God, challenging us to reach across racial and cultural barriers with the gospel. As a climax to the vision of Revelation 5, all of God's creation is drawn to authentic, God-centered worship. The bridge of theological principles for Revelation 5 is grand and cosmic in scope, and preaching on this passage serves as a good reminder that it's not all about us, our needs, and our agendas.

Sermon thesis statement: A vision of God's great work in Christ will transform our weeping into worship.

Sermon outline:
1. God is working his grand plan even when our limited, human understanding keeps us from seeing his work. (Rev. 5:1–4)
2. God's great work centers in Jesus Christ and his redemptive death on the cross. (Rev. 5:5–7, 10)
3. Our prayers for God's will to be done will one day be transformed into never-ending worship for all that he has done. (Rev. 5:8–14)

Text: Revelation 12:1–12

Suggested title: A Defeated, but Still Dangerous Enemy

Context: If Revelation 11 portrays the suffering church, Revelation 12 helps explain why Satan and his forces oppose the people of God with such intensity. The chapter opens with a woman who is about to give birth to a male child. An enormous red dragon is waiting to devour the child, but at birth the child is snatched up to God. The scene then shifts to heaven, where the archangel Michael and his angels fight against the dragon and his angels. The dragon (now explicitly called the devil or Satan) is defeated and is thrown down to earth. As a defeated foe who has had to forfeit his place in heaven, the devil pursues the woman with a vengeance and makes war against the rest of her offspring.

First-century Christians would likely have thought of the woman as the true Israel, the faithful community who gives birth to both the Messiah and the church. After giving birth to the Messiah, the woman flees to a place of spiritual refuge for a period of 1,260 days, the time of persecution between the ascension and exaltation of Christ and his future return (cf. 11:2; 12:14; 13:5). The dragon is explicitly identified in the passage as the ancient serpent—the devil or Satan (12:9). The male child most certainly represents Jesus Christ. By moving straight from Jesus' birth to his ascension and enthronement (being "taken up to God"), John stresses that Satan's evil plot has been foiled by Jesus' incarnation, life, death, resurrection, ascension, and exaltation.

The original audience would have understood the war in heaven (12:7–12) and the subsequent rage of the devil (12:13–17) as an explanation of two significant realities. First, God has defeated Satan and the victory is certain. Second, God's people on earth continue to suffer as victims of the devil's rage. This heavenly perspective helped the original audience adjust their expectations and persevere in their hostile environment. They too can appropriate the victory and overcome the devil "by the blood of the Lamb and by the word of their testimony," that is, by bearing faithful witness to the gospel of Jesus Christ even if it costs them their lives (12:11).

Text thesis statement: God's people can expect to suffer from the devil's rage, but they can overcome Satan by relying on Christ's past victory and remaining faithful in their present confession.

Text outline:
1. The first heavenly sign occurs—a woman. (Rev. 12:1–2)
2. The second heavenly sign occurs—a dragon. (Rev. 12:3–4a)
3. The woman gives birth to a male child. (Rev. 12:4b–6)
4. There is war in heaven. (Rev. 12:7–9)

5. The suffering saints on earth overcome Satan. (Rev. 12:10–12)

Crossing the bridge: Revelation 12 communicates several significant theological principles:

- There is a real devil that is opposed to God and bent on deceiving and destroying God's people. Spiritual warfare is real.
- Satan has been defeated by the life and redemptive work of Christ.
- Christians can overcome the devil by enduring and faithfully proclaiming the gospel of Jesus Christ.
- Christians can expect to suffer for being faithful in their witness to Christ.

Because we live between the first and second comings of Christ, we can expect to suffer the rage of God's archenemy. Satan's attacks against us vary from those used at other times in history and in other parts of the world, but they remain real dangers. In general, churches in North America do not face overt persecution; rather, we experience the subtle but powerful temptation to compromise (e.g., immorality, idolatry, false teaching, and materialism). The passage calls on Christians to prepare themselves to suffer physically should their circumstances change.

The great challenge in preaching Revelation 12 is to communicate the twin truths that Satan is a defeated enemy but also a dangerous one and to instruct people about the true nature of spiritual warfare. Rather than caving in to an unbalanced view of Satan, this text portrays him as a defeated enemy who continues to pose a threat. This passage also connects spiritual warfare squarely with our faithfulness to the life, work, and gospel of Jesus Christ rather than with any sort of mystical knowledge or particular religious ritual.

Sermon thesis statement: Although we as Christians should expect to suffer at the hands of Satan, we can overcome him by holding fast to the finished work of Christ.

Sermon outline:
1. We should expect to be attacked by God's archenemy, Satan. (Rev. 12:3–4, 9, 12)
2. We need to be reminded that Satan has already been defeated by Jesus Christ. (Rev. 12:1–2, 5–10)
3. We can overcome Satan now by trusting in Christ's work, being faithful in our confession, and being willing to suffer. (Rev. 12:11)

Review Questions and Assignments

1. Develop a text thesis statement, a text outline, a sermon thesis statement, and a sermon outline for a passage addressed to one of the seven churches in Revelation 2–3.
2. Develop a text thesis statement, a text outline, a sermon thesis statement, and a sermon outline for Revelation 7.
3. Develop a text thesis statement, a text outline, a sermon thesis statement, and a sermon outline for Revelation 21:1–8.

Part 3
Preaching the Old Testament

Preaching Old Testament Narrative 12

> "I am God Almighty; walk before me and be blameless."
>
> **Genesis 17:1**

Without doubt, some of the most exciting, dramatic, and uplifting texts in the entire Bible are the stories of the Old Testament. These biblical narratives still have power to connect with Christians today and to impact our lives in dramatic ways. They are fascinating and gripping, and they resonate with believers today just as they have for many millennia. These stories draw us right into the action and force us to engage with the great biblical issues of life—faith, doubt, courage, love, loyalty, and holiness. Indeed, the narratives often bring us all face to face with God himself.

Over half of the Old Testament is narrative. Obviously, God thought that narrative was a good vehicle for communicating theology and changing lives. Powerful biblical preaching should include a strong, regular dose of Old Testament narrative.

Interpretive Keys

The first interpretive key is to recognize that the Old Testament narratives are not a loosely connected conglomeration of biographies or unrelated miracle stories, but a theological history of how God related to his covenant people. The narratives reflect an inseparable mix of three things: historical events, aesthetically crafted accounts of those events,

[1]Meir Sternberg, *The Poetics of Biblical Narrative* (Bloomington, IN: Indiana Univ. Press, 1987), 41–48.

and theological purpose.[1] When interpreting the Old Testament narratives, you must keep all three aspects in view. You are dealing with important historical events that have been recounted in complex (but fascinating) aesthetic literary forms. The overall purpose, of course, is affective and theological, intending to teach us about God and to change us so that we can follow him more completely.

Second, pay close attention to literary context. The stories must be placed within the larger story, and the theology that you derive from any narrative text must be one that fits smoothly into the surrounding context. For example, one of the major themes running throughout much of 1 Samuel is the contrast between Saul (the type of king the people asked for) and David (the type of king God wanted). This extended contrast dominates the latter half of the book. Thus when preaching 1 Samuel 17 (David and Goliath), it is important to note that this story is not so much about David and Goliath as it is about David and Saul—and how differently they handle the threat of Goliath. The negative example of Saul (lack of trust in God, fear, timidity, shirking responsibility) is as much part of the message as is the contrasting, positive example of David.

Third, if you are looking to interpret accurately the biblically based theology of Old Testament narratives, you must deal with fairly large chunks of text. In a sermon from Paul's letters, you can preach a paragraph at a time. Likewise, in the New Testament gospels, you can preach episodes or pericopes (usually ten to twenty-five verses). In Old Testament narrative, however, often the smallest story unit that is coherent can stretch to an entire chapter and, on occasion, run to several chapters.

A good example of this is the "ark campaign" of 1 Samuel 4–6. This story of the ark and its campaign down into Philistia runs for three chapters. Dealing with any less than the total three chapters ruins the story and misses the theological point. In 1 Samuel 4 the foolish and disobedient Israelites lose the ark of the covenant after being defeated by the Philistines. This creates serious tension in the story: Has Israel lost their God? Can God be defeated by the Philistines?

In 1 Samuel 5 the ark (i.e., the presence of God) is carried to Philistia, where God demonstrates that it was the disobedient Israelites that had been defeated by the Philistines, not the God of Israel. The God of Israel proceeds to defeat Dagon, the god of the Philistines, and to cut off his head and hands (like a conquered king). God then smites the Philistine city of Ashdod with a plague. The people of Ashdod then send the ark up the coast to the next Philistine city, Gath, whom God also strikes with a plague. These people then send the ark to Ekron, the next Philistine city up the coast, which wisely refuses to receive the ark. The Philistines then place the ark on a cart and submit gifts of gold to God, entreating him to leave Philistia. He does so, returning victoriously to Israel in 1 Samuel 6.

Indeed, the entire episode reads like a military campaign conducted not by a human army with a human commander, but by God, all by himself. He travels alone down into Philistia and first conquers the city of Ashdod, executing her "king," the god Dagon. Ashdod surrenders and God moves up the coast like an invading army. The next city Gath quickly surrenders as well, soon followed by Ekron. The Philistines pay tribute to the God of Israel, and he returns victoriously—loaded with booty from the campaign—back to Israel. It is a wonderful story about the power and honor of God in the midst of human weakness and failure.

Further tying this three-chapter unit together are two major interrelated themes. The Hebrew word for "honor" or "glory" has a close derivative form that means "heavy." A wordplay on these two concepts runs throughout the unit. This theme is tightly connected to play on the word "hand." Unlike the *heavy* (fat) ineffectual high-priest Eli, God's *hand* is *heavy* on the Philistines, even to the point of cutting off the *hands* of their god Dagon, in order that the God of Israel might be *honored*. Indeed, the twofold aspect of this interconnected theme surfaces in over a dozen verses (1 Sam. 4:3, 8, 18, 21–22; 5:4, 6, 7, 9, 11; 6:3, 5, 6, 9).

Thus, when interpreting this text, you must study the entire story and understand its context. There is conflict and tension in the story, but also powerful resolution. All of these components are important to grasping the theology that God is trying to convey to us in this story. So you need to be prepared to handle large units of text when interpreting Old Testament narrative in preparation for your sermons.

Of course, there are significant exceptions. Occasionally you will encounter short units of text that are theologically coherent by themselves (although even these must be viewed from their larger literary context). Genesis 12:1–3 (the promise to Abraham) falls in this category. This is one of the few Old Testament narrative texts where you can legitimately interpret and preach from three verses. However, this short passage drives the story throughout the rest of the Old Testament and even into the New Testament, so although you can limit your exegesis to three brief verses, it is imperative that you connect the promise to Abraham to the larger context (most of the rest of the biblical story).

A fourth interpretive key relates to the characters: The Old Testament stories are filled with colorful characters, and these characters often provide both positive and negative models for us. Frequently the narrative will contrast two characters against each other (David vs. Saul, Hannah/Samuel vs. Eli/wicked sons, etc.). Yet keep in mind that throughout most of the Old Testament narrative literature, *God is also a central character*. God is not aloof in the Old Testament, speaking only in shadows through the narrator. He is a major player. A central feature of narrative is dialogue, and God is involved in over two hundred separate dialogues in the Old Testament! If we miss God in the story, then we have missed the story.

Narrative is powerful and effective at revealing the character of the participants. One of the central purposes of this material is to reveal God to us. We are able to see God at work in numerous different situations as he deals with varied human-related problems. For example, in the story of Gideon in Judges 6–8, Gideon is not really the one who delivers the Israelites from the Midianites. The real hero in the story is God. Gideon is weak, frightened, and hesitant. God has to give him sign after sign. What does that teach us about God? Does God choose weak individuals? Of course! Is God patient with his weak servants? Absolutely—up to a point. So, don't miss God in the narratives. Treat him as a main character. Analyze his actions and his dialogue. Probe into his emotions and his reasons for acting.

A detailed discussion concerning how to read and interpret Old Testament narrative is beyond the scope of this book, but there are several helpful works that we recommend.[2] Studying and interpreting narrative requires a close reading of the text and the context, making detailed observations about time, place, plot, irony, characters, point of view, and so on.

Sermon Keys

Preaching Old Testament narrative texts can be fun, and congregations love to hear these stories. However, the mechanics of sermon preparation, especially when you are dealing with a passage that may be several chapters long, can be quite daunting. But don't despair! The rewards are worth the work, and with some practice you will be able to develop and preach powerful, relevant, and theologically accurate sermons from the great stories of the Old Testament.

As you develop your sermon, keep in mind that Old Testament narrative is an inseparable mix of historical event, aesthetically crafted presentation, and theological purpose. Your sermon should retain this balance as well.

Therefore, the first sermon key is to connect your audience into the historical setting of the narrative text you are preaching. Sermons that refer to an Old Testament narrative briefly and then zoom off immediately into a "spiritualized" or allegorical understanding of the text are, in reality, denying the historicity of the event. These preachers are well-intentioned, but they are communicating to their audiences that it really doesn't matter whether or not these stories happened; all that matters is our "spiritualized" understanding of them.

To us the intention of God is otherwise. The Old Testament narratives are neither myth nor parable. God *acted* in human history, and the Old Testament narratives are a divinely inspired proclamation of that spectacular intervention. You need to recount these events in such a way as to make them real in the lives of your audience today.

> *The rewards from preaching the Old Testament narratives are well worth the extra work.*

[2]See Duvall and Hays, *Grasping God's Word*, ch. 4 ("How to Read the Book—Discourses") and ch. 18 ("Old Testament—Narratives"). Four standard classical discussions of Hebrew narrative, although from a nonevangelical perspective, are Robert Alter, *The Art of Biblical Narrative* (New York: Basic, 1981); David M. Gunn and Danna Nolan Fewell, *Narrative in the Hebrew Bible* (Oxford: Oxford Univ. Press, 1993); J. P. Fokkelman, *Reading Biblical Narrative* (Louisville: Westminster John Knox, 1999); and Sternberg, *The Poetics of Biblical Narrative*. We prefer Sternberg's approach because he emphasizes authorial intent while the others occasionally lapse into a "reader response" approach. However, Sternberg is extremely difficult to understand. Much of the material on reading Hebrew narrative has been synthesized and presented clearly from an evangelical perspective in Steven D. Mathewson, *The Art of Preaching Old Testament Narrative* (Grand Rapids: Baker, 2002). Also helpful in this regard is Greidanus, *The Modern Preacher and the Ancient Text*.

Connecting to the historical setting tells your audience that you think the story really happened.

Certainly the issue of historicity is not the heart of the message, and if your whole sermon dwells on historical background or historical context, you have missed the point as well. But a short orientation to the historical setting—"what it meant in their town"—at the beginning of your sermon will accomplish several important things. First, it tells your audience that you believe that this story really happened. Second, it helps reinforce sound interpretive principles in the personal Bible study of your people. Third, if you do this regularly, it will educate your people about how the Old Testament fits together.

For example, there are many Christians who have been in church all their lives but don't know whether David came after Abraham or before him. They are familiar with the details of many stories (they know that David picked up five stones to kill Goliath), but they have no concept concerning where a biblical character fits into biblical history. If you are preaching to a "seeker" type audience, the need to deal with the scope of biblical history increases. A few statements of historical orientation at the beginning of every Old Testament sermon will do wonders at helping your audience get a handle on how the Old Testament fits together. This will strengthen your audience's knowledge of God's Word, regardless of whether they are long-time church members or "seekers."

The second sermon key relates to narrative aesthetics; simply put, stories communicate differently than essays do. This is important to keep in mind. This difference provides both powerful potential in preaching narrative and the biggest challenge in sermon development. The Old Testament stories are alive and colorful. They connect with people at both the emotional level and the intellectual level. You should strive to do the same with your sermon presentation. Also, Calvin Miller notes that narrative preaching comes across to today's postmodern audience as less "preachy" and thus a little less threatening than traditional style preaching.[3] Powerful narrative-style preaching of the Old Testament can quickly grip people who have not grown up in the church or who have been disillusioned by earlier negative church experiences.

However, it is not enough to merely retell the story. Your role is to connect the vivid, colorful, and exciting story to your audience

[3]Calvin Miller, "Narrative Preaching," in *Handbook of Contemporary Preaching*, ed. Michael Duduit (Nashville: Broadman & Holman, 1992), 105.

in a relevant, applicable manner that changes their life theologically. Once you are engaging in practical theology as well as storytelling, you must present practical lessons that can be drawn from the narrative. You want your sermon to pull the audience into the story and to feel the impact of the story, while at the same time pointing out exegetically valid, yet practical and relevant, theological lessons from the text. Balancing these two goals is the challenge of preaching narrative.

Pull your audience into the story.

Thus, as you study the narrative, after you determine what the text meant for them (historical and literary context), you will need to cross the interpretive river, pass through the New Testament perspective, and develop relevant theological points or lessons from the story. But when you start preaching, if you ignore the details of the story and move straight to the theological application of your points, you will have gutted the text of its aesthetic power, and your sermon will probably be boring as well.

As a result, we encourage you to preach Old Testament narrative in a narrative preaching style. Give a brief historical orientation and then plunge right into the exciting details of the story, pulling your audience into the biblical story with you. You still want to communicate your main theological points, either along the way or at the end. That is, the story plot will drive the main structure of your sermon, not the logic of your points.

Read as much of the story as you have time for, pausing every few verses—or every verse as the need may be—to explain the story. If you have a fairly short passage (e.g., Gen. 22:1–19), read the entire passage. Constantly remind your audience that the authority of your message comes from the text, not from your office as preacher. In other words, read as much of the passage as is practical and keep your audience in the text as well, following along.

Still, many Old Testament narratives are simply too long to read. For a long passage like 1 Samuel 4–6, read some verses directly from the Scriptures and then summarize the other sections of the story. The decision regarding which verses to read aloud and which to summarize should be based on the need to clearly portray the dramatic aspects of the story, the need to focus on certain verses in order to pull out your main theological points, and the need to stay within the timeframe allowed for your sermon. And be sure to make the decision regarding which verses you will read and which you will summarize *before* you get up to preach!

Related to the aesthetic aspect is the practical observation that when preaching Old Testament narrative, you do not need as many sermon illustrations or other illustrative material as you do when preaching other types of literature, especially New Testament letters. The story itself is the great picture or illustration of your main points. Sometimes illustrations are helpful in driving home specific applicational aspects of your points. For example, if one of your main points from the narrative is that God's people should love each other, while the narrative will give a good illustration of this from biblical times, it is a good idea to focus this abstract idea for your audience into a contemporary situation; relevant illustrations can serve that purpose.

The final sermon key relates to the theological purpose of the Old Testament narratives. They are written in a fascinating, aesthetically crafted manner for the purpose of maximizing their theological impact on the audience. Your sermon should have the same purpose. The stories are often fun and entertaining, but the goal is to impact lives with the reality of God and his will for us. So while your sermon will not necessarily be structured around your main points, you will, nonetheless, need to have main points. You want your sermon to be powerful aesthetically, like the narrative itself, but your purpose is theological—to elicit a life-changing response from the listeners.

Practically speaking, there are two basic approaches to how you relate your main points to the retelling of the story. One approach is to read/summarize a unit of several verses, explain the narrative up to that point, and then stop and make a contemporary theological point and application. Thus, you might have three or four main spots where you stop and make application as you move through the story. At the end you can summarize each of your main application points and focus on the central idea, driving home your most important applicational point.

The other approach is to stay in the context of the story until you have completely retold it. Then present your main theological points and application, going back with each to make sure the connection to the story is clear. Finally, pull the points together into your main overall idea and drive home the main application of the text.

Avoid changing a historical event into spiritualized allegory.

Which approach is better? In our own preaching, we prefer the former, but the choice is really one of personal preference, and both are valid and effective. Many of you will prefer the second. We encourage you to try both. Even if you find you prefer one style, you should occasionally try the other one just to keep your sermons from becoming too predictable.

Things to Avoid

One major temptation in preaching from the Old Testament narratives is the allure of skipping over the context and the authorially embedded meaning completely and rushing straight to a "spiritualized," fuzzy-feely message loosely connected to some word or phrase in the text. While the theology conveyed by these types of sermons may be true, it rarely comes from the text at hand, and thus it loses much of its text-based authority. In reality, you end up in allegory, distorting the intended meaning of the text and preaching by your own authority instead of that of Scripture. Furthermore, remember that as you preach, you are modeling Bible study methods for your people. Ignoring context and preaching allegorically suggests to your people that this is a valid way to study Scripture, and it may lead them into all kinds of incorrect theology. Context can save your bacon on this if you will only let it.

While we were writing this chapter, we came across a good illustration of someone who succumbed to this temptation. This particular preacher was sharing with us about Joshua 4, where the Israelites were commanded to build a monument of stones taken from the middle of the Jordan River, which God had dried up to allow the Israelites to cross over into the Promised Land. This preacher correctly connected the stone monument with the concept of worship, but then his wandering eye noticed that Joshua 3:17 said that the priests stood in the middle of the Jordan *on dry ground*. At this point his allegorical imagination kicked in; he cast all thoughts of context (both literary and theological) aside and began pondering the deep meanings of *dry ground*. Aha! At last he had it! A great sermon idea! The memorial stones were taken from the dry ground. Thus, his sermon message was, "Worshiping God in the Dry Times of Your Life." His message centered on urging the listeners to worship God even when things seem to be "dry" spiritually or when things are not going well.

Now, the question is not whether or not the sermon topic is true or false. Undoubtedly, Christians are still to worship God when their lives seem "dry." The critical question to ask is, "What is God trying to say in Joshua 4?" Our allegorical preacher seriously misunderstood the point of the text and of the word *dry* in this context.

In Joshua 4, God crashes into human history and spectacularly parts the Jordan River (as he had parted the Red Sea) to empower his people to pass victoriously into the wonderful Promised Land. It is a passage showing God's great miraculous power at work on behalf of his people. To twist this great story of God's powerful presence into a lesson on "dry times in your life" is to miss completely the truth that God is conveying, not only in this chapter but also throughout the book of Joshua. The term "dry" in Joshua 3–4 has nothing to do with hard times or the spiritual absence of God in one's life; rather, it has everything to do with the fact that the Israelites were not drowning in the river. The stone memorial was set up so that Israel would remember how God miraculously parted the water and how his presence powerfully led them into the wonderful Promised Land.

A second important mistake to avoid when preaching Old Testament narrative is trying to force all of the characters in the narrative to be positive role models. This warning is important because as you study and preach from these great narratives, you will derive many of your main sermon points from the behavior of the main characters. Many of these characters are presented as models for Christians today, providing patterns and examples of faithful living before God. It is essential, then, that you be able to discern the good guys from the bad guys.

One of the most common errors made in interpreting Old Testament narrative is to assume that everyone in the story is a hero, a model for Christians today to copy. This is simply not true. Many of the characters are negative characters, and you must be aware of this. If you mistake a bad guy for a good guy, you will be missing the point of the story.

Also keep in mind that most of the main characters (excluding God) contain mixtures of good and bad traits. Very few characters emerge from the story as squeaky-clean. The narrator expects you to read with sophistication and discernment. He does not identify his characters with placards that say "good guy" or "bad guy."

> *Distinguish the good guys from the bad guys!*

Examples

Text: 1 Samuel 4–6 (the ark narrative)

Suggested title: Routs and Rats: Honor and the Heavy Hand of God

Historical context: As the book of Judges ends, the theological situation in Israel is disastrous. The Israelites are not worshiping God faithfully, and they are fighting each other instead of the inhabitants of the land. As the book of 1 Samuel opens, the narrative question hovering below the surface is, "Will someone rescue Israel from their apostasy, or will God destroy them for their serious covenant violation?" The first three chapters of 1 Samuel introduce the boy Samuel, but they also underscore how corrupt the current priesthood is and how theologically bankrupt Israel is at this time.

As mentioned above (page 225), there is a running wordplay throughout 1 Samuel 4–6 on the Hebrew word translated both as "honor" and "heavy." This theme intertwines with the theme of the "hand of God" (4:3, 8, 18, 21–22; 5:4, 6, 7, 9, 11; 6:3, 5, 6, 9). Israel trivializes God in their worship, but they think they can manipulate him into giving them power and victory in battle. God shows them otherwise, letting the Israelites lose the battle but then defeating the Philistines and their god by himself, returning triumphantly to Israel.

Thus, in preaching 1 Samuel 4–6 you really need to mention a few events from 1 Samuel 2 to tie the story into its proper context

Don't miss the subtle humor of God.

(the disobedience of Eli's two priestly sons). The primary focus of this story (and your sermon) is in chapter 5, so the majority of verses that you will actually read aloud will come from that chapter. To set the background, we recommend reading aloud 2:12, 29–30, and 33. Summarize chapter 4, spending more time on verses 1–11 than 12–22. Then focus on chapter 5, reading verses 1–2, 6–7, 9, and 11. Don't miss the irony or—we believe—the subtle humor of God. Finally, read 6:5–6 as part of the conclusion to the story.

Text thesis statement: Israel, while dishonoring God in their worship, tries to manipulate him into giving them a victory over the Philistines. God, however, instead allows them to be defeated and then wins the war by himself, bringing honor to his name.

Text outline:
1. The priestly leaders of Israel dishonor and belittle God rather than honor and serve him. (1 Sam. 2:12, 29–30, 33)
2. The disobedient Israelites try to manipulate God into giving them victory; instead, they are defeated and the ark is captured. (1 Sam. 4)
3. Yet God preserves his honor by invading and defeating the Philistines by himself. (1 Sam. 5–6)

Crossing the bridge: The theological principles that emerge from this text for today's New Testament audience revolve around how Christians today honor or dishonor God, how we try to manipulate him into serving us rather than us striving to serve him, and how, regardless of our faithfulness or unfaithfulness, God is always sovereign and able to execute his will.

Sermon thesis statement: With or without us, God will carry out his sovereign plan in the world, and all people will ultimately acknowledge and honor him. In this unfolding plan, we can honor him and be honored, or we can dishonor him and be dishonored.

Sermon outline:
1. God is offended when people belittle him or dishonor him. Ultimately, he will be acknowledged and honored. (1 Sam. 2:12, 29–30, 33)
2. God cannot be manipulated into serving us or honoring us. (1 Sam. 4)
3. God is able to bring about his sovereign plan and bring honor on himself with or without us. (1 Sam. 5–6)

Text: 2 Kings 5

Suggested sermon title: The Restoration of Life

Historical context: While this passage is much shorter than the one discussed above, it is still a bit too long to read in its entirety. We suggest that you read verses 1–19 (the focal point of the sermon), but then summarize verses 20–27. Be sure to spend a few moments describing the historical background. Israel has turned away from God, and the Israelite kings have been worshiping pagan gods instead. In contrast to the royal disobedience and impotence, Elisha, the true servant of God, speaks divine truth and acts with the power of God.

Text thesis statement: The power to restore life is not in the hands of human kings and generals, but rather in the hands of God's humble and obedient servant.

Text outline:

1. Naaman, a powerful Aramaean general, is stricken with a humiliating disease. (2 Kings 5:1)
2. In contrast to the kings of Aram and Israel, who do not know anything about the power of God, a young Hebrew slave girl knows the way to find the power of God. (2 Kings 5:2–7)
3. To be restored, Naaman must humble himself and follow Elisha's specific, but easy, instructions. (2 Kings 5:8–15a)
4. In contrast to God's humble servant Elisha, who realizes that this miracle comes from God and that God alone should receive glory from it, the servant Gehazi tries to profit from the miracle, but instead receives punishment. (2 Kings 5:15b–27)

Crossing the bridge: The river of differences between their town and our town is significant in this text. The entire political/religious setting of 2 Kings is far removed from us today. The disobedient monarchy of Israel does not equate to the presidency of the United States or even to politicians in general, but rather finds parallels in the prevailing non-Christian philosophies and secular approaches to life in today's world. Likewise, one of the main points of this story is that the approach to God (restoration of life) is easy, but it must be the approach that *he* dictates, not one that *we* (or popular opinion) choose. Note also that Jesus cites this story in Luke 4:27 to illustrate that the gospel if for all people in all nations.

Sermon thesis statement: The power to restore life (eternal life and meaning in this life) does not lie in the hands of the ruling

> *The disobedient monarchy of Israel does not equate to the presidency of the United States.*

non-Christian philosophies and secular approaches of our world, but it can be found only in Christ, often through the guidance of humble, obedient Christians, and is available to all people.

Sermon outline:

1. The world does not have the power to restore life. (2 Kings 5:1)
2. Salvation is available to all people, and even a small Christian child can point out the way to powerful unbelieving men, who don't have a clue. (2 Kings 5:2–7)
3. We must come to God by the way he has determined—through Christ, by faith. It is easy but specific, and no variations or substitutions are allowed. (2 Kings 5:8–15a)
4. A truly humble and obedient servant of God will not claim credit (or pay) for life that God has miraculously restored. (2 Kings 5:15b–27)

Conclusions

The Old Testament is filled with fascinating stories through which God communicates a wealth of theological truth—truth about his character and truth about how we as Christians should live today. These dramatic stories, when interpreted properly, provide principles and exhortations that find relevance in the lives of Christians today. Preaching from the Old Testament narratives can be fun and exciting, and your audience will love you for it. But through these texts you will also be able to edify the church by strengthening your people and helping them to mature in their walk with God.

Review Questions and Assignments

1. Develop a text thesis statement, a text outline, a sermon thesis statement, and a sermon outline for 2 Kings 1:1–17.
2. Develop a text thesis statement, a text outline, a sermon thesis statement, and a sermon outline for 2 Kings 2:1–18.
3. Develop a text thesis statement, a text outline, a sermon thesis statement, and a sermon outline for 1 Kings 18:16–46.
4. Develop a text thesis statement, a text outline, a sermon thesis statement, and a sermon outline for Genesis 39:1–23.

Preaching the Law **13**

> Open my eyes that I may see
> wonderful things in your law.
> **Ps. 119:18**

How can we take the Old Testament law (the legal material in Exodus through Deuteronomy) and preach it effectively? How can we apply it to our audience today? Obviously commands in the Mosaic law are important, for they comprise a substantial portion of God's written revelation. Likewise, Jesus and the writers of the New Testament quote from this material frequently. Yet the Old Testament contains many laws that seem strange to us today (e.g., "Do not cook a young goat in its mother's milk," Ex. 34:26; "Do not wear clothing woven of two kinds of material," Lev. 19:19; "Make tassels on the four corners of the cloak you wear," Deut. 22:12). Should we preach these texts or ignore them? If we do preach them, how on earth can we communicate them to our people today?

Also, in today's world Christians violate a number of Old Testament laws with some regularity (e.g., "A woman must not wear men's clothing, nor a man wear women's clothing," Deut. 22:5; "Rise in the presence of the aged," Lev. 19:32; "The pig is also unclean; although it has a split hoof, it does not chew the cud. You are not to eat their meat or touch their carcasses," Deut. 14:8). Are we being disobedient?

Why do we adhere to some laws and ignore others?

Should we preach against eating bacon and against women wearing pants?

Furthermore, while believers tend to ignore many Old Testament laws, they embrace others, especially the Ten Commandments, as the moral underpinnings of Christian behavior (e.g., "Love your neighbor as yourself," Lev. 19:18; "You shall not murder," Ex. 20:13; "You shall not commit adultery," Deut. 5:18).

Why do we adhere to some laws and ignore others? Which ones should we preach as valid and which should we identify as invalid? Or perhaps we should simply ignore the problem? Many people (and pastors) in the church today make these decisions based merely on whether or not a law *seems* to be relevant in today's world. Surely this haphazard and existential approach to interpreting the Old Testament law is inadequate.

Yet how do we preach this material? How can we go from their town to our town and end up with a message that is biblically correct and still relevant to today's Christian?

Interpretive Keys

The first interpretive key is to recognize the limitations of the traditional and popular approach of categorizing the laws as civil, ceremonial, or moral. Under this approach neither the civil nor the ceremonial laws apply to Christians today and thus have limited, if any, contemporary relevance. The moral laws, however, are timeless and universal and thus supposedly have direct relevance to us as God's eternal law.

We discourage you from using this approach for several reasons. The categories (civil, ceremonial, moral) are arbitrary and are not indicated at all in the Scriptures. It is often difficult to classify a passage cleanly into one of these categories. All of the legal material—even the so-called "civil" or "ceremonial" texts—has theological overtones and theological purpose and therefore has "moral" connotations. We are hesitant to use the open-ended and hard-to-define categories of "civil" and "ceremonial" as a criterion to dismiss large portions of the law.[1]

[1]For a more complete discussion of this issue, see Duvall and Hays, *Grasping God's Word*, 328–36.

In our opinion the approach of categorizing the law into civil, ceremonial, and moral is too ambiguous and too inconsistent to be a valid approach to interpreting Scripture. We do not see a clear distinction in Scripture between these different categories of law. The vagueness of this distinction thus makes us uncomfortable about using such a distinction to determine whether a particular law is to be literally obeyed as law or completely ignored. We also question the validity of dismissing the so-called civil and ceremonial laws as not being applicable. *All* Scripture is applicable to the New Testament believer. We maintain that the best method of interpreting the law is one that can be used consistently with all legal texts. It should be one that does not make arbitrary, *nontextual* distinctions between verses and their applicability.

Second, recognize that the law is not presented in the Bible by itself as some sort of timeless universal legal code, but rather as part of the theological story that describes how God delivered Israel from Egypt and established them in the Promised Land as his people. The law is part of a story, and this story thus provides an important context for interpreting it. Indeed, our methodology of interpreting Old Testament law should be similar to our methodology of interpreting Old Testament narrative, for the law is contextually part of the narrative.

Third, the law is tightly intertwined into the Mosaic covenant and should be interpreted accordingly. Thus, it is important to make several observations about the nature of this covenant.

- The Mosaic covenant is closely associated with Israel's conquest and occupation of the land. The covenant provides the framework by which Israel can occupy and live prosperously with God in the Promised Land.
- The blessings from the Mosaic covenant are conditional. A constant warning runs throughout Deuteronomy explaining to Israel that obedience to the covenant will bring blessing but disobedience to the covenant will bring punishment and curses.
- The Mosaic covenant is no longer a functional covenant. New Testament believers are no longer under the old, Mosaic covenant. Hebrews 8–9 makes it clear that Jesus came as the mediator of a *new* covenant that replaced the *old* covenant.

> *The law is imbedded in the Old Testament theological story.*

Interpret the law through the grid of New Testament teaching.

• The Old Testament law as part of the Mosaic covenant is no longer applicable over us as law. Paul makes it clear that Christians are not under the Old Testament law. Now that we are freed from the law through Christ, we do not want to put people back under the law through our hermeneutical method.[2]

Fourth, we must interpret the law through the grid of New Testament teaching. According to 2 Timothy 3:16, "all Scripture is God-breathed and is useful for teaching, rebuking, correcting and training in righteousness." Paul certainly includes the law in his phrase "all Scripture." As part of God's Word, the value of the Old Testament law is eternal. You should study and seek to apply all of it. However, the law no longer functions as the terms of the covenant for us, and thus *it no longer applies as direct literal law for us.* The coming of Christ as the fulfillment of the law has changed that forever.

The final interpretive key for interpreting Old Testament law is to follow the Interpretive Journey. The Journey provides a sound, biblically-based yet applicable approach to developing sermons from the Law. The Old Testament legal material contains rich *principles* and *lessons* for living that are still relevant today when interpreted through New Testament teaching.

Therefore, to interpret and develop applicable theological principles from a particular law, first determine the meaning in their town. What did the text mean to the biblical audience? Remember that the Old Testament law is part of a larger narrative. Read and study it as you would any narrative text. Identify the historical and literary contexts. Has the particular law you are studying been given as a response to a specific situation, or is this law describing the requirements for Israel after they move into the Promised Land? What other laws are in the immediate context? Is there a connection between these laws? Does this law govern how the Israelites approach God? Does it govern how they relate to each other? Does it relate to agriculture or commerce? Is it specifically tied to life in the Promised Land? Now determine what this specific, concrete expression of the law meant for the Old Testament audience.

Next, measure the width of the river to cross. What are the differences between the biblical audience (ancient Israelites) and us (contemporary Christians)? For example, we are under the new covenant and not under the old covenant, as they were. Thus, we are no longer under the law as the terms of the covenant.

Moreover, we are not Israelites preparing to dwell in the Promised Land with God dwelling in the tabernacle or temple. We are Christians with God dwelling within each of us. In addition, we do not approach God through the sacrifice of animals. We approach God through the sacrifice of Jesus Christ. We live under a secular government and not under a theocracy (as ancient Israel did). We do not face pressure from Canaanite religion, but rather from non-Christian worldviews and philosophies. Most of us do not live in an agrarian society, and so on. The differences are often significant, and identifying them is critical if we want to develop biblically accurate sermons for New Testament believers.

The next step is to determine the theological principle in the text. Each of the Old Testament laws presents a concrete, direct meaning for the Old Testament audience, a meaning that is tied within the old covenant context. But that meaning is usually based on a broader universal theological truth, a truth that is applicable to all of God's people, regardless of when they live and which covenant they live under. What is the universal theological principle that is reflected in this specific law? That is, what is the broad principle that God has behind this text that allows for this specific ancient application? Is it a text about the holiness of God? Is it about fellowshiping with God? Is it about caring for one's fellow believer?

Now pass through the New Testament with the theological principle and filter it through the New Testament teaching regarding the principle or the specific law being studied. For example, if you are interpreting Exodus 20:14, "You shall not commit adultery," your universal principle will be related to the sanctity of marriage and the need for faithfulness in marriage. As you pass into the New Testament, you have to incorporate Jesus' teaching on the subject. In Matthew 5:28 Jesus states, "But I tell you that anyone who looks at a

> *Follow the Interpretive Journey.*

241

woman lustfully has already committed adultery with her in his heart." Jesus has expanded the range of this law. He applies it not only to acts of adultery but also to thoughts of adultery. In developing a concrete expression of Exodus 20:14 for today's audience, we must incorporate Jesus' comments on that law. The commandment for us becomes, "You shall not commit adultery, in act or in thought."

Finally determine the meaning "in our town." How should individual Christians today apply the theological principle in their lives? Take the theological principle that you have developed and apply it to specific concrete situations that individual Christians in your church encounter today.

Sermon Keys

The first sermon key is to realize that when preaching from the Old Testament law, the appropriate size of the text that you should cover can vary dramatically. You need to preach from a coherent unit of text, one that has some definable breaks in the context that identify it as a literary unit. Some passages are tightly embedded into the surrounding narrative and thus must be approached in the same fashion as narrative. Usually this involves dealing with a fairly large portion of Scripture.

However, most units within the legal material are one chapter in length or shorter. For example, Deuteronomy 6:1–25, an entire chapter, is an identifiable unit. Likewise, these twenty-five verses can be organized into a good sermon. As when preaching narrative, it may be difficult to read aloud all twenty-five verses, so you have to decide which ones are most important to your sermon thesis statement. Read the most important verses and summarize the others as you move through the text.

On the other hand, Deuteronomy 16:9–12, only four verses, is also a complete unit and should be preached as such (within the broader context of Deuteronomy). Likewise, although the Ten Commandments are spread out over twenty-one verses (in Ex. 20 and in Deut. 5), it is difficult to preach on each of the commandments in one sermon. Because of the importance of this text and the rich amount of applicable material that it contains, we would advise splitting it up into two or more sermons.

The second sermon key is to tie the passage into its literary and historical context. Even if you choose to preach the Ten Commandments one by one, it is important to tie each one into its literary and historical context. Many of the Ten Commandments are already stated in universal theological principle form ("you shall not steal"), and it is tempting to forget about their town and rush straight into application for your audience today. We would advise you to spend a few moments tying the text into the story of the Exodus and into the theological setting of the Mosaic covenant before you move on to spend the majority of your time on connecting it to the applicational situations of your audience today.

Although all of the Ten Commandments (except the Sabbath command) are already in somewhat of a theological principle form and thus fairly easy to understand, few other verses or passages in the Old Testament law follow this pattern. Most texts are rather challenging when you attempt to cross the river from their town to our town and develop timeless theology that applies today. Developing a correct text thesis statement (what it meant to them) is not generally difficult. But moving across the river to develop a sermon thesis statement can be frustrating and hermeneutically tricky. This is perhaps the major challenge in preaching passages from the legal material in Exodus, Leviticus, Numbers, and Deuteronomy. However, don't give up on preaching this important portion of God's Word!

A third sermon key is to preach Old Testament law in light of the overarching theological principles that function like themes in the legal material. For example, in Exodus, after God led the Israelites out of Egypt, he made a covenant with them. A critical part of the covenant was God's promise to dwell among them in a real, literal sense. This was a promise of God's presence, which had powerful implications for fellowship and empowerment. But if God was to dwell among them, he needed a place to stay. Thus, the entire second half of Exodus describes how to construct the tabernacle, or God's dwelling

Don't be afraid to preach from Leviticus.

place. And if the holy, awesome, powerful God was to dwell in their midst, then lots of things in the culture and society needed to change. How were they to approach him? How could a holy God live in the midst of sinful people? How could they deal with sin? How could they fellowship with God?

The book of Leviticus answers these questions—with how the Israelites were to live with the holy and awesome God in their midst. Thus, many of the laws in Leviticus are related to the holiness of God. Most of the laws that deal with the importance of keeping clean things apart from unclean things or with the need to keep different things separate have their foundational theological basis in the holiness of God and the demands placed on the Israelites by his presence. So the universal theological principle that comes out of many of these texts is that God is holy and his presence demands that his followers be holy and stay separate from unholy things.

For Christians today, however, God does not dwell in the tabernacle or temple; rather, he dwells within each believer through the Holy Spirit. We experience God's presence in a more direct and powerful way than the Hebrews did. Are there implications for us and how we live because of the indwelling of the Holy Spirit? Absolutely!

So you can preach many of the passages in Leviticus from this perspective, stressing that just as the holy God living in their midst required that the Israelites separate from "unclean" things, so today the holy God living within us demands that we be holy as he is holy. Jesus comments on this as well (Mark 7:15, 20–23), noting that in regard to the Old Testament dietary laws, it is not what goes into a person (what he eats) that makes him unclean, but what comes out (what he says).[3] The holiness of God is a huge theological theme that runs throughout the Old Testament law, and it can be somewhat easily translated into a contemporary Christian setting.

In the same manner, many of the blood sacrifices described in the legal material provide wonderful background material for understanding the sacrifice of Christ. You can preach these texts! Explain how the sacrificial system worked in the Old Testament. Explain the historical background—that is, the repetition required, the identification

[3]See the discussion of this text in ibid., 339–41.

required with the sacrificed animal, and so on—and then relate it to Christ.

Likewise, the descriptions of the Passover Feast provide a meaningful background for understanding the death of Christ. In addition, there are other feasts and nonblood sacrifices that are simply celebrations and acts of fellowship and thanksgiving. These texts can be preached with relevance to today's audience as well, addressing the contemporary issues of worship, praise, and fellowship. We don't bring grain offerings to God anymore, but certainly we need to experience celebration and thanksgiving as we fellowship with God.

Avoid legalism!

Things to Avoid

There are two extremes to avoid. First, do not put your people back under the legalism of the Old Testament law. Paul goes to great lengths to move the church out from under the legalism that was often associated with the law. So don't become legalistic and preach the Old Testament law as a "law" for Christians. Be especially careful that you do not proclaim a works-oriented theology. Instead, preach the timeless and applicable theological principles that undergirded the original law. In addition, bring the principles through the teachings of the New Testament and proclaim these truths in the context of new covenant realities for today's believers (i.e., the "law of Christ").

The opposite tendency is the danger of ignoring the original meaning and the historical/cultural context and to engage in imaginative allegory. Resist the temptation to dream up wild connections between Christ and the minute details of the Old Testament law. Much of the popular literature on "Christ in the tabernacle," for example, is inaccurate in its claim for extreme symbolism. The tent pegs holding up the exterior walls of the tabernacle, for instance, did not symbolize the cross or death of Christ. They simply kept the walls from falling over.[4]

[4]See the discussion of this text in ibid., 192–95.

There is a third common practice often made while preaching the Old Testament legal material that we caution against. In seeking parallels between the meaning in their town and meaning in our town, it is not accurate to parallel the nation of Israel with the political entity of the

United States of America. In developing principles and making connections today, the common feature that helps us cross the principlizing bridge is the concept of the "people of God." The ancient Israelites, as they entered into covenant relationship with God, became his people. Christians today can likewise be defined accurately as God's people. The law gives us theological principles on how "God's people" can approach and fellowship with a holy God. These principles translate into application for all Christians today. They cannot be taken as how America approaches and fellowships with God.

The Old Testament legal material is quoted many, many times in the New Testament, underscoring its foundational theological importance. With some work and with solid interpretive principles, you can bring this material alive to your audience. You can teach them great things about God, give them a solid background understanding of the Old Testament, and challenge them as New Testament believers to walk more closely and obediently with Jesus Christ.

Examples

Text: Deuteronomy 6:1–25

Suggested title: Family Faithfulness in the Fast Lane

Historical context: The book of Deuteronomy is presented to the Israelites right before they are to enter into the Promised Land. God has delivered them from slavery in Egypt and led them through the desert. Now as they are about to cross the Jordan and enter the land of blessing, God calls on them to remember him and keep his commandments.

The Israelites are about to undergo a drastic change in their lifestyle and culture. They were slaves in Egypt for several hundred years. After God delivered them out of Egypt, they wandered in the desert for forty years, living as a nomadic people. Now they are about to enter a land with already established and built cities, houses, wells, vineyards, orchards, and fields. For the first time, they will have close encounters with people who follow pagan gods. There will be tremendous pressure on them to accept the religious practices of their pagan neighbors. There will also be a temptation to allow the newfound affluence of settled cities to detach them from trusting in the God who gave them such blessings. Also, notice the stress in this text on children (6:2, 7, 20) and on houses (6:7, 9, 11). The call to the Israelites to be obedient and faithful as they entered the Promised Land is placed firmly in a family context.

Text thesis statement: As the Israelites prepared to move into the Promised Land, God called on them to love him wholeheartedly, to teach his commandments and saving actions to the following generations, and to be careful lest the affluence of the Promised Land tempted them to forget what he has done for them.

Text outline:
1. Moses exhorted Israel to keep God's commandments and to love him wholeheartedly. (Deut. 6:1–6)
2. Moses exhorted Israel to teach God's commandments and his saving actions to each future generation. (Deut. 6:7–9, 20–25)
3. Moses warned Israel not to let the affluence of the Promised Land lead them to forget God, nor should the pagan practices of other people in the area lead them to worship other gods. (Deut. 6:10–19)

Crossing the bridge: This exhortation to Israel comes at a time when they are about to experience a huge societal transition filled with huge new challenges to their faith in God. This challenging historical situation for Israel can be paralleled today by the often frightening and disorientating radical changes in our current society. The guidelines that God gave to Israel to help them withstand these new pressures translate fairly easily to a more universal theology of how to stay faithful to God during challenging and disorienting times.

This message is especially appropriate to Christians today. Note the tight connection in this passage between loving God and obeying God. Jesus makes this same connection when he says: "Whoever has my commands and obeys them, he is the one who loves me" (John 14:21). For Israel, blessing in the Promised Land was tied explicitly to their obedience to the commandments in Deuteronomy.

You should note carefully the change in covenant that Christians now live under and not preach "works" salvation. But Christian obedience to the commands and example of Christ is still imperative for us as believers. You might parallel Israel's blessing in the Promised Land with the "thriving" of a Christian family today.

Deuteronomy 6 can help families today stay faithful to God.

If we want our Christian families today to be strong, healthy, Christian families (i.e., ones that thrive), then we (parents especially) must love Christ wholeheartedly and translate that love into single-minded obedience to the commands of Christ. Also, keep in mind that when asked which of the commandments was the greatest, Jesus quotes this text: Deuteronomy 6:4–5.

Sermon thesis statement: We can keep our families faithful to God as our society undergoes radical change.

Sermon outline:

1. We can keep our families faithful by being obedient and by zealously and wholeheartedly loving God. (Deut. 6:1–6)
2. We can keep our families faithful by constantly telling our kids about God and about what he has done in our lives. (Deut. 6:7–9, 20–25)
3. We can keep our families faithful by thankfully remembering what God has done for us and thus resisting the cultural pressure of affluence that pulls us toward the idolatry of wealth and social status. (Deut. 6:10–19)

Text: Leviticus 19:11–18

Suggested title: Is It a Beautiful Day in *Your* Neighborhood?

Historical context: Leviticus describes how Israel was to live in response to having the holy, awesome God dwelling in their midst. Leviticus 19 is referred to as the "Holiness Code." It is introduced by the command, "Be holy because I, the LORD your God, am holy" (Lev. 19:2). Most of the Ten Commandments are integrated into this chapter. The laws in 19:11–18 are grouped together around the theme of "neighborliness," that is, how the Israelites were to treat their neighbors.[5] Keep in mind that this exhortation falls in a chapter dealing with holiness. Holy living for Israel involved not only approaching God in holiness but treating neighbors properly.

Text thesis statement: Holy living for Israel demanded that they love their neighbors and treat them honestly and fairly.

Text outline:

1. The Israelites were commanded to be honest. (Lev. 19:11–12)
2. The Israelites were forbidden to take advantage of those individuals weaker than themselves. (Lev. 19:13–14)
3. The Israelites were commanded to provide justice in the courts for all of their neighbors, regardless of social standing. (Lev. 19:15–16)

[5]Gordon J. Wenham, *The Book of Leviticus* (NICOT; Grand Rapids: Eerdmans, 1979), 267–69.

4. The Israelites were commanded to love their neighbors as themselves. (Lev. 19:17–18)

Crossing the bridge: Much of this material, similar to the Ten Commandments, is already in universal theological language, and this passage translates over into appropriate theology for the church today quite easily. The Levitical idea that holiness involved both how one treats God and how one treats one's neighbor is certainly reaffirmed in the New Testament. In fact, after Jesus quotes Deuteronomy 6:4–5 (love God) as the greatest commandment, he quotes Leviticus 19:18 (love your neighbor) as the second greatest commandment. Thus, for Christians today, it is imperative to maintain both the vertical relationship to God and the horizontal relationship to the people around us. The two cannot be separated.

One of the aspects in this passage that does not parallel neatly into today's context is the legal courtroom situation. Keep in mind that in ancient Israel most of the "courtroom" hearings were probably done in front of village elders; thus at the village level, it was very much a "neighborhood" affair and thus susceptible to being used to settle neighborhood grudges or to achieve favor with influential neighborhood people. It was quite different from our system today, where the judge and jury are usually intentionally unfamiliar with the defendant.

The issue of justice, however, still comes across as a universal principle. God holds us responsible to stand up for justice for *all* people in our communities. Being a good Christian neighbor means that we use all of our influence to ensure that all people in our community receive fair treatment by the legal and economic systems. Remember that when he was asked, "Who is my neighbor?" Jesus tells the story of the good Samaritan, teaching us that good neighbors help all people, even if, or especially if, it means crossing ethnic or other socioeconomic lines.

Sermon thesis statement: We can live a holy life by being a good neighbor.

Sermon outline:
1. To live a holy life we must always be honest. (Lev. 19:11–12)
2. To live a holy life we must never take advantage of those less fortunate than we or those employed by us. (Lev. 19:13–14)
3. To live a holy life we must be impartial and stand for justice for all people. (Lev. 19:15–16)

4. To live a holy life, we must love our neighbors as ourselves. (Lev. 19:17–18)

Conclusions

One of the keys to interpreting and preaching the Old Testament law is to avoid the breakdown into civil, ceremonial, and moral categories; instead, we should interpret each law through the exegetical method presented in the Interpretive Journey. Treat the law as part of the narrative that runs through the Pentateuch and interpret it accordingly. Recognize the change in covenants, and do not put your people back under law.

Pay attention to context and look for the universal principles that lie behind each law. Then connect that principle to the needs of your audience today. There is much rich material in the Old Testament law that can teach Christians today about God, his character, and his holiness. Likewise, the law gives us universal principles that help Christians today to relate to each other in love. A tremendous wealth of sermon material lies in the Old Testament legal material, just waiting for you to dig it out and present it with power to your congregation.

Review Questions and Assignments

1. Develop a text thesis statement, a text outline, a sermon thesis statement, and a sermon outline for Exodus 20:1–8.
2. Develop a text thesis statement, a text outline, a sermon thesis statement, and a sermon outline for Deuteronomy 16:1–8.
3. Develop a text thesis statement, a text outline, a sermon thesis statement, and a sermon outline for Deuteronomy 16:9–12.
4. Develop a text thesis statement, a text outline, a sermon thesis statement, and a sermon outline for Leviticus 22:17–25.

Preaching the Prophets

> He has showed you, O man, what is good.
> And what does the LORD require of you?
> To act justly and to love mercy
> and to walk humbly with your God.
> **Micah 6:8**

The Old Testament prophets can be both the most challenging and the most rewarding material in the Bible to preach. The prophets were preachers themselves, and they often used colorful, figurative, and emotional language that communicated their message with power, anguish, and majesty. In the hands of a skilled interpreter and a savvy pulpiteer, the power, anguish, and majesty of God's prophetic Word to Israel can be unleashed for the church today.

Interpretive Keys[1]

First, it is important to remember that most of the prophetic books in the Old Testament are anthologies. That is, they are collections of material (oracles, sermons, narrative events, visions, etc.) that are loosely grouped together by broad themes. They are not structured by tight logic like the book of Romans. Furthermore, the main themes often repeat over and over, especially in the larger books like Isaiah

[1]Much of the material in the Interpretive Keys section is taken from Duvall and Hays, *Grasping God's Word*, 368–85.

The prophets serve as God's prosecuting attorneys.

and Jeremiah. Thus, when you are trying to set the context for a prophetic passage, it is often more helpful to tie it into the overall historical and theological context of the prophetic book you are studying than to tie it into the immediate literary context as you would in a book like Galatians or Mark.

The prophets write in the theological context of the book of Deuteronomy. This book epitomizes the Mosaic covenant and defined the terms by which Israel could live in the Promised Land with God in their midst and be blessed in their service of him. Of course, as discussed below, the prophets underscore the fact that Israel and Judah have failed to keep this covenant. Historically, the prophets write in the context of an imminent invasion by either the Assyrians (against Israel) or the Babylonians (against Judah), so there is a certain urgency and grimness in their tone.

A second interpretive key relates to the function and message of the prophets. They serve as God's prosecuting attorneys, accusing and warning the people that their violation of the covenant will have serious consequences. While there are numerous nuances and subpoints to their proclamation, their overall message can be boiled down to three basic points:

1. *Repentance!* You have broken the covenant; it's time to return to God.
2. *Judgment!* Breaking the covenant has consequences.
3. *Hope!* God is faithful and will ultimately bring a new, glorious restoration.

A large percentage of the prophetic texts in the Old Testament proclaims a message that falls into one of these three categories. As you preach these texts, you will encounter similar interpretive issues with each of these points. So first we will briefly discuss each of the points; then, in the next section, we will grapple with how to make the Interpretive Journey from this message synthesis to contemporary application for people in the pews today.

(1) Under "*Repentance!* You have broken the covenant; it's time to return to God," the prophets stress how serious the nation's

covenant violations have become and the extent to which the people have shattered the Mosaic covenant. The prophets present a tremendous amount of evidence validating this charge. Evidence of this violation falls into three categories, all of which are explicitly listed in Deuteronomy. These categories reflect three major types of *indictments* against Israel that the prophets present:

a. Idolatry
b. Social injustice
c. Religious formalism

As you study the prophets you will find many, many passages that thematically fall into one of these three categories. Thus, it will be beneficial for us to examine each of these sub-themes individually, all within the broader rubric of "you have broken the covenant."

(a) *Idolatry.* This offense was perhaps the most flagrant violation of the covenant, and the prophets preach continuously against it. Israel, of course, engaged in idolatry from their political beginning, with the golden calves in Bethel and Dan. But even Judah fell into serious idolatrous worship. Syncretization was in vogue with her neighbors, and Judah felt free to create a pantheon, worshiping Baal, Asherah, and others along with the Lord God. The people attempted to maintain the ritual of worshiping the Lord in the temple while also sacrificing to the other regional gods and participating in their festivals.

Idolatry was not merely a violation of the law. It struck at the heart of the relationship between God and his people. The central covenant formula in the Old Testament is God's statement, "I will be your God; you will be my people. I will dwell in your midst." Idolatry was a rejection of this relationship. Several of the prophets stress the emotional hurt that God feels at this rejection. For God the issue is as much an emotional issue as it is a legal issue. To aptly illustrate this, several of the prophets use the faithful husband/unfaithful wife image as a central image to paint the seriousness of idolatry. The harlotry/unfaithful wife image runs throughout Jeremiah. Ezekiel too uses this relational picture in Ezekiel 16. And poor Hosea lives out the heartbreaking drama in his own life.

The Lord is concerned with justice for all.

(b) *Social injustice.* The covenant in Deuteronomy, however, bound the people to more than just the worship of the Lord. Relationship with God required proper relationship with people as well. The Lord was concerned with justice for all, and he was especially concerned with how weaker individuals were treated. Deuteronomy demanded fair treatment of workers (Deut. 24:14ff.), justice in the court system (19:15–21), and special care for widows, orphans, and foreigners (24:17–22). As Israel and Judah turned from the Lord, they also turned from the Lord's demands for social justice. The prophets consistently condemn this and cite it as a central part of the covenant violation. They frequently cite the treatment of orphans and widows as examples of the social failure of the people. They also state that this lack of social justice invalidates the sacrifices.

(c) *Religious formalism.* The nation was relying on ritual instead of relationship. They forgot that ritual was merely the means to the relationship, not the substitute for relationship. As Israel became more enamored with formalized ritual, they lost the concept of relationship with the Lord. They lost the significance of his Presence in their midst. They thought that only ritual was required of them, and they drew the illogical conclusion that proper ritual would cover over other covenant violations like social injustice and idolatry. They rationalized their social injustice and their syncretism by focusing on the cultic ritual. This is hypocritical, the prophets declared, and not at all what God wants.

Thus, the prophets call God's people to repent. They beg the people to repent and restore their relationship with the Lord. Even after they proclaim that judgment is imminent, they continue to plead for repentance. Jeremiah, for example, proclaims the inevitability of the victorious Babylonian conquest, but all the while says that it can be averted if only the people will repent.

(2) The second point of the prophetic message is "*Judgment!* Breaking the covenant has consequences." The prophets plead with the people to repent and to turn back to covenant obedience. However, neither Israel nor Judah does repent, and the prophets acknowledge their obstinacy, proclaiming the severe consequences. Much of

the material in the prophetic books delineates the terrible imminent judgment that is about to fall on Israel or Judah.

The major judgments predicted by the prophets are the horrific invasions by, first, the Assyrians, and later, the Babylonians. The most serious aspect of this is the loss of the Promised Land. God is about to drive his people out of the Promised Land as he warned them in Deuteronomy. Keep in mind that God has been extremely patient with the Israelites. He has exhorted, begged, pleaded, and threatened them for generations and generations. But sin has its consequences, and the failure to acknowledge sin and to repent leads to tragic consequences.

(3) The final point of the prophetic message is: "*Hope!* God is faithful and will ultimately bring a new, glorious restoration." The messianic promises and future predictions of the prophets comprise a large portion of this point. The prophets do not proclaim a restoration after the destruction that simply returns back to the current status quo. Their theological and relational picture of the future is different—and better. In the future, they proclaim, the relational, theological situation will be spectacularly different. There will be a new exodus (Isaiah), a new covenant (Jeremiah), and a new presence of the Lord's indwelling spirit (Ezekiel and Joel). Forgiveness and peace will characterize this new system. Relationship will replace ritual.

> *The prophets proclaim hope for the future.*

Of course, these prophecies point to Jesus Christ, who was the ultimate fulfillment of this prophetic picture. Most of the wonderful prophecies in the Old Testament prophets regarding Jesus Christ fall into this category (hope and future restoration). The prophets announce that the people have failed miserably to keep the law and the Mosaic covenant. Thus judgment is coming. However, after the destruction, there will be a glorious restoration that includes the non-Jewish peoples (Gentiles). The Messiah will come and inaugurate a new and better covenant (one characterized by grace instead of law). Thus, Christ becomes the ultimate culmination of all that the prophets predict.

Furthermore, the prophets stress, these events are not haphazard. Nor are they driven by chance or the determination of world nations. On the contrary, the prophets proclaim boldly, all of these events—the judgment and the glorious restoration—are part of God's plan, and the unfolding of these events provide clear evidence that God is the Lord over history.

Most of the prophets can be summarized by the three points discussed above. For example, Isaiah, Jeremiah, Ezekiel, Hosea, Micah, and Zephaniah contain all three points. Amos, however, focuses primarily only on points 1 and 2 (broken covenant and judgment). Not until Amos 8 does he mention any future hope and restoration. Joel virtually skips point 1, apparently assuming that the people understood that they had broken the covenant. He goes straight into judgment (point 2) and then into the future restoration (point 3). Obadiah and Nahum do not follow the typical pattern at all. They are different because they preach against foreign nations (Edom and Nineveh, respectively), not against Israel or Judah. The postexilic prophets (Haggai, Zechariah, Malachi) likewise have a different message because they write after the Exile, not before or during that time.

Jonah, however, is much more important to the basic prophetic message, even though he also preaches against a foreign city (Nineveh) and not against Israel or Judah. Our understanding of Jonah is that while the actual historical preached message was to the Ninevites, the literary message is an indictment against Israel and Judah. Jonah is a foil for the rest of the prophets. The repentance of the Ninevites stands in stark contrast to the obstinacy of the Israelites. What happens in Nineveh is what should have happened in Jerusalem but does not. For example, Jeremiah preaches in Jerusalem for decades and the response is only one of hostility. No one repents, from the greatest to the least. Jonah, by contrast, preaches a short, reluctant sermon in Nineveh (of all places!) and the entire city repents, from the greatest to the least. This book underscores how inexcusable the response of Israel and Judah is to the prophetic warning.

Sermon Keys

The first sermon key to stress is that most of your sermons from the Old Testament prophets will involve taking one or more of the three main themes or three main indictments on the Interpretive Journey from the historical context (their town) to today's situation (our town). In the following paragraphs we will discuss each of the three points and three indictments, providing suggestions on how these theological points translate into valid application for the church today.

Point 1—Repentance! You have broken the covenant; it's time to return to God. In attempting to grasp the meaning of these texts that announce covenant violation, we often find it more helpful to focus on the relational aspects that our sin, or covenant violation, affects. In the prophetic books, God chose to use the marriage analogy and the unfaithful spouse image to convey the emotional pain that he felt when Israel and Judah were unfaithful.

However, most people today tend to view sin against God in the same fashion as they view breaking secular laws—speeding laws, for example. If someone breaks a speeding law, they pay a price, but no one is hurt emotionally. Certainly, Uncle Sam doesn't have emotional feelings about our speeding tickets. This particular attitude reflects a popular theology, that is, a theology arising out of our culture rather than out of the Bible. It is a theology that has a detached, emotionally neutral, impassive God, and it is a theology that is propagated through the culture both in and out of the church.

By contrast, one of the most important universal truths coming out of the prophetic message is that when we are unfaithful to God, we damage our relationship with him, causing him to hurt emotionally. When one loves someone deeply, that person opens himself or herself up and becomes vulnerable. God has made himself vulnerable to our unfaithfulness, and we find ourselves in the incredible situation of being able to hurt God when we are unfaithful to our relationship with him. For the New Testament believer, the consequence of unconfessed sin is not a Babylonian invasion and exile, but rather a strained and damaged relationship with God, who has been hurt by our unfaithfulness.

The three indictments of *idolatry, social injustice,* and *religious formalism* likewise find needed and powerful application in the church today. The charge of *idolatry* translates into whatever it is that draws our worship and focus away from our relationship with God.

One of the major social issue themes running through-out the prophets is the abuse, oppression, or neglect of the underclass.

For many adults this is often the job, success, or the need to make more money. For younger adults, the more common idols are popularity, clothes, movies, TV, cars, sports, and even grades.

Social injustice, however, is probably more difficult to transpose into today's context. Or perhaps the expression of this concept is simply more difficult to accept once it has been transposed. The prophets preach often against social injustice, and they consider violations of social justice as serious as idolatry. They address numerous cases of social injustice—judicial bribery, marketplace dishonesty, failure to pay just wages.

One of the major social issue themes running throughout the prophets, however, is the abuse, oppression, or even the neglect of the underclass, whom the prophets identify as the widow, the orphan, and the alien or foreigner. Deuteronomy mentions this triad eight times, commanding that the people of God give them both legal justice and food (Deut. 10:18; 24:17, 19, 20, 21; 26:12, 13; 27:19). Apparently, this group did not have enough political and economic clout in the society to fend for themselves, so in Deuteronomy God commands his people to pay specific attention to caring for them. Both Israel and Judah fail miserably at keeping this command, and the prophets make this one of their major indictments against them.

So the theological principle or practical theology coming from this prophetic indictment is related to the fact that God is concerned for those who are weak, either physically or socioeconomically. Furthermore, he expects his people, since they have him living in their midst, to be actively helping and defending such people. Certainly, bringing this truth through the New Testament filter does not alter the demand for social justice. Jesus' application of the Levitical commandment to "love your neighbor as yourself" in the story of the good Samaritan gives us an indication that Jesus continues to exhort us to care for those in need, even if, or *especially* if, the one in need is racially or culturally different from us.

So you need to ask several applicational questions. Who today does not have enough political and economic clout to get justice or food? Minorities? Illegal immigrants? The poor? The elderly? Children? Abused women? The unborn? The application process is not complete until your audience comes to grips with the seriousness of the issue and until they realize that God holds his people responsible for caring for those who do not have the political or economic power to care for themselves.

The final indictment, *religious formalism*, also has relevance for the church today. Especially in Judah, the people in the preexilic period believed that maintaining the rituals of worship was all that was necessary. They believed sacrifices fulfilled their obligation to God and therefore freed them to do anything else outside the covenant they chose to do. The prophets condemn this attitude unequivocally.

However, it is important to remember that ritual in and of itself is not bad. God himself ordained many of the rituals that the prophets critique. So the prophetic message is not a blanket repudiation of ritual. The problem for Judah is that they use the ritual to *replace* the relationship rather than to *enhance* the relationship. The practical theology emerging from this indictment is that God desires relationship over ritual. Rituals have validity only in that they assist in developing the relationship.

As we cross into the New Testament, this theology is reaffirmed. The Pharisees of Jesus' day were more concerned with Sabbath observance than they were with following Jesus or with meeting the needs and hurts of people. Jesus rebukes them strongly for this. Most of the rituals of the Old Testament were dropped in the New Testament, but the church quickly began to develop its own rituals. The goal of faith, however, then as now, is to develop relationship with God. Ritual, then as now, can help God's people in the development of that relationship.

However, without the relationship the ritual is meaningless. Once the ritual becomes the end rather than the means to the end, it becomes meaningless—or worse. Once it becomes the rationalized cover for a life devoid of social justice and true relationship with God, the ritual is on the same level as idolatry. The expression of this principle for your audience today is that their Christian rituals (how they

> *Ritual should enhance relationship, not replace it.*

259

Sin is still an affront to God's holiness.

do church) are valid as long as the rituals enhance the development of their relationship with God. The rituals are the means to an end (relationship), not the end themselves.

Point 2—Judgment! Breaking the covenant has consequences. How does the theme of judgment and exile apply today? In the discussion above we indicated that, for the biblical audience, this judgment took the form of an invasion by a foreign army, the destruction of the nation, the loss of God's presence, and the loss of the right to live in the Promised Land. The theology behind this expression reflects the fact that sin is an offense against God's holiness. Furthermore, sin demands appropriate judgment. Also, because of God's holiness, continued sin places a barrier between God's people and their relationship with him as he dwells in their midst.

As you carry this theology into the New Testament, you will recognize that sin has not changed and the consequences of sin have not changed. What has changed is that God has now transferred the judgment of death for the Christian's sin onto Christ. However, sin in the New Testament believer's life is still an affront to God's holiness. God indwells each believer, and sin in the believer's life offends the holy God dwelling within us. If Christians fail to repent and turn from their sin, their relationship with God will be damaged. They will lose the right to fellowship closely with him, and numerous negative consequences will follow.

For the unbelievers, judgment and the consequences of sin are part of the gospel and must be proclaimed. For Christian audiences, however, preaching judgment can be tricky and a bit touchy. On the one hand, you must be careful not to equate the idolatry of the Israelites and their total rejection of God with mild Christian backsliding. Likewise, you should not put your people back under a load of legalism. On the other hand, your audience does need to hear (and feel) the critique and challenge of the prophets. Often they will need to respond with repentance and a true change of heart (and behavior). Obstinacy and refusal to listen to the prophetic word is serious. Continued disobedience to the Word of God will bring about consequences. God is gracious and forgiving, but he also disciplines his children when they are blatantly disobedient. Likewise, Christians who ignore God's call to holy, righteous living and who persist in their disobedience often experience a diminished presence of God in their lives.

God is in the business of forgiving and restoring people.

Point 3—Hope! God is faithful and will ultimately bring a new, glorious restoration. Finally, let's consider applying the theme of hope and restoration. Certainly it is imperative that your audience see the ultimate fulfillment of these promises in Christ, but the spectacular prophetic message of forgiveness and restoration can also be transposed up from the national level of the ancient Hebrews into a theological principle for your audience today. This theology expresses the reality that God is in the business of forgiving and restoring people. This is part of his character. As you move into the New Testament, note that forgiveness and restoration find their ultimate expression in Jesus Christ. There is no sin or situation in the lives of God's people that he will not forgive and restore if they turn to him humbly through Christ.

Therefore, as you preach the prophets, take one or more of the three main themes or the three main indictments that run throughout the prophetic books and carry those themes or indictments across the principlizing bridge and apply them with power into the lives of your audience. The prophets are fiery and emotional. They are colorful and engaging. They are scathingly critical and yet wonderfully encouraging. Your sermons from these books can challenge your audience with all of these aspects.

Things to Avoid

As with most Old Testament texts, there are two extremes to avoid. *The first is to ignore the actual Old Testament historical context.* This is true not only as you prepare the sermon but also in your presentation of the sermon. We encourage you to spend part of your sermon explaining to your people the Old Testament historical context of the passage you are preaching. This not only helps your people to understand the Old Testament better, but it will help them see much more

You are a prophetic New Testament Christian preacher, not an Old Testament prophet.

clearly the connection between the Old Testament and New Testament. Furthermore, an accurate, colorful portrayal of the historical background for the words of the prophets can add a considerable amount of dramatic effect and power to your sermon. This also helps you to keep from preaching sermons out of context.

The other extreme to avoid, of course, is staying in the old covenant for your practical, applicational theology. As in our discussion concerning preaching the law (ch. 13), you want to be careful that you do not become one of the "Judaizers" against whom Paul preaches so fervently. All of the theological principles or practical theology that you present to your people must go through the New Testament grid of Jesus Christ and his amazing grace.

Finally, remember that you are a prophetic New Testament Christian preacher, not an Old Testament prophet. God does not generally give direct divine revelation to preachers today as he did to the Old Testament prophets. Your job is to proclaim God's Word that was revealed through the prophets. Your only basis for the authority to proclaim "This is what the LORD says" is if your proclaimed message is faithful to the written Word. Thus, as you are faithful to that Word, there is a sense in which your message can be "prophetic," but that doesn't make you to be "the prophet."

Examples

Text: Jeremiah 7:1–15

Suggested title: Hiding Behind Our Rituals

Historical context: This is a good text to examine because it includes all three of the main prophetic indictments (idolatry, social injustice, religious formalism) involved in prophetic point 1, "Repentance! You have broken the covenant, it's time to return to God." Jeremiah stood in the temple itself and addressed the people of Judah worshiping there. He called on them to change their ways, that is, to repent (Jer. 7:1–3). He told them that if they treated each other justly and if they cared for the economic underclass (orphans, widows, foreigners), God would let them continue to live in the Promised Land (7:5–7).

However, Jeremiah also warned sternly that they could not continue to sin, breaking commandment after commandment and even worshiping idols, and then expect the rituals of the temple to protect them. Like robbers they were hiding from God. The irony is that they were trying to use the temple and its rituals to hide, which put them directly in the presence of God. As God earlier destroyed Shiloh, the early religious center in the northern kingdom, so he would now destroy Jerusalem and thrust the sinful disobedient inhabitants from his presence (Jer. 7:12–15).

Text thesis statement: God called on disobedient people of Judah to quit trusting in the mere ritual of the temple and to truly change their sinful ways or else lose the land and the presence of God.

Text outline:
1. The people of Judah were called to change their sinful ways of idolatry, social injustice, and other sins. (Jer. 7:1–3)
2. If they truly repented, as demonstrated by living out social justice, God would not judge them. (Jer. 7:5–7)
3. However, by continuing to sin and then by trying to hide under the temple rituals, they slandered the name of the temple, making it into a den of robbers. (Jer. 7:4, 8–11)
4. As God judged Shiloh, an early religious center in the northern kingdom, so he would judge Jerusalem, expelling the people from his presence. (Jer. 7:12–15)
5. Historically, the people of Judah did not repent or change their ways, and in 586 B.C. Jerusalem was destroyed and the people exiled (loss of the Promised Land and the presence of God).

Crossing the bridge: This passage contains several of the central theological principles of the prophetic message. Sin is a violation of God's holiness, and if not dealt with appropriately, it will separate his people from him. God calls on his people to treat each other justly and with love and kindness. Likewise, he expects Christians today to care for those who don't have the means or power to care for themselves. In addition, religious ritual does not cover sin or excuse it. Christians today cannot live in sin, ignore justice, mistreat people, worship modern idols (like money, success, popularity, etc.), and expect the ritual of Sunday worship to cover it over and make everything OK. Such sin and refusal to repent will separate your people from God, moving them away from the blessing of his presence.

For the unbeliever, of course, the ultimate consequence is eternal separation and eternal judgment. For weak, noncommitted

263

What are the idolatries of today's world?

Preach This Sermon!

believers, however, smug in the false assumption that participation in Sunday worship will cover their sinful lifestyle, the consequence is the diminishment of God's powerful active presence in their lives, a diminishing of one of the more important blessings that he gives to Christians.

Sermon thesis statement: God calls on us to turn away from the idolatries of today's world, from habitual social injustice, and from hiding behind religious ritual, and instead to lead holy, obedient lives characterized by true relational worship.

Sermon outline:

1. God calls on us to change our sinful ways of modern idolatry, contemporary social injustice, and other fashionable sin. (Jer. 7:1–3)

2. God calls on us to demonstrate true repentance, exhibited by a life characterized by a biblical concern for others and a true worship of God. (Jer. 7:5–7)

3. The rituals of Sunday worship or other church participation do not excuse us or cover the sin we commit the rest of the week. (Jer. 7:4, 8–11)

4. If we continue to trust in religious ritual and to live disobedient lives, we will diminish the relationship we have with God, losing his powerful and active presence in our lives. (Jer. 7:12–15)

Text: Ezekiel 37:1–14

Suggested title: Re-energizing Our Lifeless Lives

Historical context: Ultimately, as discussed earlier, the people of Israel failed to repent and to turn back to following the covenant in Deuteronomy. As God had promised through the prophets (and in Deut. 28), devastating judgment eventually fell on Jerusalem. At the time of Ezekiel 37, Jerusalem had been completely destroyed by the Babylonians and the people of Israel had been carried off into exile. Humanly speaking, it was the end of Judah. They had no country, no capital, no king, and no temple. For all practical purposes, the nation was dead, and they had no hope.

In this context God took Ezekiel into the valley of dry bones. This valley had apparently been the site of a fierce battle. So many had been slain that no one had buried the dead soldiers, and their bodies had been left on the ground where they fell. Scavenger animals, decay, and the beating of the hot sun had, over time, stripped the bones clean and bleached them white.

The point, of course, is that these people were really, really *dead* and totally without hope.

God told Ezekiel to prophesy to the wind to breath into these bones and give them life. (Note that the same Hebrew word is used for "wind, breath, spirit, Spirit"—a wordplay that runs throughout this passage.) Ezekiel did as God commanded, and the dead, dry bones turned into complete, live people. In 37:11–14 God explained that this event is a picture of how he is going to restore shattered Israel.

Text thesis statement: Even though Israel was completely destroyed and exiled, God gave his people hope for the future because he himself desired to restore their life and hope through his promised, powerful, indwelling Spirit.

Text outline:

1. Exiled Israel was completely lifeless and without hope. (Ezek. 37:1–3, 11)
2. God desired to give his people hope and to restore life. (Ezek. 37:4–11)
   a. The bones had form but no life.
   b. God did not desire for Israel to stay lifeless and hopeless.
   c. There was power in the prophetic word of the Lord to change things.
3. God restored life through his Spirit. (Ezek. 37:12–14)
   a. The wordplay on wind and Spirit indicates that God will empower the restoration of Israel by his indwelling Spirit.
   b. Because of God's powerful indwelling Spirit, there is always, always, always hope.

Crossing the bridge: The theology of this passage falls into the third point of the prophetic message: *But yet, there is hope! God is faithful and will ultimately bring a new, glorious restoration.* The challenge for you is to find an appropriate parallel between the historical promised restoration of Israel and contemporary situations in the lives of believers today. One option is to connect this text to the hope of eternal life that Christian believers have, a hope that is validated for them by the empowered indwelling of the Spirit.

Another option, which we prefer, is to draw parallel situations around the theme of hopelessness. The Israelites were completely without hope. Although they were in that mess because of their own sin and obstinate disobedience, Ezekiel 37 never mentions the cause. It focuses solely on the hope of future deliverance and restoration offered by God through the Spirit. The stress is on his power to deliver and restore life in totally hopeless situations. Thus, it appears to have a broader application than just deliverance from a situation that resulted from sin.

Christians today also find themselves in situations that look and feel hopeless. Sometimes the situation is a result of their own foolish, disobedient decisions; sometimes the situation is simply a part of life. This text can be used to comfort those in the church who struggle with difficult situations and the hopelessness that often creeps in, regardless of how they happened to fall into that hopelessness. How dead were those people in the valley of dry bones? How hopeless was that situation? If by the powerful Spirit of God those dry bones can be brought back to life, then certainly by the same powerful Spirit of God, who now even dwells within his people, Christians today can be brought back to "life" and be infused with energizing hope, both for today and for tomorrow.

Sermon thesis statement: No matter how bad our current situation appears, there is always hope because God himself desires to restore life and hope to us through his powerful indwelling Spirit.

Sermon outline:

1. Sometimes we feel powerless, lifeless, and without hope. (Ezek. 37:1–3, 11)
2. God desires to give us hope and to restore life. (Ezek. 37:4–11)
   a. There is power in the prophetic Word of the Lord to change things.
   b. We as Christians can have form (motions of life) without real life or hope.
   c. God, who desires to give us both life and hope, is powerful enough to bring it about.
3. God restores life (in all its richness) to us through his Spirit. (Ezek. 37:12–14)
   a. By the power of his indwelling Spirit, God gives hope and life to those of us Christians who are shattered and discouraged. This includes both hope and life for today and for the future resurrection.
   b. Such a restored life should lead us to acknowledge and praise God.
   c. Because of God's powerful indwelling Spirit in our lives, there is always, always, always hope for us, no matter how bleak the situation appears to be.

Conclusions

The Old Testament prophets proclaim the same three themes over and over. They declare that (1) God's people have broken the covenant and must repent immediately; (2) since they will not repent, judgment is coming; and (3) beyond the judgment there is a hope for future restoration and a new covenant. Likewise, the prophets underscore three main sins of the people: idolatry, social injustice, and religious formalism. Most of your sermons from the prophetic literature will revolve around one or more of these themes. These themes (and sins) translate well across the interpretive bridge and into relevant sermon points that your audiences can apply to their lives in the world today. The prophetic message is relevant for today. Preach it often and with the same fervor that those great preachers of old, such as Jeremiah and Amos, preached.

Review Questions and Assignments

1. Develop a text thesis statement, a text outline, a sermon thesis statement, and a sermon outline for Isaiah 43:1–7.
2. Develop a text thesis statement, a text outline, a sermon thesis statement, and a sermon outline for Micah 6:6–9.
3. Develop a text thesis statement, a text outline, a sermon thesis statement, and a sermon outline for Jeremiah 10:1–10.

15

Preaching Psalms and Wisdom Literature

Let everything that has breath praise the LORD.
Psalm 150:5

. . . for attaining wisdom and discipline;
for understanding words of insight;
for acquiring a disciplined and prudent life,
doing what is right and just and fair.
Proverbs 1:2–3

If you ask Christians which book in the Bible is their favorite, many of them will answer, "Psalms." Throughout history, Christians around the world have read, sung, preached, and meditated from the Psalter. They have used this book for worship and praise, and from the many beloved psalms they have been able to express to God their joy, hope, wonderment, and thanksgiving, as well as their pain, anguish, despair, and sorrow.

Although the psalms are wonderfully effective for personal devotions, it is critical that you preach them as well and bring the power of the Psalter into the congregational setting. Every Christian's relationship with God has important emotional components, and the book of Psalms focuses on these very components. They resonate with the deepest emotions in the hearts of believers. It is both a bless-ing and a tremendous boost to the strength and well-being of your church for you to proclaim from the pulpit these wonderful and crit-ical emotional dimensions of the believer's walk with God that are expressed so eloquently in the Psalter.

Today's postmodern audiences also need to hear the practical and powerful messages from the Old Testament Wisdom books (Proverbs, Job, Ecclesiastes, and Song of Songs). Many of your people know about Jesus in their heads, but seem totally disconnected to the notion that following Jesus means living a life of personal integrity. Proverbs gives guidance for living wisely and with integrity in the nitty-gritty world of the marketplace. The book of Job, by contrast, addresses one of the most frustrating questions that all Christians struggle with at some time in their life: Why do innocent people suf-fer? Ecclesiastes raises another of the most basic human questions: How does one find meaning in life? And the Song of Songs sizzles into the issue of human sexuality.

These four Wisdom books deal with huge questions that lie at the core of life itself. Preaching these books will thus have strong prac-tical applications for day-to-day living. Your goal in proclaiming them to your people is to give them that combination of knowledge and character that enables them to live in the real world in a right and godly manner. Preaching the messages of these books can broaden the Christian maturity of your congregation in important areas that are often neglected.

In this chapter we will discuss interpreting and preaching Psalms and the Wisdom books. However, the genre of Psalms and the genre of the Wisdom literature are quite different, and when you interpret and preach them, it is important to keep that difference in mind. Therefore, in the discussion sections below, we will discuss Psalms and the Wisdom books separately.

> *Proverbs gives guidance for living with integrity in our nitty-gritty world.*

Interpretive Keys for the Psalms[1]

The first interpretive key for Psalms is to understand their function. The primary function of the book of Psalms is to "give us inspired models

[1]Much of the material in this "Interpretive Keys" sec-tion is taken from Duvall and Hays, *Grasping God's Word*, 388–407.

> "The Psalms give us inspired models of how to talk and sing to God."
> —CHISOLM

[2]Robert B. Chisholm, *From Exegesis to Exposition* (Grand Rapids: Baker, 1998), 225.

[3]Gordon D. Fee and Douglas Stuart, *How to Read the Bible for All Its Worth*, 187.

[4]Walter Brueggemann, *The Message of the Psalms* (Minneapolis: Augsburg, 1984), 19.

The Psalms teach us to be honest with God.

of how to talk and sing to God."[2] In addition the psalms provide us with inspired models of how to meditate about God—that is, how to think reflectively about God and what he has done for us. Fee and Stuart write:

> The problem with interpreting the Psalms arises primarily from their nature—what they are. Because the Bible is God's Word, most Christians automatically assume that all it contains are words *from* God *to* people. Thus many fail to recognize that the Bible also contains words spoken *to* God or *about* God, and that these words, too, are God's Word.[3]

This interactive communication in Psalms between people and God can take place in numerous contexts, reflecting the wide variety of life experiences from which people encounter God. Brueggemann has suggested that the psalms can be categorized roughly into three main contexts of human life: "seasons of well-being that evoke gratitude for the constancy of blessing ... anguished seasons of hurt, alienation, suffering, and death," and seasons of "surprise when we are overwhelmed with the new gifts of God, when joy breaks through the despair."[4]

So even though Psalms is God's Word to Christians today, it does not present specific doctrinal guidelines but rather examples of how to communicate one's deepest emotions and needs to God and how to respond in praise and thanksgiving to what God has done. When a psalmist cries out in anguish and despair, for example, the point or lesson is not that Christians also should cry out in despair. Rather, the lesson is that when we find ourselves in despair, it is right and proper for us, like the psalmist, to cry out in anguish and pain to God. As believers cry out honestly to God, we can then, like the psalmist, begin to experience his comfort and indeed be lifted "out of the slimy pit, out of the mud and mire" (Ps. 40:2).

Honesty with God is an important lesson to be learned from Psalms. The psalmists tell God exactly how they feel, and it often does not sound very spiritual or mature. Christians today tend to pressure each other into suppressing any emotional outpouring to God or to each other. The Christian model for many is that of a hard stoic, like

Spock on *Star Trek*. The book of Psalms shatters this false image of Christian behavior and provides us with wonderful models of frank, honest communication with God, full of emotion, bubbling up out of good times and bad times alike.

Second, understand the poetic nature of Psalms. One of the ways that Psalms connects emotionally to readers is through poetry. Poetic language is, by design and purpose, powerful at eliciting strong responses from readers (and hearers). However, as you interpret and preach these texts, you must be aware of how Old Testament poetry works at communicating God's Word. First of all, Old Testament poetry in general, and Psalms in particular, employs parallelism as its major structural feature. That is, each thought is communicated by two lines of text in parallel to each other. Most English translations include two (on occasion, three) parallel lines per verse. For example:

> I cry aloud to the LORD;
>> I lift up my voice to the LORD for mercy. (Ps. 142:1)

Sometimes the two lines of text are synonymous (Ps. 2:4). Sometimes the second line develops further the thought of the first line (121:3). The second line can also illustrate the first or give a symbol of the first (140:7). Often the second line is in opposition or in contrast to the first line (1:6). Finally, the second line is occasionally related to the first only loosely and structurally (2:6). But in all of these situations the two lines need to be taken together as one thought.[5] Because of the poetic parallelism in the psalms, you will not be developing a line-by-line or sentence-by-sentence series of thoughts in your sermon, but rather a verse-by-verse series of thoughts, with each verse composed of at least two lines of text.

Another important feature of Old Testament poetry in the book of Psalms is the continuous use of figurative language. Nearly every line of text in this book has a figure of speech in it. To properly interpret the ancient poems it is essential that you seek to discover the imagery behind the figure of speech and to try to determine what the author was trying to communicate with that imagery.[6] It is precisely

[5] For a more detailed discussion on parallelism, see Duvall and Hays, *Grasping God's Word*, 349–51.

[6] See the discussion on figures of speech in ibid., 352–60.

the images painted by the psalmist that communicate so powerfully to the hearts (and heads) of God's people today.

Third, categorize the psalm you are studying by form and content. Based on both form and content, most psalms fall into one of three categories. First, there are *praise psalms*. These psalms often begin or end with the statement, "Praise the LORD!" In these psalms the author calls on other people (or himself) to praise God because of God's divine attributes, his character, his name, or his actions. These psalms stress God's role as creator and sustainer of the universe, the one who brings order to the chaos of the world and thus brings assurance to his people. Psalms that fall into this category are Psalms 8, 19, 104, 148 (God as creator); 66, 100, 111, 114, 149 (God as protector and benefactor of Israel); and 33, 103, 113, 117, 145–147 (God as Lord of history).[7]

Second, many psalms can be categorized as *laments*. These psalms are addressed directly to God. They are characterized by an opening cry to God for help. In these psalms the writer is expressing pain, suffering, confusion, and even despair. Sometimes God seems distant to him or unresponsive. Nonetheless, the psalmist cries out to God to deliver him from his suffering, often ending on a positive note of hope in God's (still future) deliverance. These psalms can reflect either individual suffering or corporate suffering (e.g., Israel in exile). Examples include Psalms 3, 22, 31, 39, 42, 57, 71, 120, 139, 142 (individual); and 12, 44, 80, 94, 137 (corporate).[8]

The third major category of psalms is that of *thanksgiving*. Like the lament psalms, these songs recognize that there is pain and suffering in the world. However, thanksgiving psalms are written from the view of one who has already been delivered by God. Thus, while in the psalms of lament the writer is currently suffering and crying out for future deliverance, in the thanksgiving psalms the writer is looking back at how God has delivered him from pain and suffering. In this sense they function like contemporary testimonies, a time to share how God has acted in one's life and delivered one from a difficult time. As with the laments, these thanksgiving psalms can be either corporate/community (Ps. 65, 67, 75, 107, 124, 136) or individual (18, 30, 32, 34, 40, 66, 92, 116, 118, 138).[9]

[7]Fee and Stuart, *How to Read the Bible*, 195; Gerald Wilson, *Psalms* (NIVAC; Grand Rapids: Zondervan, 2002), 65.

[8]Fee and Stuart, *How to Read the Bible*, 194; Wilson, *Psalms*, 65.

[9]Fee and Stuart, *How to Read the Bible*, 194–95; Wilson, *Psalms*, 65–66.

In addition to the three main categories discussed above, there are several other subcategories that are less well-defined and even sometimes disputed. There are *royal psalms* (Ps. 2, 18, 20, 21, 45, 72, 101, 110, 144) and *enthronement psalms* (24, 29, 47, 93, 95–99) that deal with "royal rule," both that of the present human Israelite king and the future ultimate rule of God as king. There are also *wisdom psalms*, which like the book of Proverbs challenge the listener to live a wise life (e.g., Ps. 119). So one of the main interpretive keys for understanding Psalms is to determine the type or category of each psalm and recognize the similar themes and structure running through each psalm of that category.

For some psalms it is helpful to note the historical setting given in the superscription. Keep in mind that the superscriptions (e.g., "A psalm of David") prior to verse 1 are not modern editorial remarks but are part of the psalm. In the Hebrew Bible these superscriptions comprise verse 1. Sometimes the historical setting given in these psalms provides the critical (and colorful) setting for the psalm that you will need to incorporate into your sermons. In Psalm 51, for example, David cries out to God, confessing his sin and pleading for forgiveness. The setting given in the superscription is revealing— right after David's sin with Bathsheba.

Fourth, be sure to keep literary context in mind. Traditionally, most expositors of Psalms treated each psalm as an independent unit, in isolation from its literary context. In recent years, today's leading scholars have noted what appears to be a literary context flowing through the book as a whole, and many of them are advocating that interpreters and preachers pay more attention to that context.[10]

In some cases, two or more adjacent psalms relate to each other theologically (e.g., Ps. 103 and 104, or Ps. 22 and 23). It is instructive to note that Psalm 1 and Psalm 2 introduce the book as a whole with a call to obedience, and Psalm 150 concludes it with an extended climactic call to praise. Throughout the book there is a clear movement from lament (which is the dominant theme in Ps. 3–41) to praise (which dominates the latter psalms),[11] suggesting that Christians today also move (slowly but surely) from their honest cry of pain and

> *In the thanksgiving psalms, the writer is looking back at how God has delivered him from pain and suffering.*

[10]See especially the pastorally oriented commentaries such as James Limburg, *Psalms* (Westminster Bible Companion; Louisville: Westminster John Knox, 2000); James L. Mays, *Psalms* (Interpretation; Louisville: Westminster John Knox, 1994); and J. Clinton McCann, "The Book of Psalms," in *The New Interpreter's Bible*, vol. 4 (Nashville: Abingdon, 1996).

[11]Limburg, *Psalms*, xvii.

The purpose of the Wisdom books is to develop character in God's people.

suffering to a shout of praise to their God who delivers them and reigns forever.

The final interpretive key for Psalms is proper Christological emphasis. Most of the psalms are not directly messianic, but several have strong prophetic, messianic elements (Ps. 22, 110), and many, especially the royal/enthronement psalms, have historical meaning that finds ultimate fulfillment for Christians in the eschatological reign of Christ. In interpreting these psalms it is appropriate and helpful to move from the psalm into the New Testament and to note how that psalm finds ultimate fulfillment in Christ.

Interpretive Keys for the Wisdom Books

The imperatives of the Wisdom literature—listen, look, think, reflect—combine to focus on the overarching purpose of these books: to develop character in God's people. The Wisdom books are not a collection of universal promises. They are a collection of valuable insights into godly living, which, if taken to heart (and head), will develop godly character, a character that makes wise choices in the rough-and-tumble marketplace of life.[12] Wisdom literature makes the subtle suggestion that godly living involves solid, common sense choices. Likewise, living in a foolish, naive, or cynical fashion is a reflection of ungodly living.

The first interpretive key for the Wisdom books is to note that the four books balance each other theologically, and any one of them read out of the context of the others can be easily misunderstood. Each of the four Wisdom books (Job, Proverbs, Ecclesiastes, and Song of Songs) makes a different contribution to the believer's education in wise living. It is important to see the different roles of each, but also be able to see how they integrate together to form the broad literary context of wisdom. Basically, Proverbs presents the rational, ordered norms of life, while the other three books present the exceptions and limitations to the rational, ordered approach to life.

Second, regarding Proverbs, perhaps the most critical thing to remember when studying and preaching this book is that the individual

[12]William P. Brown, *Character in Crisis: A Fresh Approach to the Wisdom Literature of the Old Testament* (Grand Rapids: Eerdmans, 1996).

proverbs reflect general nuggets of wisdom, not universal truths. To interpret each proverb as an absolute promise from God is to misunderstand the intent of the author. Proverbs gives guidance for life, addressing situations that are normally true. For example, consider Proverbs 10:4:

> Lazy hands make a man poor,
>   but diligent hands bring wealth.

This proverb is generally true. If you work hard, you will most likely prosper, and if you are lazy, you will most likely not prosper. This lesson was true especially in ancient Israel, where most people were involved in farming. Likewise, this is good advice for any person today in their job. The lesson is clear—don't be lazy! Be a hard worker! However, in today's economy there is hardly a direct correlation between how hard one works and how much money one makes. Farmers, factory workers, construction workers, and loggers work every bit as hard as lawyers, doctors, and stockbrokers, but their "blue-collar" income is but a fraction of that enjoyed by the "white-collar" workers. In our current world of e-commerce and stock trading, millionaires can be made overnight, and while hard work often plays a role, it is not always the major ingredient. We have to be careful not to interpret Proverbs 10:4 as a universal promise that guarantees monetary reward to hard work in every situation.

Third, the book of Job is a strong counterbalance to the book of Proverbs, dealing with one of life's great exceptions to the norms expressed in Proverbs. In Proverbs the world is rational and ordered. If we serve God faithfully, work hard, and treat others correctly, we will have a blessed and prosperous life. Job's experience, however, is in complete contrast to Proverbs. He does all of the good things that Proverbs commands, but instead of receiving blessing, he enters into a nightmarish world of dead children, economic ruin, endless physical suffering, and harsh criticism from close friends. Most of the time your people live in the world that Proverbs describes; inevitably they also spend some of their lives hurting and asking questions in the world of Job.

Inevitably your people spend some of their lives hurting and asking questions in the world of Job.

Of utmost importance for interpretation and application is the literary context. The book of Proverbs is comprised largely of short, unrelated proverbial statements. The book of Job, by contrast, is a story. It has movement, time sequence, and plot. As we seek to understand various passages in the book, it is critical to place those smaller passages into the context of the complete story reflected in the entire book. Major misinterpretations will emerge if we pull verses from Job out of context and try to interpret them as we do the independent verses in Proverbs.

This is especially true for the many chapters in the middle of the book in which Job's friends speak. There are several lessons to be learned from the misguided friends of Job, but only if we interpret their words within the total context of the book. Job's friends try to explain his tragedy through the misapplication of traditional "Proverbs-like" wisdom. Thus, they make two central assumptions: (1) Through wisdom they have access to all the information they need to analyze the problem, and (2) through wisdom, and based on this information, they can correctly understand the problem. Both assumptions are wrong!

Thus, the limitations of wisdom are underscored. Working off of wrong assumptions, the friends make numerous mistakes. Kidner writes, "They overestimate their grasp of truth, misapply the truth they know, and close their minds to any facts that contradict what they assume."[13] After some initial sympathy, they distance themselves above Job and his sufferings. They do not seek to comfort; rather, they seek to explain. Comforting and explaining are quite different. While the basic theology of the friends is not bad, their application of it is incorrect. Thus, as Kidner notes, the rebuke of the friends by God does not dismiss the basic theology of Proverbs as much as it "attacks the arrogance of pontificating about the application of these truths, and of thereby misrepresenting God and misjudging one's fellow men."[14] The friends are thus negative characters and not models of behavior for our audiences. Much of what they say is true, but they say it at the wrong time and apply it to the wrong situation.

[13]Derek Kidner, *The Wisdom of Proverbs, Job & Ecclesiastes* (Downers Grove, IL: InterVarsity Press, 1985), 61.

[14]Ibid.

Fourth, Ecclesiastes is an intellectual search for life that presents another exception or qualification to the ordered norms of Proverbs. Ecclesiastes is perhaps the strangest and the least straightforward book in the Bible.[15] It is similar to Job in that the literary context of the entire book must be considered in analyzing any of its smaller parts. Ecclesiastes must be interpreted as a whole. The book is not a collection of guidelines for living as Proverbs is. Rather, the book is an intellectual search for meaning in life. Most of the search is futile; the true meaning is not discovered until the end. Therefore, the interpretation of any of the intermediate parts of the book must be understood in light of the entire search and the ultimate answer found at the end.

The conclusion in Ecclesiastes, not disclosed until the final verses, is that the only way to find meaning in life is to be in relationship with God. Logic and rational thought (wisdom) can help you on a day-to-day basis, but ultimate meaning in life requires relationship with God. While the author acknowledges that being wise is better than being stupid, he concludes that wisdom does not by itself provide meaning to life. Also, while Job told the story of one exception to the norms of Proverbs, the cynical analysis in Ecclesiastes chronicles numerous exceptions to the thesis of an ordered, rational universe.

Fifth, the Song of Songs speaks openly and joyfully of human sexuality. It is a collection of love poems between a young man and a young woman (called the Shulamite). Thus, it is one of the most shocking books in the Bible. Unlike Proverbs, the Song of Songs is organized into three logical, sequential units: the Courtship (1:2–3:5), the Wedding (3:6–5:1), and the following Life of Love (5:2–8:14).[16] In some sections the man and woman are describing their love for each other; in other sections they are describing how beautiful or handsome their spouse is. The woman—who does most of the talking—also describes the dreams she has of her husband while he is away, and she shares how much she misses him. The book is highly emotional and is full of figurative imagery as the man and woman use a wide range of colorful analogies to describe their wonderful mates and the wild and crazy love that they have for each other.

> *The Song of Songs speaks openly and joyfully of human sexuality.*

[15] William P. Brown, *Ecclesiastes* (Interpretation; Louisville: John Knox, 2000), 17.

[16] The major features of this outline are taken from Dennis F. Kinlaw, "Song of Songs," in *The Expositor's Bible Commentary* (Grand Rapids: Zondervan, 1991), 5:1214.

The church has often struggled with how to interpret and apply such an unusual book. Starting from the third century A.D. and continuing on throughout much of church history, the prevailing approach to Song of Songs has been to explain it as an allegory of Christ and his love for the church. However, this method breaks down when you read the text closely and pay attention to context. Scholars today are virtually unanimous in rejecting the allegorical interpretation of this book. Christians today also recognize that sexuality in marriage is a big part of life, and if the Wisdom literature is to address the major issues of life, then Christians should not be surprised (or shocked) to see a frank discussion of the joys associated with marital intimacy.

Of course, it is also important to note that the lyrics of the Song of Songs are addressed to the man or the woman in the story and not to God. If we assume this to be part of wisdom and part of the teachings about character and living rightly, we conclude that the book also provides a model for how a husband and wife are to feel toward one another and how they are to express their feelings. As mentioned above, the wisdom of Proverbs presents a model to ancient Israel of a quiet, thoughtful, somewhat reserved wise person who acts dignified in the public world. This image changes in the Song of Songs. The wise, righteous person is now seen as madly in love with his or her spouse, spouting out line after line of mushy compliments and praises, many in regard to sexuality.

Sermon Keys for the Psalms

The first sermon key for Psalms is to develop your sermon along the lines determined by the form/structural category that the psalm falls in. The three main categories of psalms—praise, thanksgiving, and lament—provide you with helpful keys for sermon development. Most of your sermons from this book will fall into one of these three thematic categories, and most of your sermons should likewise focus on one of those themes (i.e., praise, thanksgiving, or lament). It is also helpful to remember that many of the psalms are directed to God and are models for us to employ in worshiping God.

Especially when preaching from a praise psalm, you may want to try occasionally preaching Psalms directly to God as you lead the congregation in praise. In this sense preaching from the praise psalms can be quite different than preaching from other books of the Bible. Your primary goal might not be to send your congregation home intent on praising God all week long; rather, you might lead your congregation to praise God *now*, through your exposition of this praise psalm. Likewise, your main focus will not be on "six ways you can successfully praise God in your life" (implying that this is something they will do later on) but rather, "Here are six fantastic ways by which we will praise God this morning." You do not have to preach Psalms in this way (i.e., directly addressed to God), but we suggest that you try it occasionally. Not only the praise psalms, but also the laments and the thanksgiving psalms can be preached successfully in this manner.

Likewise, when preaching the lament psalms, it is important to reflect the tone and the essential message of pain, despair, and frustration of these psalms. Those in your church who are hurting (and there are always quite a few of these) need a valid biblical way to express this hurt and to cry out to God. It is true that the lament psalms usually end on a statement of trust and hope in God, and you will likewise want to lead your people through the cry of lament into the same trust and hope.

But don't be too quick to skim over the real suffering present in these psalms. In many churches the preaching style and the standard preaching themes have ignored or dismissed the peoples' biblically mandated need to mourn. Too often preachers move quickly from painful, inexplicable tragedy to "God works all things together for good," without letting the people cry out in pain or confusion or even mourn adequately. This implies it is wrong for Christians to hurt or to question God in tragic situations, so those people who are hurting tend to withdraw to themselves rather than share their pain with the church and express that pain together to God. Yet the lament psalms lead Christians to approach God honestly and to express their hurt and frustration openly.

> *Those in your church who are hurting need a valid biblical way to express this hurt and to cry out to God.*

Second, each psalm usually expresses a complete unit of thought, so generally it is advisable to preach an entire psalm. Most psalms are just about the right length for a sermon. Of course, Psalm 119 is a little long to preach in one sermon; for extra long psalms, we suggest preaching one of the subunits (e.g., 119:1–8). However, as mentioned above, you do need to pay attention as to whether the psalm you are preaching is connected to the psalms around it. Psalm 1, for example, introduces the entire book, setting the stage for our understanding of the rest of the book. You should point that out while preaching Psalm 1. Likewise, it is helpful to observe the literary and theological connection between Psalm 22 (the suffering at the cross) and Psalm 23 (protection and deliverance from death).

Sermon Keys for the Wisdom Books

The first sermon key for the Wisdom books relates to Proverbs and involves deciding which text and how much text to use in your sermon. The answer depends on which section of Proverbs you are preaching from. Proverbs 1–9 is comprised of longer poetic units than just the two-line parallelism of normal proverbs. So while this section is part of the book of Proverbs, it does not contain any of the small, two-line units we call *proverbs*. This section contains reflections on life, usually followed by examples and admonitions. So all of Proverbs 5, for example, must be kept together and preached as a unit, for it comprises a complete unit—one that warns its readers of the dangerous consequences of sexual immorality. So when we preach from Proverbs 1–9, we must structure our sermons to include the appropriate literary unit (usually about a chapter long).

Likewise, toward the end of the book, Proverbs 30:1–31:9 (the sayings of Agur and King Lemuel's mother) also contains units of text that stretch to several verses and should be preached as units. In the same fashion, the unique closing unit (31:10–31), which describes the woman of true, wise character, should be kept as a unit and covered in one sermon.

In the middle of Proverbs, however, things are different. Proverbs 10–29 is the section that contains the literary form that is traditionally called a *proverb*—usually two short lines of poetry expressing one general truth of wisdom. Most of these proverbs are somewhat random in their placement, and there is no apparent structured order throughout most of this section. Therefore, unlike the entire rest of the Bible, in Proverbs 10–29 the larger unit (chapter, paragraph, etc.) does not play a role in literary context. These proverbs each stand by themselves against the context of the entire book and the rest of the wisdom books; they do not relate to the verses immediately preceding and following. Proverbs 10–29 is the only section of the Bible where you can preach one verse while ignoring the verses that come before and after.[17]

Nevertheless, it can be challenging to preach an entire sermon from one verse in Proverbs. So when preaching from Proverbs 10–29 we recommend that you preach themes. Choose one of the major themes that recurs over and over throughout this section of the book, gather three to five relevant and thought-provoking proverbs that relate to this theme, and then structure your sermon around those texts, focusing on the unifying theme. Major themes running throughout Proverbs 10–29 that make good compact, succinct preaching topics include: hard work/laziness, honesty, good speech, gossiping, encouragement, friendship, concern for the poor, justice, marriage, modesty, and discretion. Likewise there are broader themes that can be profitably explored in your sermons: the nature of wisdom, the fool, the scoffer, the naive, money matters, and the fear of God.[18]

Second, the book of Job is a story with a dramatic and somewhat unexpected ending. It is hazardous to preach small parts of the book without placing that small part firmly in the context of the entire story. We recommend that you have at least one sermon in which you preach the book of Job as a whole. In fact, your first sermon from Job should probably deal with the entire story. Retell the story of Job 1, reading a few critical verses. Job initially responds to his tragedy piously. Then summarize the wrong approach of Job's friends in chapters 3–37. Note also from these chapters that Job departs from his patient, accepting manner and begins to accuse God of injustice. Finally, focus

[17]Paul Koptak points out that sometimes the proverbs in this section are grouped around word repetitions or themes and that such groupings do provide a "context" of sorts by which to interpret the proverbs. See Paul E. Koptak, *Proverbs* (NIVAC; Grand Rapids: Zondervan, 2003), 284.

[18]See the topics for study listed and discussed by Derek Kidner, *The Proverbs* (TOTC; Downers Grove, IL: InterVarsity Press, 1964), 31–56; and Tremper Longman III, *How to Read Proverbs* (Downers Grove, IL: InterVarsity Press, 2002), 117–55.

Ecclesiastes teaches us that life is not a puzzle to be understood, but a gift to be enjoyed as we walk by faith.

on God's response to Job in chapters 38–41, followed by the conclusion of the story in chapter 42.

Theological principles that should emerge from your study and your sermon include:

- God is sovereign and we are not.
- God knows all and we know little.
- God is always just, but he does not disclose his explanations to us.
- God expects us to trust in his character and his sovereignty when unexplained tragedy strikes.

On any given Sunday, there will probably be several people who are hurting and questioning God about some inexplicable tragedy in their lives. Furthermore, all Christians probably find themselves in this situation at some time in their lives. The message of Job is an important one to proclaim.

You could also preach a series of sermons from Job 38–42, focusing on one or two of these principles in each sermon and placing each sermon into the story context of the entire book each time (i.e., summarizing the familiar story at the beginning of each sermon).

Third, any passage in Ecclesiastes must be preached in light of the overall message, especially the ending. Although smaller units of Ecclesiastes can be preached coherently (e.g., 2:1–11), it is important to preach these smaller units in the context of the overall message of the book in view of the important ending (12:9–14). The book as a whole teaches us three main points:

- Apart from God, life is meaningless. Wisdom is not bad, but it does not provide ultimate meaning in life.
- Wisdom does not explain the contradictions of life; it only points them out. Therefore people should simply trust God (the same meaning as Job).
- Life, therefore, is not a puzzle to be completely understood but a gift to be enjoyed (similar to Song of Songs) as we walk by faith.

Thus, when preaching from smaller units within Ecclesiastes, it is critical to tie that message into the overarching message of the book. You need to present a brief overview of the entire book and tell your people that this book reflects an intellectual search for meaning. You can connect the "Teacher's" search for meaning with the search that people today are making; just be sure to point out the Teacher's final conclusion (the three points above).

Fourth, sermons from Song of Songs are appropriate for preaching series that deal with marriage. The main theological principle emerging from many of the passages in the Song of Songs is that the married Christian today who is seeking to live a wise, godly life should be madly in love with his or her spouse and should express this love in strong, emotional (even sappy and mushy) terms. Also, in contrast to Proverbs, where you will often be preaching individual verses, and to Job and Ecclesiastes, where you will usually be preaching in the context of the entire book, in Song of Songs you will find numerous paragraph-size and chapter-size units that are appropriate to preach, either by themselves or in a series on love and marriage.

Things to Avoid—Psalms

When preaching Psalms, be sure to keep in mind that we are no longer under the old Mosaic covenant of law but under the new covenant of grace. As with any Old Testament text, it is important to identify the river of differences (covenant, culture, language) that must be crossed, and then to cross over that river and move through the New Testament. Thus, psalms such as Psalm 119, which extol the keeping of the law, can still be preached, but for the Christian today obedience needs to be understood in the context of following Christ (who has imputed righteousness to us) rather than obeying Torah (in order to achieve righteousness).

We would also caution you against making the difference between present tense verbs and future tense verbs in texts from Psalms a big issue in your sermon or a part of one of your main points. The Hebrew imperfect can be translated either as present ("the LORD reigns") or

> *Proverbs gives us guidelines and norms for wise living and character building.*

future ("the LORD will reign"), and it is often difficult for the translators to know which English tense to use.

Finally, as mentioned above, when preaching in Psalms, do not force your people to put on dishonestly pious masks before each other and to try to act as if everything is just fine when in reality they are suffering and struggling. Allow them to hurt and to mourn, and lead them to express their feelings to God through the lament psalms. This expression is also worship.

Things to Avoid—Wisdom Books

As mentioned earlier, when you preach from the Wisdom books, it is critical to understand how they balance each other. Thus, as you preach the ordered, rational world of Proverbs, you at least need to acknowledge the stark exceptions declared in the other Wisdom books. Also, remind your people that most of the proverbs are not universal promises from God to be claimed, but rather guidelines or norms for wise living and character building.

Be careful in Job and in Ecclesiastes about pulling verses out of context. Job's friends are mistaken in their analysis of Job; don't use their speeches as models for theology. The "Teacher's" search for meaning is futile until Ecclesiastes 12. Be sure that you see and communicate that futility if you are preaching passages from earlier in the book.

Finally, don't allegorize the Song of Songs into a book about Christ and the church. Let the book speak to building strong marriages.

Examples

Text: Psalm 142

Suggested title: When No One Cares about You

Historical context: The superscription of this psalm refers to a time when David was hiding in a cave, probably a reference to 1 Samuel 22:1, when David flees from Saul and hides in the cave of Adullam. So David has some real enemies who want to kill him. His psalm is written as if composed in the cave, but it is addressed to other faithful people who at some time in the future will join him in worship.

Text thesis statement: David, helpless before his enemies, cried out to God, trusting him for deliverance.

Text thesis outline:

1. David addressed the congregation, declaring that he would pour out his troubles before God. (Ps. 142:1–2)
2. David addressed God (Ps. 142:3–7)
   a. David's laments; his foes sought to kill him and no one cared. (Ps. 142:3–4)
   b. David expressed his confidence in God, his refuge. (Ps. 142:5)
   c. David petitioned God to rescue him, acknowledging his own weakness. (Ps. 142:6)
   d. David looked forward to praising and worshiping God because of his deliverance. (Ps. 142:7)

Crossing the bridge: This is a typical lament in which the psalmist pours out his heart and expresses his fear and his feelings of aloneness and helplessness. These feelings—fear, aloneness, helplessness—are certainly universal and are issues that your people today struggle with frequently. So the basic problem of the psalmist translates well across the bridge to today's situation. Likewise, the psalmist honestly pours out his heart before God and expresses his aloneness and hopelessness. This also translates across the bridge as a model for believers.

The cause of David's trouble is unique. He is being pursued by bad people who want to kill him. This is an important difference to note. In fact, throughout the psalms, often the trouble is caused by dangerous "enemies," usually tied into the historical context of David as king or in conflict with Saul. Today you must find a parallel situation for your people. Few of them have political or military opponents that actually seek to kill them. But practically all of your people face serious problems at one time or another that can create the same feelings of helplessness and aloneness. In our statement below we have generalized this as an "overwhelmingly difficult situation." You will need to develop specific illustrative situations that apply to your audience and connect their fear and helplessness to that of the psalmist, who pours out his heart to God and then trusts in God for deliverance.

> *The psalmist expresses fear, aloneness, and helplessness—feelings that your people also frequently experience.*

Sermon thesis statement: When we feel alone and helpless before overwhelming circumstances, let us pour out our hearts to God and trust him to deliver us.

Sermon outline:

1. O God, sometimes we encounter overwhelmingly difficult problems and we feel all alone and helpless. (Ps. 142:1–4)
2. Yet we turn to you, O God, for refuge. (Ps. 142:5)
3. O God, rescue us and set us free from this overwhelmingly difficult situation we are in. (Ps. 142:6)
4. We look forward to praising you, O God, because of how you will deliver us. (Ps. 142:7)

Text: Job (using the entire book)

Suggested title: When We Question God

Historical context: Remember our discussion above. Job is an exception to the norms of Proverbs and deals with the issue of how to respond when bad things happen to good people.

Text thesis statement: Job learned that because God is sovereign, all-wise, and just, he could trust him in all situations, even those he did not understand.

Text outline:

1. Job was stricken with a terrible and inexplicable tragedy. (Job 1:1–2:10, summarize the story)
2. As time passes Job began to question (and accuse) God.
   a. Job thought that an injustice had been committed and that if he could present his argument to God, he would be acquitted. (Job 23:1–9; 24:1)
   b. Job accused God of committing injustice. (Job 27:2)
   c. Job demanded that God give him his day in court. (Job 31:35)
3. God answered Job from the storm and questioned him.
   a. God declared that he is sovereign and Job is not. (Job 38:1–5)
   b. God declared that he is all-wise and Job is not. (Job 38:18–21)
   c. God declared that his justice should not be challenged. (Job 40:8)
4. Conclusions.
   a. Job was not really rebuked by God, but he did learn not to question the way God runs the universe.
   b. Job learned to trust God even when he didn't understand.

Crossing the bridge: As discussed above, much Wisdom literature is written in a language that is practically universal already.

Thus, while Christians today do not find themselves in the exact same situation as Job (loss of children, wealth, etc., all at the same time), they do find themselves in similar situations. They face terrible inexplicable tragedy and begin to question God. The lessons Job learned apply almost directly to today's audience.

Don't overlook the Wisdom books.

Sermon thesis statement: Because God is sovereign, all-wise, and just, we can trust him even in the darkest inexplicably tragic situations.

Sermon outline:

1. We often face terrible, inexplicable tragedy. (Job 1:1–2:10, summarize the story)
2. As the tragedy persists, we tend to question (even accuse) God.
   a. We often want to argue with God about the tragedy. We want to know "why." (Job 23:1–9; 24:1)
   b. Sometimes we accuse God of injustice. (Job 27:2)
   c. We want our day in court to "straighten God out" about how he runs the universe. (Job 31:35)
3. God answers us with the same answer he gave Job.
   a. He is sovereign and we are not. (Job 38:1–5)
   b. He is all-wise and we are limited in our knowledge. (Job 38:18)
   c. God is just and does not like his justice to be challenged. (Job 40:8)
4. Conclusions.
   a. We need not question how God runs the universe.
   b. We should trust God even when we don't understand.

Conclusions

As you make out your preaching schedule for the year, be sure to include several sermons from Psalms. As you preach the psalms, you will be able to connect with those of your congregation who are hurting and crying out in pain and confusion. You will be able to help them to feel accepted, to cry out honestly to God, and then to move on to acknowledging God's great promised deliverance. Likewise, you can preach the psalms as worship, leading your people to praise God for his wonderful and mighty acts of salvation for both those in the Bible and for his people today. And don't overlook the Wisdom books. These books speak especially to today's postmodern audience, giving God's advice for godly living—guidelines for those searching for meaning in life, for direction in ethical behavior, and for strong, healthy marriages.

Review Questions and Assignments

1. Develop a text thesis statement, a text outline, a sermon thesis statement, and a sermon outline for Psalm 3.
2. Develop a text thesis statement, a text outline, a sermon thesis statement, and a sermon outline for Psalm 111.
3. Develop a text thesis statement, a text outline, a sermon thesis statement, and a sermon outline for Proverbs 31:10–31.

Conclusion

Our goal in *Preaching God's Word* has been to instruct and encourage you to stand before your congregation having carefully handled the biblical text and incorporated the relevant exegetical information into a sermon. We sought to take you step-by-step from the exegesis of a text to sermon development based on that exegesis. We shared insights on communicating with a specific audience in a specific life situation. We offered helps on how to apply, illustrate, and deliver the sermon so it will connect powerfully with your audience. We outlined key elements in interpreting and developing sermons from the primary types of biblical literature because we believe that literary genre plays a central role in interpreting and communicating the biblical message.

We know that just reading a book like ours does not ensure biblical preaching. We do hope, however, that you will become a better preacher as a result of using *Preaching God's Word*.

Why is it critical that preachers preach biblical sermons? First, week after week people gather in buildings everywhere to hear a word from God. They are convinced that that word is somehow connected to the Bible; as a result, a preacher who claims (implicitly or explicitly) to be speaking on behalf of God should seek to ensure that connection. That weighty responsibility calls for a plan that will produce a biblical sermon. We have tried to provide such a plan.

Second, congregations learn by observation. They spend hours listening to preachers interpret and communicate God's Word. On a weekly basis, whether preachers realize it or not, they are teaching by example how to interpret and apply the Bible. When people turn to personal Bible study, they tend to mimic what they have observed from their preacher. Knowing how to handle the Word yourself is invaluable to this education-by-example opportunity.

Finally, we are convinced people are truly interested in what the Bible has to say to them. The preacher must do some work to discover that message and communicate it effectively. We believe the sermons that result from using the method presented in *Preaching God's Word* will not only meet your audience's needs but also satisfy their interest as well.

Now what? Preaching requires great effort on the part of the preacher, and that means you must now put into practice what you have learned in this book. We do not want to sound arrogant by claiming we have discovered the secret to preaching for all preachers. We have merely tried to offer some helpful guidelines that have assisted us in developing and delivering biblical sermons.

God has chosen to use preaching as a primary method of broadcasting his written revelation. He has called some to that task, and you are probably one of those "called ones." God's call, the gospel, your congregation, and the needs of the world are reasons enough to take the task of preaching seriously and to do your best to improve your preaching. We encourage you to never stop learning how to preach better sermons. We sincerely hope that something you have seen in *Preaching God's Word* will help you become more effective as a preacher.

So preach! Then evaluate your sermon, improve a little at a time, and preach again. Week after week, preach faithfully to the congregation God gives you. And for you beginners, remember this: Preaching has a characteristic that we call the grace factor. Sometimes you will prepare and preach a sermon that doesn't go as well as you had expected. But guess what? You'll get another chance next week to do a better job. So keep trying, keep improving. In preaching it helps to think "little-by-little" since learning how to preach is a lifelong process. Take the biblical text seriously and make sure every sermon you preach reflects both the meaning of the text and its relevance to your audience.

Scripture Index

Subject and Name Index

A

actions and roles of God and people in Scripture, 49

age of audiences, 95

animated delivery of sermons, 161–62

application of biblical messages to real life, 31; avoiding oversimplification in, 128–29; balanced, 129–30; bridges to behavior and, 125–26; exegesis and, 120–21; general, 120–21; importance of, 117; and the Interpretive Journey, 119–28; and the New Testament letters, 177–78; potential pitfalls for preachers in sermon, 128–30; pragmatism versus, 130; real-world scenarios and, 124–25; reluctance in, 118–19; and Revelation, 214; specific, 121–28; whole-person, 127

articulation, 157–58

Art of Storytelling, The (Walsh), 147

audiences: ages of people in, 95; biblical, 59–60, 62–65, 199, 241; culture of, 92–94; evaluating illustrations effects on, 144–45; exegesis of sermon, 85–88; maturity of, 88–90; men and women in, 95–96; preachers' knowledge of, 90–92, 126–27; size of, 95; targeting sermon applications to various, 126–27

B

Baker Exegetical Commentary, 57

Bell, Rob, 133–34

Bible Speaks Today Commentaries, 57

body language: eye contact and, 160–61; facial, 160; hands and feet, 159–60; importance of paying attention to, 158–59

book or theme series, 25

Braga, James, 144

bridges to behavior, 125–26

Brown, H. C., 22, 152

Buttrick, David, 35, 136

C

calendar, church, 25

Campolo, Tony, 21, 150–51

Carson, D. A., 181

casual biblical sermons, 23

Cat's Cradle (Vonnegut), 28–29

cause and effect in Scripture, 46

Chapell, Bryan, 157, 163

ChristianityToday.com, 142

Clinard, H. Gordon, 152

clothesline concept, 110

combination biblical sermons, 23

commentaries, Scripture, 56–59

comparisons in Scripture, 46

computer projections technology, 165–66

conclusions to biblical sermons, 32

conditional clauses in Scripture, 48, 77–78, 78

congregational needs, 25

conjunctions in Scripture, 47

connections between passages in Scripture, 49

context: historical, 52–54, 73–75, 175, 178, 192–93, 205–6, 227–28, 243, 245, 261–62; literary, 50–52, 79–81, 193–94, 206–7, 224, 243, 273–74, 276; theological, 75–76; understanding original, 50–54, 62–64

contrasts in Scripture, 46

conversational preaching style, 163

corrupted biblical sermons, 23

Cox, James, 164, 166

Craddock, Fred, 35, 162

creative writing, 141

culture: and cultural language, 72–73; sermon audience, 92–94

D

DeBrand, Roy, 158, 159, 160–61

deductive versus inductive model of preaching, 33–37, 97

delivery of biblical sermons: animated, 161–62; articulation and, 157–58; avoiding monotony in, 163; body language and, 158–62; computer projections technology and, 165–66; conversational, 163; correct grammar in, 164; extemporaneous style and, 154–55; eye contact during, 160–61; facial movements in, 160; hands and feet movement in, 159; importance of effective, 151–52; length of sermons and, 166–67; manuscript preaching style and, 153–54; memorization style and, 154, 164–65; natural, 152; pace of, 156; phonation and, 155–56; preaching style and, 153; vocal elements and, 155–58; volume of speaking and, 156–57. *See also* preaching styles; sermons

dialogue in Scripture, 48

direct biblical sermons, 22–23

Duvall, J. Scott, 122–23, 153–54

E

elements of biblical sermons: application, 31; conclusion, 32; explanatory, 30–31; illustrative, 31; introductory, 27–29; main points, 30, 103–8, 109–11; text reading, 26–27. *See also* sermons

emotional terms in Scripture, 49

English-only fallacy, 180

enthronement psalms, 273

evaluation of illustrations, 144–45

exegesis: and application of biblical messages to real life, 120–21; of

Grasping God's Word Workbook

A Hands-On Approach to Reading, Interpreting, and Applying the Bible

J. Scott Duvall and J. Daniel Hays

This workbook is designed for use with *Grasping God's Word*. While the textbook shows you the principles and tools of interpretation, the workbook lets you try them out by applying them to specific genres and contexts. Together, these books will help you get a grip on the solid rock of Scripture—how to read it, how to interpret it, and how to apply it. Features include:

- Emphasis on real-life application
- Supplemented by a website for professors providing extensive teaching materials
- Updates corresponding to the second edition of the textbook, including new exercises, 3-hole punched and perforated pages

Zondervan Get an A! Study Guides
Grasping God's Word Laminated Sheet

J. Scott Duvall and J. Daniel Hays

Whether studying for exams or delving into the Scriptures, Bible students will love how this Zondervan Get an A! Study Guide puts critical information at their fingertips. Portable and durable, this laminated, three-hole-punched study resource is ideal for obtaining a quick overview of Scott Duvall and Daniel Hays' *Grasping God's Word* for exam preparation and last-minute review, or as an aid in Bible study.

Available in stores and online!

Journey into God's Word

Your Guide to Understanding and Applying the Bible

J. Scott Duvall and J. Daniel Hays, Authors of Grasping God's Word

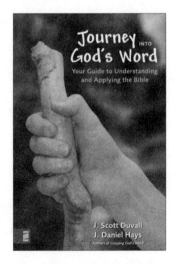

Life is a journey, and like any journey, it requires an accurate, reliable roadmap to get us where we need to go. God has provided such a guide in his Word. But just as a navigator needs to learn how to interpret all the contours and symbols of a map, so also we need to be able to understand how the Bible communicates its directions to us. *Journey Into God's Word* helps Bible readers acquire these skills and become better at reading, interpreting, and applying the Bible to life.

This abridgment of the bestselling college/seminary textbook *Grasping God's Word* takes the proven principles from that book and makes them accessible to people in the church. It starts with general principles of interpretation, then moves on to apply those principles to specific genres and contexts. Hands-on exercises guide readers through the interpretation process, with an emphasis on real-life application.

Dictionary of Biblical Prophecy and End Times

J. Daniel Hays, J. Scott Duvall, and C. Marvin Pate

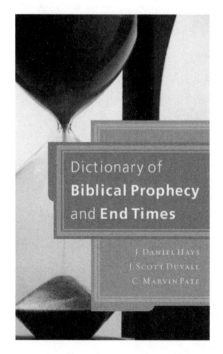

All you ever wanted to know about biblical prophecy from A to Z, the *Dictionary of Biblical Prophecy and End Times* is a comprehensive reference tool. It is written for those who truly desire to understand prophecy and the end times. Starting with "Abomination of Desolation" and continuing through hundreds of articles until "Zionism," this book provides helpful and interesting discussions of the entire range of biblical prophecy, all at your fingertips.

This exhaustive work contains articles on a broad sweep of topics relevant to the study of biblical prophecy and eschatology. The articles are based on solid scholarship, yet are clear and accessible to the lay reader, illuminating even the most complicated issues. The authors balance their presentation by laying out differing positions along with each position's strengths and weaknesses. They do not push any specific theological or interpretive agenda, but have a firm commitment to seeking to understand the Scriptures. This is a valuable tool you will refer to time and again.

Available in stores and online!

We want to hear from you. Please send your comments about this book to us in care of zreview@zondervan.com. Thank you.

ZONDERVAN.com/
AUTHORTRACKER
follow your favorite authors